TOP TRAILS
ARIZONA

INCLUDES GRAND CANYON, PETRIFIED FOREST,
MONUMENT VALLEY, VERMILION CLIFFS, HAVASU
FALLS, ANTELOPE CANYON, AND SLIDE ROCK

MW01148176

by Eric Henze

Gone Beyond Guides
Publisher

Parks Covered in This Book

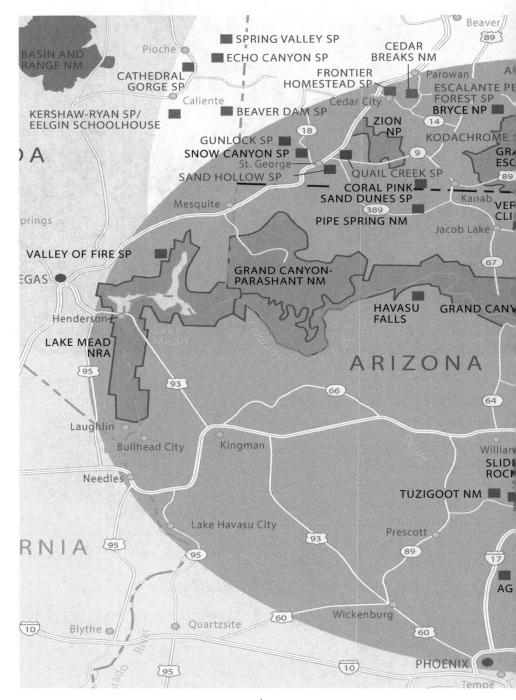

BASIN AND RANGE NM

Pioche

SPRING VALLEY SP

ECHO CANYON SP

CEDAR BREAKS NM

Beaver

89

CATHEDRAL GORGE SP

Caliente

FRONTIER HOMESTEAD SP

Parowan

A

KERSHAW-RYAN SP/ EELGIN SCHOOLHOUSE

BEAVER DAM SP

Cedar City

ESCALANTE PE FOREST SP

BRYCE NP

D A

GUNLOCK SP

SNOW CANYON SP

St. George

SAND HOLLOW SP

18

ZION NP

KODACHROME

14

9

GR ESC

QUAIL CREEK SP

89

Mesquite

CORAL PINK SAND DUNES SP

Kanab

VER CLI

389

prings

PIPE SPRING NM

Jacob Lake

VALLEY OF FIRE SP

67

EGAS

GRAND CANYON- PARASHANT NM

Henderson

HAVASU FALLS

GRAND CANY

LAKE MEAD NRA

Lake Mead

Colorado

A R I Z O N A

95

93

66

64

Laughlin

Bullhead City

Kingman

Willia

SLIDE ROCK

Needles

TUZIGOOT NM

RNIA

95

Lake Havasu City

93

Prescott

95

89

17

10

Blythe

Quartzsite

60

Wickenburg

AG

95

10

60

PHOENIX

Tempe

4

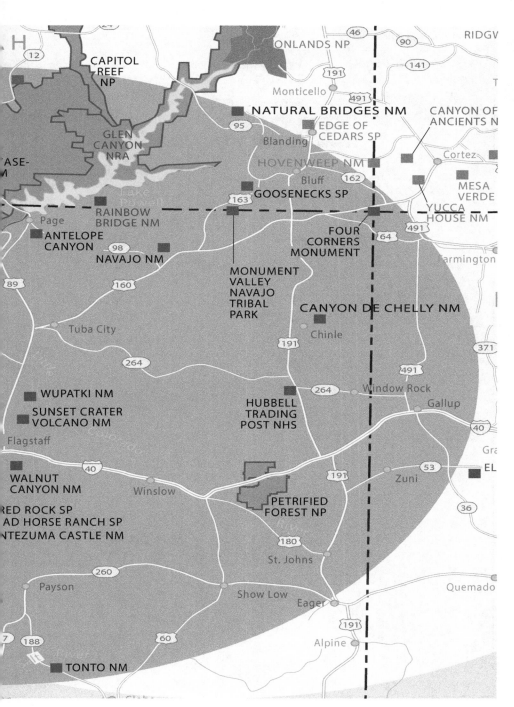

H
12
CAPITOL
REEF
NP

ONLANDS NP
46
90
RIDGV
191
141
Monticello
491
NATURAL BRIDGES NM
CANYON OF
ANCIENTS N
95
EDGE OF
CEDARS SP
GLEN
CANYON
NRA
Blanding
Cortez
ASE-
M
HOVENWEEP NM
MESA
VERDE
Bluff
162
GOOSENECKS SP
163
YUCCA
HOUSE NM
RAINBOW
BRIDGE NM
FOUR
CORNERS
MONUMENT
491
64
Page
ANTELOPE
CANYON
98
Farmington
NAVAJO NM
MONUMENT
VALLEY
NAVAJO
TRIBAL
PARK
89
160
CANYON DE CHELLY NM
371
Tuba City
Chinle
191
264
491
WUPATKI NM
264
Window Rock
SUNSET CRATER
VOLCANO NM
Gallup
Flagstaff
40
Gra
WALNUT
CANYON NM
Winslow
HUBBELL
TRADING
POST NHS
53
EL
191
Zuni
RED ROCK SP
AD HORSE RANCH SP
NTEZUMA CASTLE NM
PETRIFIED
FOREST NP
36
180
St. Johns
260
Payson
Show Low
Quemado
Eager
7
188
191
60
Alpine
TONTO NM

Lake
Powell

PARKS OF THE GRAND CIRCLE

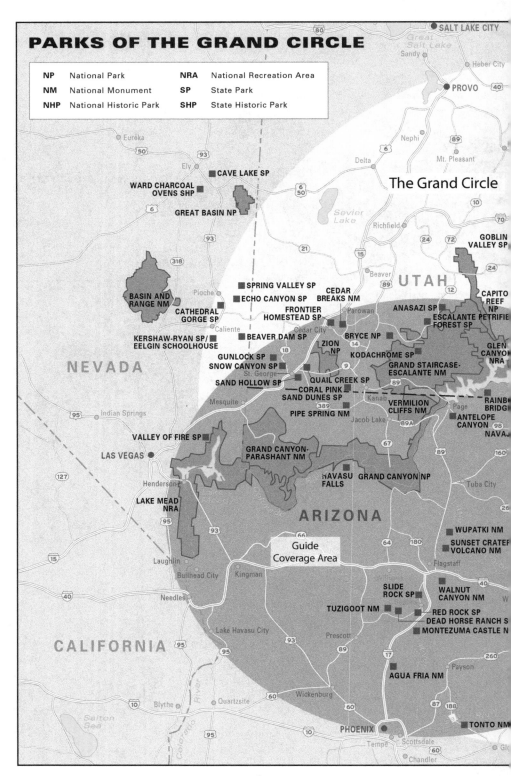

NP	National Park	**NRA**	National Recreation Area
NM	National Monument	**SP**	State Park
NHP	National Historic Park	**SHP**	State Historic Park

The Grand Circle

SALT LAKE CITY

Great Salt Lake

Sandy

Heber City

PROVO

Eureka

Nephi

Mt. Pleasant

Ely

CAVE LAKE SP

Delta

Richfield

WARD CHARCOAL OVENS SHP

Sevier Lake

GOBLIN VALLEY SP

GREAT BASIN NP

UTAH

Beaver

CAPITOL REEF NP

BASIN AND RANGE NM

Pioche

SPRING VALLEY SP

CEDAR BREAKS NM

ANASAZI SP

CATHEDRAL GORGE SP

ECHO CANYON SP

FRONTIER HOMESTEAD SP

Parowan

ESCALANTE PETRIFIE FOREST SP

Caliente

Cedar City

BRYCE NP

KERSHAW-RYAN SP/ EELGIN SCHOOLHOUSE

BEAVER DAM SP

ZION NP

KODACHROME SP

GLEN CANYO NRA

NEVADA

GUNLOCK SP

St. George

GRAND STAIRCASE-ESCALANTE NM

SNOW CANYON SP

QUAIL CREEK SP

SAND HOLLOW SP

CORAL PINK SAND DUNES SP

Kanab

VERMILION CLIFFS NM

Page

RAINB BRIDG

Mesquite

PIPE SPRING NM

Jacob Lake

ANTELOPE CANYON

NAVAJ

VALLEY OF FIRE SP

Indian Springs

GRAND CANYON-PARASHANT NM

LAS VEGAS

HAVASU FALLS

GRAND CANYON NP

Tuba City

Henderson

ARIZONA

LAKE MEAD NRA

WUPATKI NM

Laughlin

Guide Coverage Area

SUNSET CRATER VOLCANO NM

Bullhead City

Kingman

Flagstaff

Needles

SLIDE ROCK SP

WALNUT CANYON NM

TUZIGOOT NM

RED ROCK SP

CALIFORNIA

Lake Havasu City

Prescott

DEAD HORSE RANCH S

MONTEZUMA CASTLE N

AGUA FRIA NM

Payson

Blythe

Quartzsite

Wickenburg

Salton Sea

Colorado River

PHOENIX

TONTO NM

Tempe

Scottsdale

Chandler

6

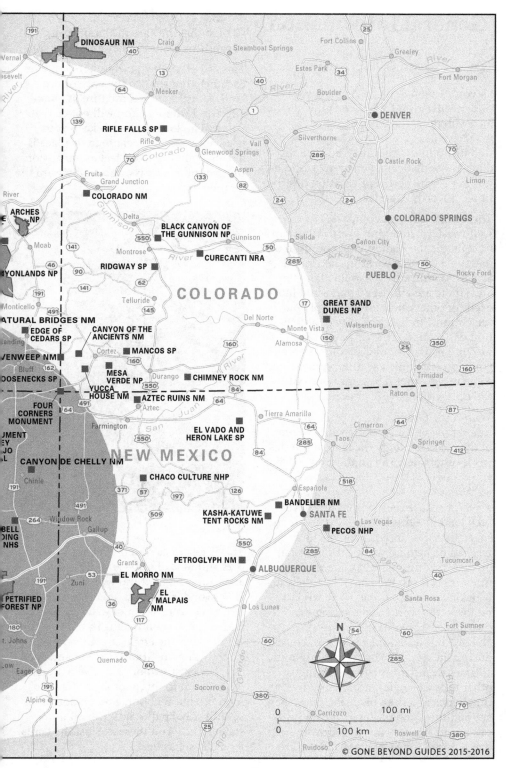

DINOSAUR NM
Craig
Steamboat Springs
Fort Collins
25
Greeley
Vernal
osevelt
191
River
Fort Morgan
Estes Park
34
40
13
40
River
Boulder
DENVER
Meeker
64
Colorado
139
RIFLE FALLS SP
Silverthorne
70
285
Castle Rock
70
Rifle
Vail
Glenwood Springs
Fruita
Grand Junction
Aspen
133
Limon
River
Grand Junction
82
COLORADO NM
24
24
COLORADO SPRINGS
Delta
ARCHES
NP
141
Moab
BLACK CANYON OF
THE GUNNISON NP
Gunnison
Salida
Cañon City
50
550
Montrose
CURECANTI NRA
50
Rocky Ford
YONLANDS NP
90
RIDGWAY SP
285
PUEBLO
River
46
141
62
COLORADO
Monticello
491
Telluride
145
17
GREAT SAND
DUNES NP
350
TURAL BRIDGES NM
Del Norte
Walsenburg
EDGE OF
CEDARS SP
CANYON OF THE
ANCIENTS NM
Monte Vista
150
25
160
Alamosa
anding
Cortez
MANCOS SP
160
River
160
ENWEEP NM
162
MESA
VERDE NP
Durango
CHIMNEY ROCK NM
Trinidad
Bluff
OSENECKS SP
YUCCA
HOUSE NM
550
84
FOUR
CORNERS
MONUMENT
491
AZTEC RUINS NM
64
Raton
87
Aztec
San
Juan
Tierra Amarilla
MENT
EY
JO
L
Farmington
EL VADO AND
HERON LAKE SP
64
Cimarron
64
550
Taos
NEW MEXICO
285
Springer
412
CANYON DE CHELLY NM
84
518
191
Chinle
CHACO CULTURE NHP
Española
371
57
197
126
BANDELIER NM
491
264
Window Rock
509
KASHA-KATUWE
TENT ROCKS NM
SANTA FE
Las Vegas
BELL
ING
NHS
Gallup
40
550
PECOS NHP
Pecos
285
84
Tucumcari
PETRIFIED
FOREST NP
Grants
PETROGLYPH NM
ALBUQUERQUE
40
53
180
EL MORRO NM
Zuni
36
EL
MALPAIS
NM
Santa Rosa
t. Johns
Los Lunas
ow
117
Fort Sumner
Eager
N
54
60
191
Quemado
60
285
Alpine
380
70
Socorro
0
100 mi
Carrizozo
0
100 km
Roswell
380
25
Ruidoso
© GONE BEYOND GUIDES 2015-2016

General Information

What is the Grand Circle?

So you've been done an Arizona vacation, maybe even Colorado and Utah, but have you done the Grand Circle? You may have heard of it and likely know it well if you live within it. For those that don't know the term, you aren't alone, as it is one of the best kept vacation destinations in North America.

The Grand Circle encompasses five southwestern states but more importantly, contains the highest concentration of national and state parks in the United States. Within this 500-mile diameter area, there are almost 80 parks and hundreds of other attractions. Simply put, the Grand Circle is a bounty of a vacation destination. This isn't about going to Zion or the Grand Canyon, it's about going on a lifetime vacation, something so incredible that it becomes one of the top things you have ever done.

Within the Grand Circle are attractions found nowhere else in the world. Some of these seem to defy the laws of physics while others defy the boundaries of what you thought was possible. I've taken folks into areas where nobody spoke a word because they simply had never seen land like this before. They were in speechless awe and its true, the journey can be beyond works, the land can be that striking. Within it are timeless monoliths, thousands of arches, delicately balanced rocks, some of the wildest rapids in the world and the deepest canyons. It contains the darkest skies in North America and the brightest colors during the day. The land is a symphony, at times thunderous and deafening, at other times a single soft note trailing into the silence of a deep blue sky. Here there are hoodoos, goblins, fins, tall alpine peaks and slot canyon so narrow there is barely room for one person. There are red rock cliffs, sheer vertical walls or rock so high that they are the emotional equal in sandstone what Yosemite is in granite.

This is a place that resets a person. One can't help but slow to the pace of the land. A visit here is a mixture of relaxation and wonder. You will notice that you will no longer need to keep your head above water because in its place is a realization that your feet are firmly on the ground. Such is a vacation within the Grand Circle.

Reverse Handprint at Hovenweep

This is a land carved by water and wind over millions of years and the results are astounding natural works of art. It is no wonder that this area contains the largest concentration of national parks and national monuments in the United States. Sure, the circle contains the nationally known Grand Canyon and Zion, but that's just two of its twelve national parks. Add to this another 30 national monuments, 3 national recreation areas, several tribal parks and over 30 more state parks. And these are just the lands formally set aside.

By the numbers, most of the parks that make up the Grand Circle are within Utah and Arizona, but the full magnitude of the circle encompasses lands within Nevada, New Mexico and Colorado as well. The imaginary circle is about 500 miles in diameter or roughly 126 million acres of land. As daunting as that sounds, one can comfortably visit 7-8 of the most popular national parks (and several other parks along the way) in 10 days. Of course, the more one is able to slow down, the more one will see, but the point is, if you are looking for natural wonder, you can experience a large and varied amount in a relatively short amount of time.

Historically, the Grand Circle was a term created when the Southwest National Parks were just beginning. The NPS worked with the Union Pacific Railway and created trips by rail and bus up until the 1970's. Back then, a trip to the Grand Circle was a time of great adventure and romance. There were dance bands at the stops and as your tour bus would drive away from the lodge, employees would line up and "sing away" the visitors. Today, it remains one of the best vacations in North America that one can take. This is a vacation destination of adventure, relaxation and wonder. It is a land that humbles, inspires and refreshes the spirit and for those that know of it, have the Grand Circle as a bucket list place to experience at least once in their lives. The term Grand Circle could not be more perfect to describe this land.

When to Go

There are really only two factors on when to go, do you like temperate climates or would you prefer less people. The two are both related to temperature but in different ways.

In general, the Grand Circle is blistering hot in the summer, starting in mid to late June and going full force through August. That doesn't seem to keep folks away,

particularly if you have kids out for the school year. Temperature wise though, the best time to go is during the spring, early summer, fall and early winter. Other considerations on temperature is elevation. High elevation parks such as Bryce and Great Basin are typically cooler in the summer than say Canyonlands or Lake Powell.

In terms of going at a time when the crowds have thinned, the best times to go are the dead of winter, followed by the dead of summer. Winter receives a lot fewer crowds for the obvious reasons. It's colder, snowier and wetter. In fact, it tends to be the antithesis of what folks have in mind when they think of say, the Grand Canyon. That said, these parks in winter are perhaps when they are at their most special. There is something transformative about a dusting of snow across the layered mesas and canyons or topping each hoodoo of Bryce. In fact, for places like Bryce, which receive tons of visitors each summer, the arguably best time to go is winter. I've been out on trails covered in snow on a crisp clear cold day with the entire park practically to myself.

Winter at any of the parks can be magical, but it does run the risk of being miserable. In fact, you could get snowed in, which isn't the worst thing that could happen to a person, but can be difficult if your boss is expecting you back at work. The dead of summer is a good second choice as it is usually too hot for most. That said, there are many whose lifestyles gives them nothing else to work with, so it can still be crowded. The parks in summer can be too hot to hike in during the heat of the day, so for those that take this tactic, get in the habit of hitting the trails in the cool of early morning.

Where to Go

If you think about it, there is a fair amount of irony in guide books that tell you the best places to go to avoid crowds.

They are basically saying, we've learned all these secret cool places that no one goes to and we are now publishing this information in a guide book for anyone to read. If you see one of these sections, don't believe it, the word's already out on all these "secret places". In fact, places like Havasu Falls are so impacted, it is nearly impossible to get a permit to hike the trail.

That said, there are some general tips to getting an otherwise crowded national park or monument to yourself. Take the Grand Canyon for example. This park receives some 4.5 million visitors to the South Rim alone. The vast majority of these folks don't hike any farther than to the overlook. So simply getting out on any trail cuts the population of the park down by about 90%. If you've purchased this book, you are on good footing right from the start.

to yourself. If the trail is a short little flat ditty with interpretive signs, be prepared to share it. If it is one of the routes described in these guides, so rugged there isn't even a trail, be prepared to survive on your own because you are likely the only people out that way.

The same can be said about weather. Heat, rain, snow and cold tend to filter out a fair amount of people. What's amazing about this is sometimes inclement weather will bring out the most unique views of a trail you will likely ever see. Now keep you in mind that you should add in a large degree of common sense. You don't want to have a slot canyon "all to yourself" in a thunderstorm or hike in the direct heat of a summer's day unless you are fully prepared and acclimated. Don't be stupid in your quest to have the place to yourself. The point here is, in general I've found a rather obvious truth. If a guide book says it's

Monument Valley

There are other tips to share. In general, I've found that the more strenuous the hike is, the harder the trail is to get to, and the longer the trail's length is, the greater the chances you will have the trail

secret, it isn't. The more remote a place is, the longer the hike, the steeper the inclines, the more extreme the journey, these all act as filters to minimizing the crowd factor.

Being Prepared

Hiking in the Grand Circle can be highly rewarding. But don't let the desert fool you, this is an extreme environment and one shouldn't just venture out without some forethought and preparation. This section seems pretty straightforward, but as the rangers at the Grand Canyon can attest to, there are literally dozens of people that venture out into the wilderness with nothing more than enthusiasm. Since enthusiasm alone can really put a damper on your hike, here are some tips to make your hikes safer and more enjoyable.

Water

Rule of thumb, bring three quarts per person per day. Some folks prefer two 1.5 liter bottles; some find they can balance their day or backpacks out better with three 1.0 liter bottles. Make sure the bottles do not leak by turning them upside down to see if water comes out. If it's only a drip, it's still a problem.

If you are traveling with small children, you will likely need to carry their water for them beyond one quart. Keep this in mind as you are packing.

Clothing

Bring layers as appropriate for the hike. This means if its colder when you are at rest, bring a layer or two to keep you warm. Windbreakers are great allies in keeping warmth in and cold out and are also lighter weight. A good beanie helps as well as some 15% of your body temperature is lost through your head. If it looks like rain, bring a waterproof version of that windbreaker.

In the heat, most folks go with the t-shirt and shorts, which is fine, but definitely bring a hat. The heat can be oppressing, especially with no shade and that hat will definitely help. I also recommend a full brimmed hat over a baseball cap. This will provide more shade and definitely helps keep the back of your neck from getting sunburned.

In either hot or cold, bring another warm layer if you can. This is your emergency backup layer should you find yourself having to overnight for whatever reason. A windbreaker that can be rolled up or a long sleeve t-shirt can make a big difference if you find yourself with nothing but a t-shirt and shorts at 3am on a summer trip. I've also found it to be a good loaner for others that may need some warmth on say a spring hike.

Boots, Tennis and Water Shoes

Most people will tend to go for their tennis shoes because they are comfortable and easier to lace up. That said, boots are preferred because they offer a lot more protection, especially around the ankles. Tennis shoes are great for flat surfaces, but boots are made for uneven terrain. It's like taking a sedan tire on a 4WD road instead of an all-terrain tire. You wouldn't do it to your car, don't do it to your feet. Where a good boot and also, be the boot. Wear it in before you start your hiking adventures so you don't get blisters.

If the trail involves some hiking in water, it really helps to have a pair of water shoes. They are lightweight and keep your boots dry. A dry boot makes for a happy hiker, whereas a wet boot can destroy your feet in short order.

Daypack

A decent no nonsense day back to hold everything. There are fancier daypacks with hydration systems and such. At the end of the day, you just want something that will last a long time. The more parts the pack has, the more parts that can fail. Zipper quality is number one. Most otherwise solid daypacks fail because of the zipper.

Vermilion Cliffs

Also, a little tip on the daypack. If you get one that zips like an upside down U, put the zippers on one side or the other, not at the top. I have seen and personally had a branch find its way between the two zippers and open the entire contents of the pack onto the trail. In my case, it opened on brushy 30-degree slope and I watched my lunch and water roll downhill out of sight forever.

Other Gear

At this point, you've got three quarts of water, a bunch of layers, some food and no room for anything else right? Well, it can seem that way. What to bring is a balancing act. On the one hand, you want to be lightweight. The more stuff you have on your back, the more burdensome it will feel. On the other hand, you do want to be prepared. In the excellent book, Climbing Ice by Yvon Chouinard, he says something that is about as true a piece of advice I've ever heard in this context.

If you bring it, you will use it.

What this means is if you bring a sleeping bag, you will likely spend the night in it. If you bring rope, you will likely use that rope. So start with packing only what you need for the hike.

Essentials include:

- Water and some food

- A hat

- Extra clothing as appropriate

- Sunscreen

- A map and possibly the trail guide book (if you feel you will need it to navigate the trail)

On top of this, I would seriously consider also bringing:

- Some form of fire, a lighter or fire starter of some kind

- Compass

- Small first aid kit, a whistle and reflector mirror (for emergencies)

- A sharp knife

12

- Moleskin (for blisters)
- Ibuprofen (to help if you aren't acclimated to the heat)
- Water purification tablets
- Small flashlight
- Cell phone
- GPS device

It's hard to come up with a list that works under all conditions and the above list is more geared towards summer hiking than winter, so be adjust for cold, rain or snow. Also, be sure to bring something fun, a little treat goes a long way and is much better appreciated on the trail. This falls under "being kind to yourself" which is described below.

Know Yourself

Gung Ho-ness

A lot of these trails are steep and long. Add in that you are at high elevations and the temperatures are hot means many of the hikes in this book can be challenging. With that in mind, choose a hike that is appropriate for you. You will enjoy the hike more and plus; you will be able to go on another hike the next day. Know your physical limitations and don't test them to the point that you will need to be rescued.

Find your pace

Great hiking partners are not only experienced; they are great for each other because they both travel at the same pace. Start by finding your own pace and if you are the partner that can travel faster, slow down to the page of the other person or group.

Take Breaks, Eat Snacks

Taking a ten minute break every hour actually improves your stamina, allowing you to enjoy the hike more and go longer.

The reason for this is simple, well, simple if you remember your biology course. When your body is at rest, it gets most of its energy in part from the air you breath. When you are in motion, that production of energy continues to work, but as you have likely noticed, you breath harder as you increase that motion. At some point, you can't get enough air, but your body still needs more energy, so it kicks in another mechanism for creating it. This mechanism, (I'm trying to keep this in layman's terms, but I can't help it, it's called anaerobic metabolism) is much less efficient, creating all manner of waste products. These waste products build up in your muscles and cause pain. One of these waste products is called lactic acid.

Resting helps remove the metabolic waste products and your body is pretty good at flushing them out. Eating snacks and drinking fluids helps refuel your body for the continued efforts of both the aerobic and anaerobic metabolic processes.

Time Flies

Being stuck on the trail after the sun sets isn't much fun, well unless there's a full moon out and no canopy to block the light. That can actually be a lot of fun and is highly recommended. Wait, the point I'm trying to make here is if you are out in the wilderness, watch your time and be aware of how long it took you to get to your turn around point. If the trail starts as a major descent, some of the steeper trails require twice as much time for returning up then it took getting down. The Grand Canyon is a good example of this. Being stuck in areas where the temperature drops dramatically at night is also a concern. The Narrows hike is a great example of this. Also, if you think you might be caught out in the dark, having a little flashlight, per person, can be a lifesaver.

Don't be afraid to abort the trip

If you or another hiker are showing signs of exhaustion, heat stroke, hypothermia or if the weather doesn't look like its adding up right, don't hesitate to turn back. Typically, these trips are planned far in advance and there is plenty of anticipation and excitement, but nothing is worth serious health issues or worse from not making the right decision. If someone doesn't feel they are up to a hike or someone in the group feels they may be putting themselves in danger, take their concerns seriously. Heat stroke and hypothermia can get serious and can lead to death.

Hypothermia, altitude sickness and heat exhaustion have nothing to do with physical ability. I've seen first hand the symptoms of each of these health issues and everyone that experienced them started out in terrific shape. It can hit hard and quickly. The typical "first signs" that I've seen are loss of mental sharpness and generally just out of it. The victim appears drunk and off, but otherwise may seem "themselves" at times. Don't second guess here, if your buddy isn't acting like his or her normal self; stop, assess and remediate the issue. Don't keep pressing on.

The Hazardous H's + Altitude Sickness

The below is put out by the National Park Service and gives a good over of some of the health issues to look out for while hiking. Since some of the trails within the Grand Circle are at altitude, a description of altitude sickness or acute mountain sickness (AMS) is also included

Heat Exhaustion

The result of dehydration due to intense sweating. Hikers can lose one or two quarts (liters) of water per hour.

Symptoms: pale face, nausea, vomiting, cool and moist skin, headache, cramps.

View within Petrified Forest National Park

Treatment: drink water with electrolytes, eat high-energy foods (with fats and sugars), rest in the shade for 30-45 minutes, and cool the body by getting wet.

Heatstroke

A life-threatening emergency where the body's heat regulating mechanisms become overwhelmed by a combination of internal heat production and environmental demands. Your body loses its ability to cool itself. Grand Canyon has two to three cases of heatstroke a year. Untreated heat exhaustion can lead to heatstroke.

Symptoms: flushed face, dry skin, weak and rapid pulse, high core body temperature, confusion, poor judgment or inability to cope, unconsciousness, seizures.

Treatment: the heatstroke victim must be cooled immediately! Continuously pour water on the victim's head and torso, fan to create an evaporative cooling effect. Immerse the victim in cold water if possible. Move the victim to shade and remove excess clothing. The victim needs evacuation to a hospital. Someone should go for help while attempts to cool the victim continue.

Hyponatremia (water intoxication)

An illness that mimics the early symptoms of heat exhaustion. It is the result of low sodium in the blood caused by drinking too much water and losing too much salt through sweating.

Symptoms: nausea, vomiting, altered mental states, confusion, frequent urination. The victim may appear intoxicated. In extreme cases seizures may occur.

Treatment: have the victim eat salty foods, slowly drink sports drinks with electrolytes, and rest in the shade. If mental alertness decreases, seek immediate help!

Hypothermia

A life-threatening emergency where the body cannot keep itself warm, due to exhaustion and exposure to cold, wet, windy weather.

Symptoms: uncontrolled shivering, poor muscle control, careless attitude. Look for signs of the "umbles" - stumbling, mumbling, fumbling, grumbling.

Treatment: remove wet clothing and put on dry clothing, drink warm sugary liquids, warm victim by body contact with another person, protect from wind, rain, and cold.

Altitude Sickness

Altitude sickness is your body not being able to acclimate to altitude. If untreated, it can lead to high altitude pulmonary oedema (HAPE) which is a life threatening condition where your lungs fill with fluid, making it difficult to breath. It can also lead to high altitude cerebral oedema (HACE), which is a build up of fluid in your brain. Both can cause death within hours if not treated.

Symptoms: The most common symptom is typically a headache similar to that felt with a hangover. Some folks will feel nausea and may vomit as well as a general malaise feeling, and dizziness.

Treatment: Altitude sickness is not uncommon, especially if you have ascended in elevation too fast, starting at elevations of 8200 feet (2500 m). While it is common, some people are only slightly affected, while others feel so bad they have to turn around. For all, even those slightly affected, be self aware as it can lead to pulmonary and cerebral oedema, which are very serious conditions.

If You Get Lost

Daniel Boone once said, "I have never been lost, but I will admit to being confused for several weeks." If you do get lost, you will quickly realize you aren't Daniel Boone and wished you had of paid more attention to all those nifty tricks you might have seen on those survival shows. Never fear, this book might just save you. Read the following tips if you happen to get lost.

- Stay calm. The sun's setting, you still haven't even found the trail, let alone your car. This is not a time to freak out. Take some deep breaths and stay calm. You will get through this.

- Ration water and food. Stay hungry, ration your water, don't eat and drink everything at once.

- Readjust your schedule to maximize for hydration. Water loss has now become your biggest enemy. This means hiking during the cool of the morning and evening, while hunkering down at mid-day. Aim for shade and stay put during the heat of the day. Remember, the power of threes when it comes to survival. Though you will be incredibly hungry, you can survive three weeks without food. For water, it is only three days (and for air, three minutes). Water loss is the biggest barrier to you surviving or not if you are lost in the desert.

- Make a plan. If you have a compass, see a landmark, can get a sense of direction from the sun, use all these things to help make a plan of action. This starts by stay-ing calm. With calmness, you can think. In thought, you can assess what you know (and what you don't know). From this catalog of observations, you can make a plan. Try to remain rational and fact based in your observations, it's okay to make an assumption, but assess how confident you are of these assumptions.

- Stay at an even calm pace, pick your path. Scout ahead to where you want to go, aim for paths of least resistance and effort versus paths that are harder if possible. Don't rush your walking, stay calm.

- Follow a road, a trail, or a route. If you see a road or a trail, take it. You have greatly increased your chances of being found or finding a way out yourself.

- Stay off the ground during the day. Finding shade is important when resting as the ground temperature can by 30 degrees hotter than the air temperature.

- Hike together at the pace of the slowest member, only separate if someone is injured.

- Stay with your car. If you are near your car, stay with it. It will make finding you easier and will provide shade, shelter and hopefully some food.

Northern Arizona

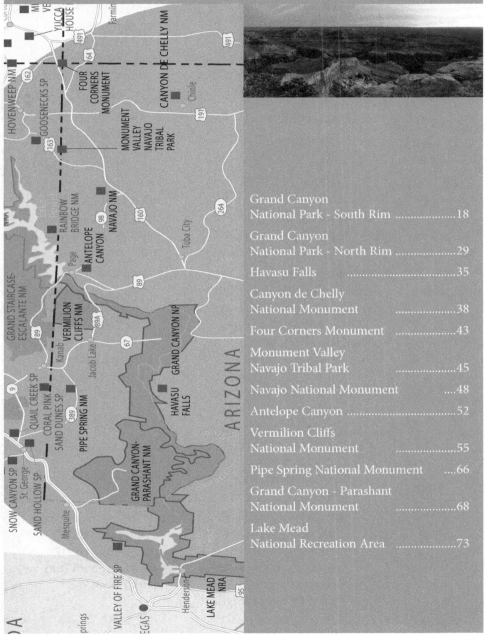

Grand Canyon National Park - South Rim

Quick Facts

Official Park Website:
http://www.nps.gov/grca

Visitor Center:

- General Visitor Information: (928) 638-7888
- Backcountry Information Center: (928) 638-7875

Park Accessibility:

- Okay for 2WD and RVs
- Day and Overnight Use

Experience Level:

- Family Friendly – Backcountry Hiker

Camping in Park:
Reservations strongly recommended at (877) 444-6777 or online at the http://www.recreation.gov/

- Mather Campground: 309 T/RV, open year round, drinking water, flush toilets, pull-thru sites, laundry and showers, no hookups, 30-foot total vehicle length, group sites available.
- Trailer Village RV: 80 RV, open year round, hookups, drinking water, flush toilets, accommodates vehicles up to 50 feet in length, pull-thru sites, shower and laundry
- Desert View: 50 T/RV, first come–first served, closed in winter, drinking water, restrooms, 30-foot total vehicle length, typically fills be early afternoon in summer.

Lodging in Park:

- 7 lodges in the South Rim, including Phantom Ranch. Go here for full details: http://www.nps.gov/grca/planyourvisit/lodging.htm. Reservations strongly recommended

Dining in Park:

- Multiple restaurants and markets for groceries. Go here for full details: http://www.nps.gov/grca/planyourvisit/restaurants.htm

Nearest Town with Amenities:

- Tusayan, AZ is less than 2 mi / 3 km from park

Getting There:

- From Flagstaff, AZ: take I-40 to US-180 North to South Rim park entrance

What Makes the South Rim of the Grand Canyon Special

- Hiking in one of the most amazing natural wonders on the planet
- Knowing that if you make it the canyon floor, you are amongst rock that is 2.2 billion years old, some of the oldest exposed rock on earth
- The grandeur of the mesas, the magnitude of the various rock layers, the sheer immensity, it's the Grand Canyon!

Hiking in the South Rim of the Grand Canyon

Rim Trail

Easy – (13.0 mi / 21.0 km), one way, time varies on route taken, elev. Δ: 200 ft / 61m, trailhead at viewpoint at Grand Canyon Village and along Hermit Road

The Rim Trail is great for just strolling in the Grand Canyon with the view slowly changing before you. The trail starts at the South Kaibab Trailhead and extends to Hermit's Rest. It can be picked up from any overlook, and by utilizing the shuttle system one can pick up the trail and drop off it with a great deal of convenience. The trail is mostly paved and well traveled. For quieter moments, try walking it in tune to the sunrise or meander along its route in the late afternoon into dusk.

Bright Angel Trail

Strenuous – (12.0 mi / 19.3 km to Plateau Point), round trip, allow 5-8 hours, elev. Δ: 3,039 ft / 926 m, trailhead west of Bright Angel Lodge

Strenuous – (17.6 mi / 28.3 km to Colorado River), round trip, allow 5-8 hours, elev. Δ: 4,888 ft / 1,490 m, trailhead west of Bright Angel Lodge

Bright Angel is a very well defined trail that ultimately leads to the Colorado River itself. While it is possible to do this in one day, as mentioned above, this is an all-day hike and not for the casual hiker. The thing to realize about Bright Angel is it is very inviting and gives wonderful views as you immerse yourself into the depths of the canyon. However, the trail is steep, which gives you the impression that you are "cooking with gas" as you travel downward. It is only on the return that you realize just how steep this trail is. Allow twice as much time for the return trip and bring twice as much water for this hot, exposed trail.

For groups with small children, going to the first switchback offers a good experience without subjecting little feet to the steeper bits just ahead. For those not looking to do a full 12-mile (19 km) hike, going to Indian Gardens offers great views and a nice stopping point before turning around. There is water to refill your canteen and even a ranger on duty most of the time. Indian Gardens is 9 miles (14.5 km) round trip. If you decide

From the bottom of the canyon

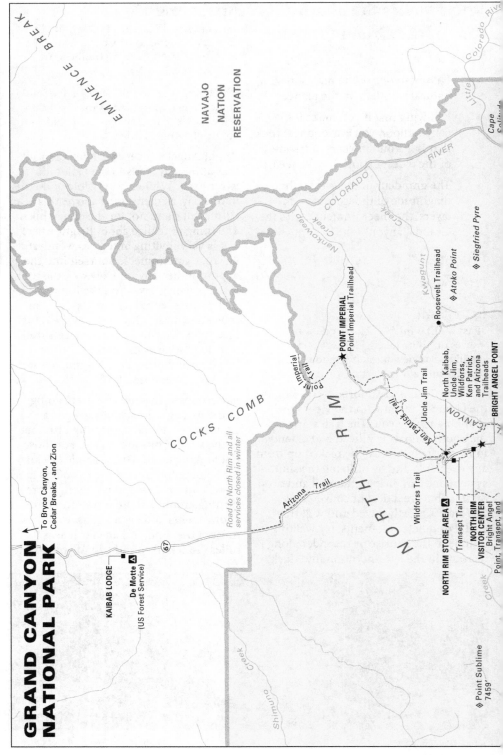

GRAND CANYON
NATIONAL PARK

To Bryce Canyon,
Cedar Breaks , and Zion

KAIBAB LODGE
De Motte
(US Forest Service)

67

Road to North Rim and all
services closed in winter

Arizona   Trail

EMINENCE BREAK

NAVAJO
NATION
RESERVATION

Colorado River

Little

Cape
Solitude

COLORADO   RIVER

Creek

Nankoweap

COLORADO

Creek

Kwagunt

Siegfried Pyre

Atoko Point

Roosevelt Trailhead

COCKS   COMB

Point   Imperial   Trail

POINT IMPERIAL
Point Imperial Trailhead

R I M

N O R T H

CANYON

Ken Patrick Trail

Uncle Jim Trail

North Kaibab,
Uncle Jim,
Wildforss,
Ken Patrick,
and Arizona
Trailheads

BRIGHT ANGEL POINT

Wildforss Trail

Transept Trail

NORTH RIM STORE AREA

NORTH RIM
VISITOR CENTER
Bright Angel
Point, Transept, and

Point Sublime
7459'

Creek

Shinumo

Creek

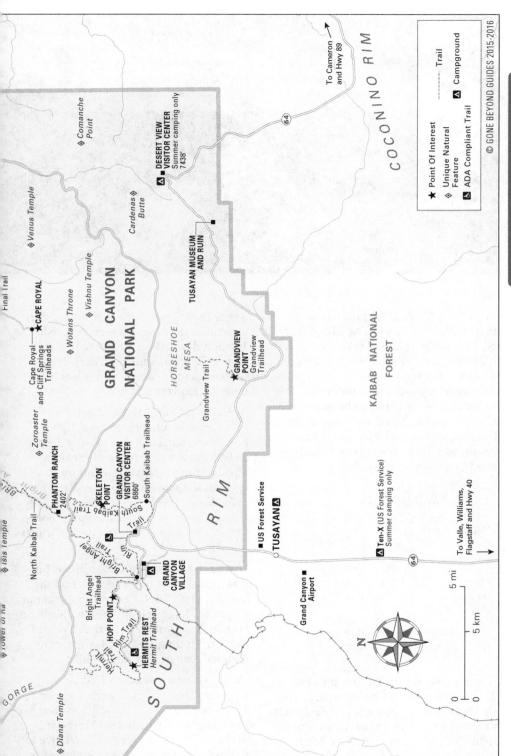

Grand Canyon - South Rim

NORTHERN ARIZONA

© GONE BEYOND GUIDES 2015-2016

★ Point Of Interest   ------- Trail
◇ Unique Natural   △ Campground
  Feature
⧖ ADA Compliant Trail

GRAND CANYON NATIONAL PARK

KAIBAB NATIONAL FOREST

COCONINO RIM

SOUTH RIM

To Cameron and Hwy 89

◇ Comanche Point
◇ Venus Temple
Cardenas Butte
△ DESERT VIEW VISITOR CENTER
  Summer camping only
  7438'

64

TUSAYAN MUSEUM AND RUIN

◇ Vishnu Temple
◇ Wotans Throne
★ CAPE ROYAL
Cape Royal and Cliff Springs Trailheads
Final Trail

HORSESHOE MESA

★ GRANDVIEW POINT
  Grandview Trailhead

Grandview Trail

◇ Zoroaster Temple
PHANTOM RANCH
2402'
■ SKELETON POINT
GRAND CANYON VISITOR CENTER
6860'
South Kaibab Trailhead
South Kaibab Trail

North Kaibab Trail

◇ Isis Temple

Bright Angel Trail

Bright Angel Trailhead

△ GRAND CANYON VILLAGE
★ HOPI POINT
Rim Trail
★ HERMITS REST
  Hermit Trailhead
Hermit Trail

◇ Tower of Ra
◇ Diana Temple
GORGE

■ US Forest Service

△ Ten-X (US Forest Service)
  Summer camping only
TUSAYAN △

■ Grand Canyon Airport

64

To Valle, Williams, Flagstaff and Hwy 40

N

0   5 mi
0   5 km

21

to go the 1.5 miles (2.4 km) farther to Plateau Point, you won't be disappointed. This fairly level trail takes you to a nice viewpoint of the Colorado River and surrounding canyon. This is a great spot to get a good understanding of the immensity, grandeur, and beauty of the Grand Canyon. You'll see how far you've traveled, and upon looking at the river below, you'll see how far you would still need to go, which is humbling.

South Kaibab Trail

Strenuous – (6.0 mi / 9.7 km to Skeleton Point), round trip, allow 4 -5 hours, elev. Δ: 2,011 ft / 613 m, trailhead at Yaki Point off Desert View Drive

Strenuous – (12.0 mi / 19.3 km to Colorado River), round trip, allow 8 -10 hours, elev. Δ: 4,800 ft / 1,463 m,

From South Rim to Phantom Ranch: 6.9 mi / 11.1 km, to North Rim: 20.9 mi / 33.6 km

It is possible to take the South Kaibab Trail to the river and even connect over to Bright Angel, but most people do this as a multi-day trip due to the strenuous nature of the journey. Just like Bright

Angel Trail, South Kaibab is steep, offers incredible views, and is very exposed. The first destination along the trail is Ooh-Aah Point, which offers an expansive view of the canyon and is less than 2 miles (3.2 km) round trip.

By the way, Ooh-Aah Point gets its name from an uncommon, nearly prehistoric language that is hotly debated by linguists as to its exact meaning. This is a rough translation, but most agree that "Ooh-Aah" means either "Wow!" or "The-Place-of-Amazing-Selfie-with-View-of-Grand-Canyon-About-One-Mile-From-Rim." You decide which translation works best for you.

There is a restroom at Cedar Ridge, but that is the extent of the facilities on the South Kaibab Trail. Cedar Ridge is about 1.5 miles (2.4 km) from the rim. Skeleton Point offers great views of the river and the surrounding area and is the recommended turnaround for day hikers.

On the question of South Kaibab versus Bright Angel, South Kaibab's fewer amenities means it is slightly less traveled than Bright Angel. That said there are very few hikers on these trails relative to the vast number of people looking over

Panorama of the Grand Canyon

the canyon's edge at the rim. If you are looking to escape into your own personal experience of the canyon, either trail will get you there.

Hermit Trail

Strenuous – (17.8 mi / 28.6 km to Colorado River), round trip, allow 8-12 hours, elev. Δ: 4,340 ft / 1,323 m, trailhead at Hermits Rest

The Hermit Trail begins at Hermit's Rest and, like all the trails described here, is accessed via shuttle. This trail is great for many reasons if you are an experienced hiker looking for something a little more rugged. It was originally built by horse thieves during the nineteenth century and is today considered a threshold trail, which means the National Park doesn't actively maintain it. There is water to be found along the trail, but it needs to be treated. Some of the trail has rutted out in areas and, in some cases, rock slides covering the trail require one to do a little scrambling to navigate around them. The point here is, if you are an experienced hiker, the Hermit Trail offers just about everything, including an endpoint worthy of the journey. It is 8.9 miles (14 km) down to the river, but if you are able to make it, you are rewarded with Hermit Rapids, perhaps the strongest hydraulics and biggest waves of any set of rapids in the canyon. The Hermit Rapids help to motivate any hiker and do not disappoint. You hear them before you see them and in seeing them there is nothing but gushing awe and respect.

It cannot be overstated that this is a trail to be taken seriously. Plan—bring the right gear, including plenty of food and water, and start early if you do plan to take on this all-day hike. There is a primitive campground at the river's edge and most folks do this as an overnight trip.

Grandview Trail

Strenuous – (6.0 mi / 9.7 km to Horseshoe Mesa / Toilet Junction), round trip, allow 4-5 hours, elev. Δ: 2,500 ft / 762 m, trailhead at Grandview Point along Desert View Drive

Grandview is one of the quickest ways to get down into the canyon. It is very steep in some places and during the winter is dangerously icy. Crampons or some other means of traction for your footwear is required in winter. The trail offers deep views into the canyon as well as ruins of historic mining structures. Another feature of the trail is the placement of log "cribs" in some of the vertical sections of the Kaibab/Toroweap section. Many of these log supports were swept away during a landslide in the winter of 2005, but there are a few examples of these historical trail structures still around.

The Grandview Trail is not as well maintained as either Bright Angel or South Kaibab Trails. There are steep drop-offs in some areas. Use caution when hiking this trail.

River Rafting

Rafting down the Colorado is not only a popular activity, for many it is a bucket list item, something they have to do before they head on to the big national park in the sky. As a result, don't expect to show up and get on the river. Rafting is by permit only in the Grand Canyon and, depending on the activity, can take one to two years to receive a permit. The Park has made an effort to streamline the types of trips available and the permitting process for each.

That said, rafting down the Colorado through the Grand Canyon is truly a defining moment in anyone's life. It is an experience that moves beyond words, resets your definitions of awe and wonder, brings a restful peace to the soul and at times puts you in moments of unholy

terror that—on getting to the other side of—help remind you just how awesome it is to be alive. It is worth the planning and the wait.

One Day Commercial River Trips:

Half day and full day smooth water river trips are available through park concessionaire Colorado River Discovery. You can purchase tickets at any of the park's lodges. The smooth water river trips are the only trips that do not require a permit and as the trip never encounters rapids, is open to all ages from four years old and up.

While these trips are gentle and without the excitement of white water, they are a great way to see the park and are highly recommended. Bring food and water, sunscreen, a hat and, of course, your camera. On a side note about the camera, yes, it's okay to bring a camera on the trip that isn't waterproof as it is unlikely you will get wet. That said, use caution. In the summer, you won't need a towel as in the heat of the day you will dry off pretty quickly. In the spring and cooler seasons, bring layers. As you will be entering at the Glen Canyon Dam, which is inside the protection of Homeland Security, you will be checked for weapons, including pepper spray and pocket knives. These will not be allowed, so don't bring them. Transportation from the lodge to the dam is included.

3- to 18-Day Commercial River Trips

For those who are looking for white water rapids and adventure, there are hosts of river concessioners that provide full service guided trips. Each company offers its own suite of trips and many cater to the different experiences visitors are looking for. Trips can last for as little as a few days to up to 18 days.

The upside of a guided trip is that, first and foremost, you don't need to be-

A dory in Hance Rapids

come an expert in white water rafting. The domain of the rafter is a world unto itself. They have their own language, and while they are a friendly, tightly knitted group, it's an investment of time and money to enter their world and walk, err—paddle—among them. A guided trip comes with the security that you are riding down the Colorado with an expert at the helm. Plus, the thoughts of where to camp, what to eat, and even where to do your business are pretty much taken care of for you. The downside is the cost and the fact that reservations need to be made one to two years in advance.

Details on what trips are offered, in what type of raft, duration and other amenities are numerous. The best place to start is the Grand Canyon NPS page, which lists all of the river concessionaires. Go to: http://www.nps.gov/grca/planyourvisit/river-concessioners.htm

2- to 5-Day Noncommercial River Trips

Permits are available to the general public starting one year in advance and are assigned on a first come, first served basis. Two noncommercial permits are authorized each day launching from Diamond Creek. Each trip is limited to a maximum of 16 people. There is no fee for the permits and they can be obtained by filling out a permit application and mailing it to the NPS permits department. While the NPS does not charge a fee for the permit, the Hualapai Tribe does charge a fee for crossing their land.

The permit can be found by going to: http://www.nps.gov/grca/planyourvisit/upload/Diamond_Creek_Application.pdfYou can also call directly: (800) 959-9164 or (928) 638-7843.

As mentioned above, you are crossing both National Park Service land and Hualapai tribal land. Hualapai means "people of the tall trees" in reference to the Ponderosa Pine. This small commu-

nity of about 2,000 individuals primarily bases its economy on tourism. One way they do that is to charge a fee for each person (including drivers) and each vehicle traveling Diamond Creek Road, which they own. Cost is $64.20 for each person and vehicle, (example: 16 passengers, 2 drivers and 2 vehicles will cost $1284 total). Camping on the south side of the river (river left) above the high water mark will also require a permit from the Haulapai. More information can be had by calling the Haulapai directly at (928) 769-2219.

The NPS permits authorize you and your group to travel for 2 to 5 days from Diamond Creek in the Lower Gorge of the Colorado River. This 52-mile (84 km) section is spectacular and includes both smooth water and some decent rapids to shoot as well as culturally significant areas. River users are asked to treat these cultural areas with respect so that future generations can enjoy them. Camping is limited but is free on the north side (river right).

One word of note: acceptance. The river has changed since the days of Powell. You will be sharing the river with many other users, especially at the launch and take-out areas. You will find motorized upstream and downstream travel from Lake Mead and even see a helicopter or two. There will be moments that are all yours, but there will also be moments that are shared with others

12- to 25-Day Noncommercial River Trips

This type of self-guided river trip travels among the rugged section between Lees Ferry to Diamond Creek and is for those fully experienced in river rafting. The permits are made available through a weighted lottery. For more information, start here: http://www.nps.gov/grca/planyourvisit/overview-lees-ferry-diamond-ck.htm.

Mule Trips

The mule rides offered by park concessionaire Xanterra are a classic way of seeing the Grand Canyon. The day trips offered change seasonally, and new offerings open up at the whim of the concessionaire. Most rides are typically 3-hour, 4-mile (6.4 km) rides. You don't need prior experience riding a mule, and your tour will include a fair amount of interesting interpretation about the geology and human history along the trail.

Overnight tours are also offered, and this ride is on par with rafting down the Colorado River in terms of generating incredible memories. You will ride your mule to Phantom Ranch located near the river. Lunch is provided and the steak dinner at the ranch is hearty and very welcome after the day's journey. As with the day trips, the overnight trips are full of interpretive narration on nearly all aspects of the park. The overnight trip to Phantom Ranch has been a high water mark for many visitors.

The downsides to the mule trips are the expense and the fact that you need to reserve the event well in advance. There is a wait list for day-before cancellations; however, the chances of people canceling are very slim. As of June 2014, it cost $548.84 for one person or $960.01 for two to ride a mule to Phantom Ranch and spend the night there.

Mule rides from the South Rim can be reserved through:

Xanterra Parks & Resorts (303) 297-2757, (888) 297-2757

Virtual Caching

For those who have never heard of this, virtual caching is the delightful marriage of treasure hunting and technology. Specifically, a "cache" is a term that denotes a bunch of stuff stowed somewhere in the wilderness.   With virtual caching, a visitor uses his or her GPS system to find the cache. The reward is in part the journey and in part finding the cache, which— being virtual—means what you find is a cool location.

The National Park Service has done a wonderful job of offering an interesting way to explore the park.

You will need a GPS device (or smart

phone with GPS), the park map, which is located inside the park's official newspaper, The Guide, and a copy of the instruction sheet, titled "Story of Grand Canyon." The instructions can be picked up at the Grand Canyon Visitor Center, where different coordinates are listed. Input the coordinates into your GPS device and take the shuttle or walk to the various destinations. None of the virtual caching is done off trail; everything can be found on the paved rim of the park and on the trails. Along the way, the instruction sheet acts as an educational pamphlet on different aspects of the park. Virtual caching is a cool way to discover new things about the park, and if you are navigationally challenged, perhaps a way of discovering a bit about yourself as well!

You will need to keep a record of all your coordinates, which will be necessary to solve the final clue. It takes about 4–6 hours to complete this puzzle, and the tour will take you over a good deal of the park along the way. You can, in the end, receive a certificate of completion. See the visitor center for more details.

Driving Around

Like Zion NP and Bryce NP, Grand Canyon receives too many visitors to make driving around the park practical. The NPS offers a fairly robust shuttle system to get you around, and it is not only highly recommended to use the shuttle system; it is the only method year round for some roads and during peak season for others.

In general, the shuttle system is divided into two loops, the Village Route and Kaibab Rim Route. The Village Route goes to the west and stops at Mather Campground, Trailer Village, Market Plaza, Grand Canyon Visitor Center, Shrine of the Ages, Train Depot, Bright Angel Lodge and Trailhead, and Maswik Lodge. The Village Route also stops at the Hermit's Rest Transfer, which is where you pick up the Hermit's Rest shuttle during peak season.

The Kaibab Route winds to the east and stops at the Grand Canyon Visitor Center, South Kaibab Trailhead, Yaki Point, Pipe Creek Vista, Mather Point and Yavapai Geology Museum.

Grand Canyon - South Rim

Grand Canyon with clouds overhead

You can drive on Hermit's Rest Road during the winter months and, to the east, the Desert View is a wonderful drive that ultimately takes you to the East Rim of the Grand Canyon.

There is so much to do in the South Rim of the Grand Canyon

There is a tremendous number of things to do and see, more than this little all-inclusive guidebook of seven National Parks can manage to describe in detail. Here are a few places worth exploring further:

Kolb Studio

Art gallery, photo gallery, bookstore and place of historical interest run by the Grand Canyon Association. Near the Bright Angel Lodge

El Tovar Hotel

Built in 1905, this hotel is on the National Register of Historic Places. It is noted for its Arts and Crafts as well as Mission style interior and exterior and is an incredible example of early twentieth century National Park lodge architecture.

Yavapai Geology Museum

A great place to learn everything you wanted to know about the geology of the Grand Canyon. Many exhibits, three dimensional models and photographs along with the outdoor nature and geology "Trail of Time" where each meter traveled on the trail represents one million years of the geology of the Grand Canyon. If you think about it, the "Trail of Time" took about 2 billion years to make, so it is well worth seeing.

Desert View Watchtower

Located on the East Rim of the park, the four story, 70-foot-high (21m) stone building was built in 1932 by Fred Harvey Architect Mary Colter. Mary Colter designed many of the buildings in the Grand Canyon, including Hopi House, Lookout Studio, Bright Angel Lodge, the Phantom Ranch buildings and Hermit's Rest (but not El Tovar Lodge). Patterned after the Pueblo kivas and watchtowers, the watchtower has a unique touch in its design.

Desert View Watchtower

Skywalk

The Skywalk is managed by the Hualapai Tribe and is located on their tribal lands. It is a horseshoe-shaped walkway securely bolted into the canyon walls such that is juts out over the canyon itself. With the floors and sides made of glass, the structure juts out about 70 feet (21m) from the canyon rim, giving the feeling that you are suspended in air over the canyon. It is one of the most famous attractions within the western portion of the Grand Canyon. There is a separate fee for this attraction. Skywalk reservations: 1-888-868-9378 or 1-928-769-2636

Quick Facts

Official Park Website: http://www.nps.gov/grca

Visitor Center:

- General Visitor Information: (928) 638-7888
- Backcountry Information Center: (928) 638-7875

Park Accessibility:

- Okay for 2WD and RVs
- Day and Overnight Use (seasonally)

View from the North Rim

Experience Level:
- Family Friendly – Backcountry Hiker

Camping in Park:
Reservations strongly recommended at (877) 444-6777 or online at the http://www.recreation.gov/
- North Rim Campground: 90 T/RV, seasonal (closed in winter), drinking water, flush toilets, pull-thru sites, no hookups, dump station, group sites available.

Lodging in Park:
- North Rim Lodge, closed in winter. Reservations strongly recommended at (877) 386-4383.

Dining in Park:
- Multiple dining options and market at North Rim Lodge, closed in winter.

Nearest Town with Amenities:
- Jacob Lake, AZ is 44 mi / 71 km from park

Getting There:
- From St George, UT: take I-15 North to UT-59 South to AZ-389 East, turn right onto US-89A South to AZ-67 South to North Rim park entrance

What Makes the North Rim of the Grand Canyon Special

- The less crowded, more intimate side of the Grand Canyon
- For those that have done the South Rim, knowing you are about to hike new trails within one of the most scenic places on earth
- The better side to start a "rim to rim" day hike because the longer of the two sides is downhill if you come from the North Rim

Granted the North Rim is a bit harder to get to and is closed during the winter season, but the reward is far fewer people. It brings the ability to see the Grand Canyon more on your terms and pace, receiving around 500,000 visitors annually. The North Rim is higher in elevation and thus can be cooler. This side of the canyon is up to 1800 feet higher, making day trips down to the river and back longer than the South Rim.

Hiking the North Rim of the Grand Canyon

Bright Angel Point Trail

Easy – (0.5 mi / 0.8 km), round trip, allow 30 minutes, elev. Δ: 200 ft / 61m, trailhead near visitor center

Bright Angel Point is a nice walk from Grand Canyon Lodge and nearby visitor center. There are examples of marine fossils within the rocks along the way. Be sure to pick a park brochure, which shows the location of the fossils and gives a good historical backstory of the lodge and this historic trail.

Transept Trail

Easy – (3.0 mi / 4.8 km), round trip, allow 1 - 2 hours, elev. Δ: 150 ft / 46 m, trailhead near North Rim Lodge

The Transept Trail starts at the Grand Canyon Lodge and follows the rim of the canyon to the North Rim Campground. Great views along the way.

North Rim with cloud play

Ken Patrick Trail

Strenuous – (10.0 mi / 16.0 km), one way, 5 - 6 hours, elev. Δ: 600 ft / 183 m, trailhead north of visitor center at North Kaibab trailhead

The Ken Patrick Trail is named after a ranger killed in the line of duty. He is buried within the Grand Canyon, but worked at Point Reyes National Seashore and was killed by poachers in 1973.

This there and back trail is best accomplished with two cars. Starting from the North Kaibab Trailhead, the Ken Patrick Trail starts off clearly for the first 2 ½ miles but can become very difficult to find after reaching the Old Bright Angel Trail sign post. If you are an experienced hiker and this sounds appealing, simply keep north and don't go too far from the rim. Once you pick up the Cape Royal Road, the trail becomes easier to find and maintains close to the rim all the way to Point Imperial.

Lower Ribbon Falls

Uncle Jim Trail

Moderate – (5.0 mi / 8.0 km), round trip, allow 2 - 3 hours, elev. Δ: 100 ft / 30 m, trailhead north of visitor center at North Kaibab trailhead

This trail starts from the same parking lot as the North Kaibab Trailhead and meanders through the Kaibab Plateau forest to Uncle Jim's Point, which overlooks Bright Angel, Roaring Springs and an overall spectacular view of the canyon.

Bridle Trail

Easy – (1.2 mi / 2.0 km), one way, allow 1 hour, elev. Δ: 161 ft / 49m, trailheads at viewpoint at North Rim Lodge and at North Kaibab Trailhead

A gentle trail that parallels the road from the Grand Canyon Lodge to the North Kaibab Trailhead. The Bridle Trail is a great after dinner hike to take in the peace of the canyon.

North Kaibab Trail

Strenuous – (14.0 mi / 22.5 km), one way, allow 6-10 hours, elev. Δ: 5,780 ft / 1,762 m, trailhead north of visitor center at North Kaibab trailhead

Note that while the total distance to the river is shown, it does not include the distance back. This is because the total distance to the Colorado River and back is 28 miles and is definitely not recommended as a day hike. Folks do use the North Kaibab Trail as the starting point for a rim-to-rim hike, primarily because the trip for the longer leg of the two sides is downhill if you start on from the North Rim.

The North Kaibab Trail is special because it is starts at a higher elevation than either South Kaibab or Bright Angel trails. The 1,000-foot increase in elevation is such that a hike down the North Kaibab Trail to the Colorado River means you will pass through every ecosystem found between Canada and Mexico. It is the least visited of the maintained trails and is also the most strenuous. It is definitely a serious day hike at 28 miles (45 km) round trip and is typically done as a backpacking trip. There are a few restroom facilities and seasonal water available, though the water will need to be treated.

The trail heads steeply down at first until it flattens out a bit as you enter into the base of Bright Angel Canyon. At 5.0 miles (8.0 km), you encounter Roaring Springs, which is a short side trip that is easily visible from the trail. Here you can see water coming directly out of the cliff, typically with a nice flow, creating a little island of moss and ferns within the desert. Roaring Springs flows into Bright Angel Creek as you continue down the trail. This is an important water source, delivering the drinking water for every visitor within Grand Canyon NP. If you make it to the Colorado River, you can see the pipe going over the river on the underside of Bright Angel Trail's Silver Bridge.

Just a little farther down at 5.4 miles (8.7 km) is a structure known as the Pumphouse Residence, or Aiken Residence. From 1973 to 2006, Bruce Aiken was an artist, NP employee, and pump mas-

ter, overseeing the water supply for the park. He and his wife Mary raised three children at the canyon bottom and lucky hikers were greeted with lemonade from the children from time to time. Aiken's work reflects a fine-tuned harmony with the area of the Grand Canyon. Working mainly in oil, the light, balance, and overall portrayal of rock and water are testimonies to living within the Grand Canyon, raising a family and experiencing nearly each day of one's life for 33 years inside its walls.

Another treasure on the North Kaibab is Ribbon Falls at 8.5 miles (13.7 km). It is a little grotto in the desert cascading gently on the west side of Bright Angel Creek. It is a great place to get out of the heat of the day, which can be intense in the summer. Between the Cottonwood Campground and Bright Angel Campground, you enter the Inner Gorge, which is a narrow canyon of the 2 billion-year-old Vishnu Schist. If you make it this far, you are now walking among rock roughly half as old as the earth itself. You can connect to either the South Kaibab or Bright Angel Trail over the two bridges that cross the Colorado at the canyon bottom.

South of Point Imperial

At this point you may be thinking North Kaibab is a gem of a trail, (which it is), and thus wondering if you could do a rim-to-rim adventure. The good news is you can. Trans Canyon Shuttle offers two rim-to-rim shuttles daily (go to http://www.trans-canyonshuttle.com for more info). The not-so-good news is getting reservations at one of the primitive campgrounds is a challenge. In addition, the shuttles depart early morning and early afternoon, so factor in an overnight stay at the opposing rim or hoofing it out to make the shuttle on the last day.

Widforss Trail

Strenuous – (10.0 mi / 16.0 km), round trip allow 4 – 5 hours, elev. Δ: 400 ft / 122 m, trailhead north of visitor center west of North Kaibab trailhead

The Widforss Trail may just be the longest interpretative trail in the entire Grand Circle. Be sure to pick up a brochure at the trailhead. The trail hugs the canyon rim for the first half of the hike and then heads into a forested area to end at Widforss Point. The expansiveness of the Grand Canyon from this vista is impressive and it was a favorite of Gunnar Widforss, an early twentieth century landscape artist.

Arizona Trail

Strenuous – (12.6 mi / 20.3 km), one way, allow 5 - 6 hours, trailheads at North Kaibab trailhead and Kaibab National Forest boundary

The Arizona Trail is an 800-mile adventure that starts in Mexico and heads northward until it ends in Utah. A part of the trail leverages the existing north and south rim to rim trails of Grand Canyon NP. From the North Kaibab Trail, it continues through the park for another 10 miles before hitting the park's boundary. This portion roughly follows Highway 67, traveling through forest canopy and the Harvey Meadow.

Point Imperial Trail

Easy – (4.0 mi / 6.4 km), round trip, allow 1.5 - 2 hours, elev. Δ: negligible, trailhead at end of Point Imperial Road

This is an easy hike through an area recovering from a wildfire in 2000 and is great way to take in the tenacity of nature recovering from devastation. On the way, one will see young Aspens and innocent wildflowers starting anew from the aftermath of the fire. This is a great hike for a sunrise at Point Imperial.

Roosevelt Point Trail

Easy – (0.2 mi / 0.3 km), round trip, allow 30 minutes, elev. Δ: negligible, trailhead at Cape Royal Road

More of a pleasant walk than a hike, this little ditty leads to a nice bench with great views of the canyon.

Cape Final Trail

Easy – (4.0 mi / 6.4 km), round trip, allow 1.5 - 2 hours, elev. Δ: 150 ft / 46 m, trailhead at Cape Royal Road

An easy trail that ends at one of the higher elevation views of the Grand Canyon at Cape Final. As this trail is not often used, it provides good promise if you are looking for a secluded and peaceful hike. Cape Final is at 7,850 feet. Be careful if you decide to go onto the ledge's edge, it's a long way down.

Cliff Springs Trail

Easy – (1.0 mi / 1.6 km), round trip, allow 45 – 60 minutes, elev. Δ: 150 ft / 46 m, trailhead at end of Cape Royal Road

A refreshing hike through a wooded ravine to a rocky overhang containing a seeping spring. The water is not suitable for drinking directly as tempting as it may seem. The spring holds an ecosystem for ferns and moss and can provide some nice shade from the day's sun. Look for the remains of a granary from the original inhabitants of the area early into the hike.

Cape Royal Trail

Easy – (0.6 mi / 1.0 km), round trip, allow 30 minutes, elev. Δ: 40 ft / 12 m, trailhead at end of Cape Royal Road

An easy, flat walk that allows views of Angels Window arch, the Colorado River, and if you look through the arch at the right angle, you can see both at the same time! Great photo opportunity and easy to access. There are interpretative markers along the way.

Ewe in the canyon

Grand Canyon's Three Sets of Rocks

Layered Paleozoic Rocks	Grand Canyon Supergroup Rocks	Vishnu Basement Rocks
1. Kaibab Formation (Fm)	12. Sixtymile Formation	16. Schists
2. Toroweap Formation	13. Chuar Group	17. Granites
3. Coconino Sandstone	14. Nankoweap Fm	18. Elves Chasm Gneiss
4. Hermit Formation	15. Unkar Group	
5. Supai Group		
6. Surprise Canyon Fm		
7. Redwall Limestone		
8. Temple Butte Fm		
9. Muav Limestone		
10. Bright Angel Shale		
11. Tapeats Sandstone		

Layered Paleozoic Rocks

The Great Unconformity

Tonto Group

Grand Canyon Supergroup Rocks

Vishnu Basement Rocks

	Layer age in millions of years	Layer thickness in feet
1	270	350'
2	273	250'
3	275	300'
4	280	300'
5	285–315	1,000'
6	320	0–75'
7	340	500'
8	385	0–50'
9	505	450'
10	515	350'
11	525	0–200'
12	<740	200'
13	740–770	5,200'
14	900	370'
15	1,100–1,200	6,800'
	1,680–1,840	Unknown

Paleozoic — Permian, Pennsylvanian, Mississippian, Cambrian

Precambrian — Proterozoic

The geology of the Grand Canyon

Quick Facts

Official Park Website: http://www.havasupai-nsn.gov/tourism.html

Visitor Center:

- Contact Havasupai Tourism at: P.O. Box 160 Supai, AZ, 86435, Phone: (928) 448-2121 or (928) 448-2141, (928) 448-2174, or (928) 448-2180

Park Accessibility:

- Okay for 2WD, RVs not recommended
- Primarily Overnight Use

Experience Level:

- Casual Hiker, some exposure

Camping in Park:

- Havasu Falls Campground: Reservations required, call Havasupai Tourism numbers listed above, (keep trying if no answer), 250T, drinking water, restrooms, no campfires, day ranger on duty in season

Lodging in Park:

- Havasupai Lodge, located on the trail 8 miles from trailhead in the town of Supai. Reservations required: (928) 448-2111 or (928) 448-2201.

Dining in Park:

- Supai Café, near Havasupai Lodge

Nearest Town with Amenities:

- Besides Supai, which is along the trail, Seligman, Arizona, 91 mi / 146 km from trailhead

Getting There:

- From Flagstaff: take US I-40 west to Historic Route 66 west at Seligman and turn right onto Indian Road 18 for 65 miles to trailhead at Hualapai Hilltop.

Havasu Falls

What Makes Havasu and Mooney Falls Special

- Soft turquoise waters leading to healthy flowing 100 foot and 210 foot waterfalls in a peaceful canyon setting

- Ability to swim, camp and chill in this amazing area

- Getting a postcard to your family and friends partially via mules!

Within the entirety of the Grand Circle, Havasu and Mooney Falls are arguably the pinnacle of destinations. It is the soul of the Southwest, willing to accept all those that travel to it and yet the area continues to retain a serene simplicity and purity. If ever there should be an item at the top of your bucket list of places to go within the Grand Circle, this is that place.

Hiking Havasu and Mooney Falls

Havasu and Mooney Falls
Strenuous – (24.0 mi / 38.6 km), round trip, 2-day backpacking trip

First things first, get reservations and pay the fees. One will need to pay a $35 entrance fee plus an environment fee of $5, (each fee is per person). Camping is an additional $17 per person per night. Your entire party will be billed double this amount if you come without reservations, assuming there is availability. There is also a 10% tax on all purchases and a $5 Environmental Care Fee. Total for one night camping is $62.71 per person and $81.41 for two nights. The season opens on February 1st each year and 300 permits are given each day.

Now that you know the particulars on permits and camping, the next thing you will need is luck. The word is out on Havasu Falls and it is very difficult

to get a permit. The best approach is to mark your calendar for February 1st and then start dialing every number listed repeatedly until you get through. It is not unheard of for multiple folks trying from different phones to take several days to finally get through. As rough as this sounds, many do get through on the first day. The only good news here is this is the same process whether you are hiking alone or are booking for a professional tour company.

If you do have a group helping you to get the permits, have a plan A, B and C for dates and make sure you have a communication system for when you finally do get through. The season usually books out within weeks, but there is always hope that there will be a cancellation if you don't want to wait until next February to get in line.

Located within the Havasupai Reservation, the trip does get a lot of visitors during peak season. Start by finding a parking spot near the trailhead, which is situated about 1,000 feet off the canyon bottom. Right from the trailhead, you will see you are in a special place. The views down and around are amazing.

The hike heads steeply down to the valley floor via a series of switchbacks. There are plenty of mules along this trail and one needs to be especially diligent on this part. If you see mules coming, stick to the canyon wall side and not the cliff side. The mules often travel at a decent clip giving the backpacker little time to react. Hugging a wall in these instances tends to fair better than clinging to the edge of a cliff. This is especially true in a narrow section later on. The mules have the right of way on this trail.

Most of the hike travels along the wash, with great views of towering orange-red walls on either side. At about mile 7 into the journey, the trail narrows. Be especially aware of mules here. The hiking here is shadier and thus cooler unless you are doing this stretch at high noon.

The slot canyon opens into Havasu Creek and shortly thereafter to the peaceful village of the Supai People. The town holds 208 residents, give or take and is officially the most remote inhabited community in the lower 48. Besides flying in by helicopter (or as the locals call it, "cheating"), the only way in is via the Havasupai Trail. It is the last community in the United States to have its mail delivered by mule.

Havasu Falls are 2 miles from the town of Supai. These two miles deeper into the canyon are utterly sublime. The water is a light blue green turquoise. The distinctive hue comes from the strong reflection of the underlying limestone creek bed. It's not just the falls that are this color, the entire creek from Supai on are a gem like color of paradise found.

Havasu Falls and Mooney Falls further on are tall, roaring sheets of water and simply beyond words. Both are amazing and both must be seen. Getting to Mooney Falls requires a Class 3 descent to the bottom, some 210 feet below. Aids include a tunnel, ladders, handholds, railings, and footholds. This section is quite steep and exposed in areas and not for those that have a fear of heights. In addition, these areas become bottlenecks and one may have to stand in place as they wait for folks to come up or down. Finally, it should

not be attempted when the conditions are wet or otherwise unfavorable, as sections can get very slippery. There is a campground in between the Havasu and Mooney Falls.

If you do want to send a post card home from Supai, note that the post office is closed on weekends. If you do go on a weekend, some locals are willing to mail it for you for a nominal fee. The novelty of mailing anything from the community is knowing that the first leg (pun intended) is by mule, the last community in the United States to move mail in this manner.

The sublime waters of Havasu Falls

37

Canyon de Chelly National Monument

Quick Facts

Official Park Website: http://www.nps.gov/cach

Visitor Center:

- (928) 674-5500

Park Accessibility:

- Okay for 2WD and RVs
- Day and Overnight Use

Experience Level:
- Family Friendly – Casual Hiker

Camping in Park:
- Cottonwood Campground: 93 T/RV, flush toilets, drinking water, dump station, no hookups, some pull thru sites, first come-first served

Lodging and Dining in Park:
- None

Nearest Town with Amenities:
- Chinle, AZ is 1 mi / 1.6 km from park

Getting There:
- From Flagstaff, AZ, take I-40 East to AZ-87 North to Indian Route 15. Turn left on AZ-77 to Indian Route 15 to AZ-191 North to Indian Route 7 for 183 mi / 294 km to park

Looking down into Canyon de Chelly

What Makes Canyon de Chelly National Monument Special

- Arguably the oldest continuously inhabited location in the United States

In writing about nearly 80 parks, all of them remarkable, there are a few that are truly unique. Canyon de Chelly is one of these places. The land was established by the National Park Service in 1931, but is not federally owned. Chelly is a Spanish interpretation of the Navajo word Tséyi' which means "inside the rock". This series of finger canyons have been home to a history of people for over 5,000 years. Today, 40 Navajo families live and farm the land. In many respects, the ways of the past are the way of the present here. To peer over the edge is to catch a glimpse of the ancient past. To take a guided tour is to bring this past into the present.

Canyon de Chelly is entirely operated by the Navajo Nation and is the only park to be operated in this manner. As it is also home to 40 families and as such, there are restrictions in visiting the park. In visiting, the most common approach is to take one of the two scenic drives and gaze over one of the ten overlooks. That said, private tours offer a more immersive experience. There are many tour operators and many options, including overnight camping, horseback riding, and backcountry backpacking with guide and jeep tours. To ensure you are able to get the tour you want, it is highly advisable to make reservations. There is no entrance fee to the park.

White House Trail is the only established hike in the park. All backcountry travel must have a backcountry permit and be accompanied by an authorized guide. Off road vehicles are prohibited in the park. All this is to protect the privacy of the residents.

On the subject of privacy, don't be frustrated if you are asked not to photograph the residents and their homes, etc. This is living cultural preserve. To allow a window into the lives of these people is rare enough, enjoy the tour for what it is. If that doesn't work, imagine what your life would be like if you had a parade of people coming to your house in jeeps and horses to watch your activities every single day. It makes sense when you turn this experience around. This is a very unique experience from that context. If you are a photographer, it is very frustrating as there are some amazing shots. That said, be respectful of their wishes.

The 800 foot spire named Spider Rock

Canyon de Chelly

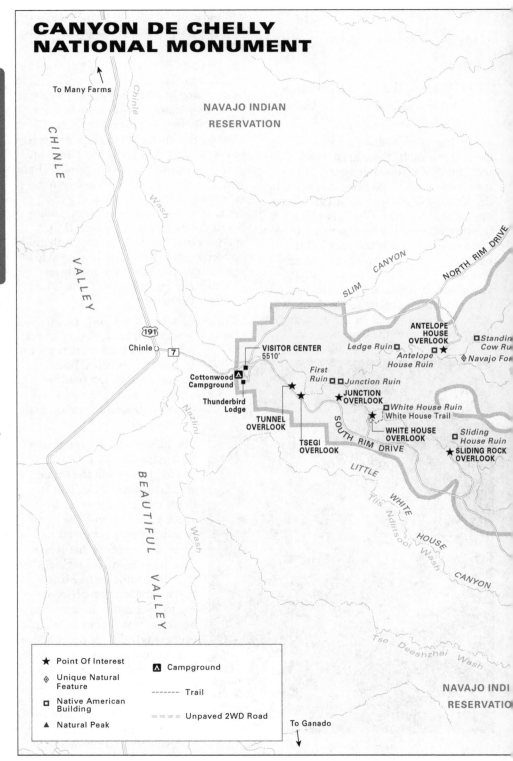

CANYON DE CHELLY
NATIONAL MONUMENT

NORTHERN ARIZONA

Canyon de Chelly

To Many Farms

NAVAJO INDIAN
RESERVATION

Chinle
CHINLE

Wash

VALLEY

191

7

Chinle

VISITOR CENTER
5510'

Cottonwood
Campground

Thunderbird
Lodge

TUNNEL
OVERLOOK

TSEGI
OVERLOOK

First
Ruin

Junction Ruin

JUNCTION
OVERLOOK

Ledge Ruin

Antelope
House Ruin

ANTELOPE
HOUSE
OVERLOOK

Standin
Cow Ru

Navajo For

White House Ruin
White House Trail

WHITE HOUSE
OVERLOOK

Sliding
House Ruin

SLIDING ROCK
OVERLOOK

SLIM   CANYON

NORTH RIM DRIVE

SOUTH RIM DRIVE

LITTLE

WHITE

HOUSE

CANYON

This Ndittsooi   Wash

Nazlini

BEAUTIFUL

VALLEY

Wash

Tse Deeshzhai Wash

NAVAJO INDI
RESERVATIO

Legend

★ Point Of Interest

◇ Unique Natural Feature

◻ Native American Building

▲ Natural Peak

🅰 Campground

------- Trail

==== Unpaved 2WD Road

To Ganado

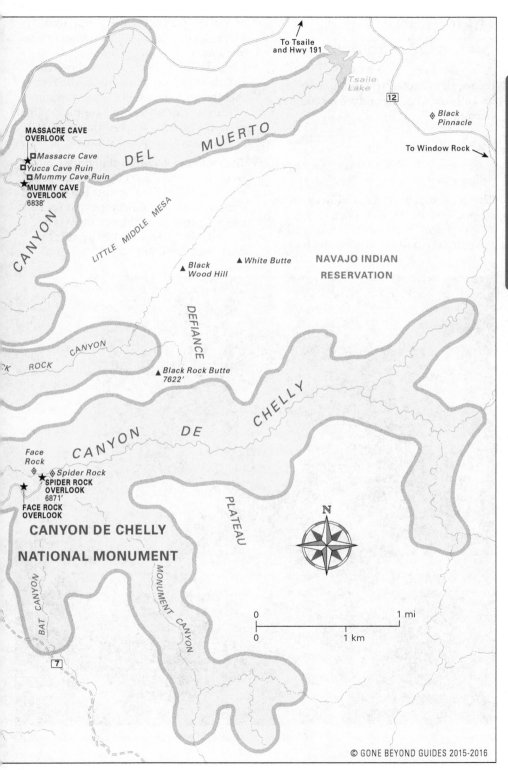

To Tsaile
and Hwy 191

Tsaile
Lake

12

◇ Black
Pinnacle

To Window Rock →

DEL MUERTO

MASSACRE CAVE
OVERLOOK
□ Massacre Cave
□ Yucca Cave Ruin
□ Mummy Cave Ruin
MUMMY CAVE
OVERLOOK
6838'

CANYON

LITTLE MIDDLE MESA

▲ Black
Wood Hill

▲ White Butte

NAVAJO INDIAN
RESERVATION

DEFIANCE

CANYON

CK ROCK

▲ Black Rock Butte
7622'

CANYON DE CHELLY

Face
Rock

◇ Spider Rock
SPIDER ROCK
OVERLOOK
6871'
FACE ROCK
OVERLOOK

CANYON DE CHELLY

NATIONAL MONUMENT

PLATEAU

N

BAT CANYON

MONUMENT CANYON

7

0 _____ 1 mi
0 _____ 1 km

© GONE BEYOND GUIDES 2015-2016

Hiking Canyon de Chelly National Monument

As stated above, except for the trail listed below, all backcountry hiking requires an authorized guide and a backcountry permit.

White House Trail

Strenuous – (2.5 mi / 4.0 km), round trip, allow 2 hours

This there and back trail follows a series of switchbacks 600 feet down to the canyon floor. There is one tunnel and a bridge at the bottom to cross, with the end of the trail being the magnificent White House Ruins. What makes this set of ruins so stunning is the sheer water stained cliff wall that towers above the cliff dwelling and floor ruins. The ruins themselves are well preserved and some of the exterior walls still have the original plaster. There is a fence at the perimeter of the ruins to help protect them.

The fresh green colors of mature Cottonwood trees and cacti create an uplifting and peaceful setting against the reds and dark stains of the sandstone that frame them. Bottom line, though there is but one hike in Canyon de Chelly, this one does not disappoint.

Come for the ruins, stay for the water stained cliff murals

Four Corners Monument

Come on, you know you want to stand here!

Official Park Website: http://www.navajonationparks.org/htm/fourcorners.htm

Visitor Center:

None in park, contact: Four Corners Monument Park Office, P.O. Box 861, Teec Nos Pos, AZ 86514, Phone: (928) 206-2540

Park Accessibility:

- Okay for 2WD and RVs
- Day Use Only

Experience Level:

- Family Friendly

Camping in Park:

- None

Lodging and Dining in Park:

- Seasonally open snack stand

Nearest Town with Amenities:

- Cortez, CO is 41 mi / 66 km from park

Getting There:

- From Moab, UT: Take US-191 South to UT-262 East to US-160 West to NM-597. Total distance is 145 mi / 233 km to park

- From Cortez, CO: Take US-160 West/US-491 South to NM-597. Total distance is 41 mi / 66 km to park

- From Gallup, NM: Take US-491 North to US-64 West to US-160 East to NM-597. Total distance is 124 mi / 200 km to park

- From Flagstaff, AZ: Take US-89 North to US-160 East to NM-597. Total distance is 227 mi / 365 km to park

What Makes Four Corners Special

- The only place you can play a game of four state Twister!

- Being in the center of the Grand Circle! (Well, not really, in fact, not at all, but go with it)

- Trying to find that unique Four Corner keepsake from stall after stall of folks selling the same thing

If there is an anchor to the Grand Circle, it is the Four Corners. It isn't the center of the circle, which is a shame from a perfect symmetry standpoint, but it is the symbolic center. In this one spot are captured four of the five states that make up the Grand Circle, namely Utah, Colorado, New Mexico and Arizona. Part of the overall allure of the Grand Circle is "Where does that highway lead to?" The answer to this question here is it leads to a magical place where one can stand in four states at the same time.

The park is run by the Navajo Nation and consists of a large marker indicating the location of the four corners, suitable for family photos and what not. Surrounding this marker on all four sides is a row of vendor stalls. Each stall is run by a local merchant selling the usual collection of jewelry, carved stones, arrows, feathered earrings, dream catchers, and spirit animals. While it would seem that the initial intent was to have New Mexico crafts on one side and Colorado goods on the other, at this point all of the merchants are for the most part selling Navajo crafts. Sometimes there is some Zuni and Hopi representation as well.

The flea market vibe aside, the merchants are all great folk and perhaps the best part of the monument. They come each day; they all know each other and are worth getting to know a little. Most are willing to share a little of their life with you if you invite them into a conversation. There is Navajo bread and other goodies for sale and basic bathroom facilities, however true to being the center of nowhere, there is no electricity, phone service, or running water here.

Time isn't used, it's experienced ~ Hopi proverb

Monument Valley Navajo Tribal Park

Monument Valley

Quick Facts

Official Park Website:

- http://www.navajonationparks.org/htm/monumentvalley.htm

Visitor Center:

- Contact Monument Valley Navajo Tribal Park at: PO Box 360289, Monument Valley, Utah 84536, Phone: (435) 727-5874, (435) 727-5879, (435) 727-5870

Park Accessibility:

- Okay for 2WD and RVs
- Day and Overnight Use

Experience Level:

- Family Friendly – Casual Hiker

Camping in Park:

- The View Campground: 90 T/RV, no water, no hookups, restrooms, shower, reservations: (435) 727-5802

Lodging in Park:

- The View Lodge, reservations: (435) 727-5555

Dining in Park:

- The View Restaurant

Nearest Town with Amenities:

- Oljato-Monument Valley, UT – adjacent to park

Getting There:

- From Flagstaff, AZ: take US-89 North, US-160 East and US-163 North to Monument Valley Rd in Olja-to-Monument Valley
- From Moab, UT: take US-191 South to Oljato-Monument Valley
- From Cortez, CO: take UT-162 West and US-163 South to Oljato-Monument Valley

What Makes Monument Valley Special

If you have ever watched the classic movie Stagecoach, one of the top westerns of all time, you will notice one thing. No matter where that stagecoach is heading, they are always passing through Monument Valley. The movie was John Wayne's breakthrough role and arguably put Monument Valley on the map for America. From 1939, when the movie was made, to present, Monument Valley has become THE definitive icon of the Southwest.

The problem with any icon is it tends to become larger than reality itself and we are let down when we finally meet it. The good news with Monument Valley is it will not disappoint in this way. It is as sweeping and epic in real life as it is on film. It is a place where time seems to slow down and watching the late afternoon sun slowly slip off the monuments is a memory that will stick with you for life.

Monument Valley is easy to drive through, but to capture the impact of this area it is recommended to stay overnight. The campground set up by the Navajo Tribal Park offers some of the best viewing real estate in the park. The campsites sit on a sandy hill overlooking many of the most recognized monuments, including the Mittens. The View Hotel nearby is also recommended. The famed Goulding's Lodge is another favorite place to stay and was home for the cast and crew of the movie Stagecoach and other westerns.

In terms of hiking, the land is privately owned and actively used by the Navajo. The Wildcat Trail is the only hike that a visitor can take without a Navajo escort in the park. The trail is a 3.2-mile loop that goes completely around the West Mitten. The trail starts at The View Hotel and once down in the valley is fairly flat. Allow 2 – 3 hours to complete this hike and bring water.

There is also a 17-mile scenic drive on a maintained unpaved road, which is highly recommended. The drive is suitable for most cars and is open for day use only. If you are looking for more immersion, you can take a guided tour. These tours are really the only way to see some of the places within the park. All of the official tour operators are listed here: www.navajonationparks.org/htm/monument-valleytours.htm

West Mitten Butte, Monument Valley

MONUMENT VALLEY NAVAJO TRIBAL PARK

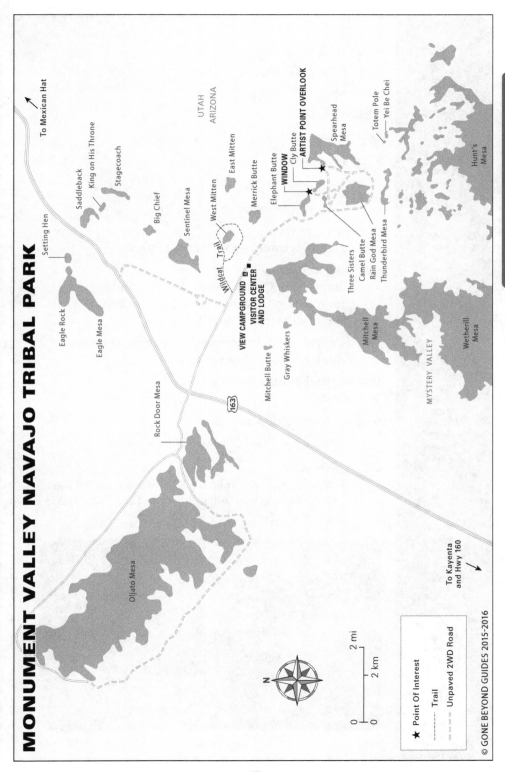

To Mexican Hat

Setting Hen

Saddleback
King on His Throne
Stagecoach

Eagle Rock

Big Chief

Eagle Mesa

Sentinel Mesa

West Mitten

East Mitten

Merrick Butte

Elephant Butte

Cly Butte

WINDOW

ARTIST POINT OVERLOOK

Spearhead Mesa

Totem Pole

Yei Be Chei

Hunt's Mesa

UTAH
ARIZONA

Wildcat Trail

VIEW CAMPGROUND
VISITOR CENTER
AND LODGE

Three Sisters
Camel Butte
Rain God Mesa
Thunderbird Mesa

Rock Door Mesa

163

Mitchell Butte

Gray Whiskers

Mitchell Mesa

MYSTERY VALLEY

Wetherill Mesa

Oljato Mesa

To Kayenta
and Hwy 160

N

★ Point Of Interest

------ Trail

= = = Unpaved 2WD Road

0   2 mi
0   2 km

© GONE BEYOND GUIDES 2015-2016

NORTHERN ARIZONA

Monument Valley

Navajo National Monument

Quick Facts

Official Park Website:

- http://www.nps.gov/nava

Visitor Center:

- (928) 672-2700, park is open seasonally

Park Accessibility:

- Okay for 2WD and RVs
- Day and Overnight Use

Experience Level:
- Family Friendly – Experienced Hiker

Camping in Park:
- Sunset View Campground: 33 T/RV, drinking water, restrooms, no hookups, some pull thru sites, no fee site, first come-first served
- Canyon View Campground: 14T, compost toilets, no water, first come-first served

Lodging and Dining in Park:
- None

Nearest Town with Amenities:

- Tsegi, AZ is 18 mi / 11 km from the park

Getting There:
- From Flagstaff, AZ: take US-89 North to US-160 East to AZ-564 North to Indian Route 221 for 140 mi / 225 km to the park

Large alcove protecting Betatakin ruins

NAVAJO NATIONAL MONUMENT

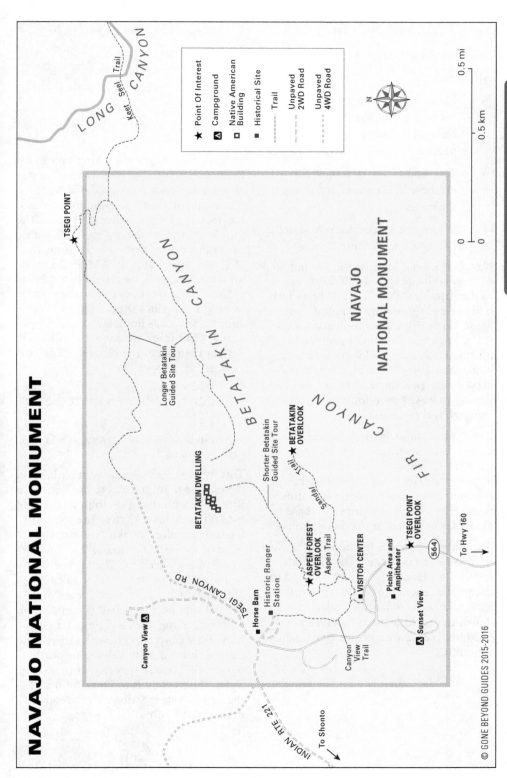

Legend:
- ★ Point Of Interest
- ◩ Campground
- ◻ Native American Building
- ◼ Historical Site
- ------- Trail
- ------- Unpaved 2WD Road
- ------- Unpaved 4WD Road

0 — 0.5 km
0 — 0.5 mi

N

LONG CANYON
Keet Seel Trail
TSEGI POINT ★

BETATAKIN CANYON
Longer Betatakin Guided Site Tour
Shorter Betatakin Guided Site Tour
BETATAKIN DWELLING ◻
★ BETATAKIN OVERLOOK

FIR CANYON

NAVAJO NATIONAL MONUMENT

Sandal Trail

★ ASPEN FOREST OVERLOOK
Aspen Trail

◼ Historic Ranger Station
◼ Horse Barn

TSEGI CANYON RD

Canyon View ◩

◼ VISITOR CENTER
Picnic Area and Ampitheater
★ TSEGI POINT OVERLOOK
564
To Hwy 160

Canyon View Trail

◩ Sunset View

INDIAN RTE 221
To Shonto

49

What Makes Navajo National Monument Special

- Knowing that you are arguably at the best preserved cliff dwelling ruins of the Ancestral Pueblo people
- That first view of the massive rock rainbow-like alcoves that protect the ruins
- Taking the guided tours and not having to pay a dime

Navajo National Monument is comprised of three well-preserved cliff dwellings of the Ancestral Puebloans. While there had been a fair amount of plunder at Mesa Verde prior to its protection, this set of ruins was put under protection in a better state. Keet Seel is considered by some archaeologists to be the best-preserved cliff dwelling in the Southwest and Betatakin wasn't even found until after the park was created.

Besides the cliff dwellings, the redrock canyon setting and even the alcoves themselves are worth the visit. These alcoves are giant grand arcs of rock, with the centerpiece within being the ruins themselves. The first glimpse of these alcoves is breathtaking in their own right.

There are free ranger led tours of the Keet Seel and Betatakin sites. The third site, Inscription House, is currently closed to the public. There is also a short 1-mile walk to an overlook of Betatakin ruins. Amenities include two small campgrounds, picnic area, visitor center, and museum.

Hiking Navajo National Monument

Shorter Betatakin Guided Site Tour

Strenuous – (3.0 mi / 4.8 km), round trip, allow 3 – 4 hours

This is a free ranger led hiking tour to the Betatakin Ruins. The tour follows Sandal and Aspen Trails down to the bottom of the canyon. With an elevation loss of 700 feet, the hike is rather strenuous. The tour is offered seasonally, so check with the visitor center first on exact time. In 2015, the tour was at 10 AM. Folks meet for a briefing with the ranger behind the visitor center and then follow the ranger as he/she describes the people and their culture, as well as flora, fauna and geography. Visitors are welcome to walk back at their own pace. The ranger will be last person out.

Longer Betatakin Guided Site Tour

Strenuous – (5.0 mi / 8.0 km), round trip, allow 3 – 5hours

This free tour takes a different path, using the old Tsegi Point Road to the Betatakin Ruins. As with the other tour, it is ranger led and quite informative. The tour is offered seasonally. To take this tour, start in front of the visitor center at 8:15 AM for a preliminary briefing. Then, the group will need to take their vehicle to end of the navigable portion of Tsegi Point Road. From here, the road becomes trail, following along a wide peninsular portion of the canyon's rim, with alcoves and canyon floor on both sides. This portion of the hike is quite spectacular in its own right. The road ends at Tsegi Point and then climbs steeply down to the canyon floor and the ruins.

Keet Seel

Strenuous – (17.0 mi / 27.4 km), round trip, full day or overnight backpacking trip

It is possible to visit the ruins of Keet Seel. This is considered by some to be the best-preserved cliff dwelling in the Southwest. The ruins are laden with artifacts, both in volume and variety. These include pieces of jewelry, arrowheads, and corncobs. Many of the rooms have the original ceiling beams and exterior plaster still intact. There is a ranger on site who will lead you around once you arrive. For visitors that feel 17 miles is too long for a day hike, there is a primitive campground nearby.

The park limits the number of visitors to Keet Seel to 20 per day. Advanced reservation and a backcountry permit are required. Before receiving a permit, one must listen to orientation, which is held daily at 8:15 AM and 3:00 PM. Keep the permit with you at all times as you hike. Fortunately, it is not difficult to obtain a permit due to the monument's location and the trail's distance.

The route starts in a similar manner as the "Longer Betatakin Guided Site Tour". A permitted visitor takes Tsegi Road to Tsegi Trail down to the canyon floor. From there, look for signs indicating the side canyon for Keet Seel. This primitive trail heads up canyon, crossing the stream multiple times and passes a 100-foot, awe-inspiring waterfall.

Keet Seel is not open in the winter and early spring. In addition, during the summer monsoon season, the park may cancel reservations due to potential flash flooding in the park.

Sandal Trail

Easy – (1.0 mi / 1.6 km), round trip, allow 30 minutes

A paved and accessible trail that leads to an overlook of Betatakin cliff dwelling and surrounding canyon.

Aspen Trail

Moderate – (0.8 mi / 1.3 km), round trip, allow 30 minutes

A spur trail off Sandal Trail that heads lower into the canyon and an old growth grove of Aspen trees.

Canyon View Trail

Easy – (0.4 mi / 0.6 km), round trip, allow 30 minutes

This is an easy walk along the rim, leading from the visitor center and campground to the historic ranger station

Betatakin ruins

Antelope Canyon

Antelope Canyon

Quick Facts

Official Park Website:

- http://navajonationparks.org/htm/antelopecanyon.htm

Visitor Center:

- Contact Lake Powell Navajo Tribal Park Office, P.O. Box 4803, Page, AZ 86040, Phone: (928) 698-2808

Park Accessibility:

- Okay for 2WD and RVs
- Day Use Only

Experience Level:

- Family Friendly – Casual Hiker

Camping in Park:

- None

Lodging and Dining in Park:

- None

Nearest Town with Amenities:

- Page, AZ – most tours begin in Page.

Getting There:

- From Flagstaff, AZ: take US 89 North to Page, AZ
- From Cortez, CO: take US 160 West to AZ 98 West to Page, AZ
- From Kanab, UT: take US 89 South/East to Page, AZ

It really is this beautiful

What Makes Antelope Slot Canyon Special

- One of the most stunning and easily accessible slot canyons in the Grand Circle

- Knowing you are taking photographs that are typically seen in art studios

- Special enough to be one of the only attractions in this book that is not a national or state park!

Antelope Slot Canyon is, on the surface, one of the most incredible and beautiful sights one can see on a trip to the Grand Circle. If you are fortunate enough to book a high noon tour, when the beams of sunlight shine down onto the sands of the canyon floor, the experience is transcendent. Antelope Slot Canyon is a delight to the eye, with narrow water carved walls of multihued sandstone, towering high above into an infinitely blue sky. The contrast of light combined with shadow play brings out an experience that is certainly worth the trip and is often a highlight of any vacation to the southwest.

This is despite the downsides of the slot canyon. Once an unknown secret canyon revealed occasionally by photographers in desert themed coffee table books, the canyon is now wide open to the public via tours given by the Navajo. Herein lies the flipside of this heavenly experience. The narrow canyon is packed with tourists. Look up and the views are stunningly divine. Look at eye level and it's like being at Times Square on New Year's Eve. Adding to this is the equally dichotomous Navajo sentiment towards the site; a people torn between guarding a place held sacred and exploiting this "outdoor church" for money.

This is not in any way meant to discourage one from going; the trip is definitely

High noon sunbeams

worth it. In addition, what is described above is reflective of peak season traffic. If you go in the off-season, the experience can be more intimate.

There are almost as many tour groups going to the slot canyon as there are layers of sandstone in the canyon. Some are recommended below. There are also two major sections to visit, the upper and lower slot canyons. Most tours go to the upper canyon due to access and popularity. The lower canyon can be more intimate though it too is getting more crowded with each passing year.

The best time to go for photography and effect is during the high noon tour. There is direct sunlight into the canyon at this time and the guides will toss sand high up which brings out filtered streams of light, which make for incredible photos. (Wait until the dust settles a bit for the best photos). The canyon is so narrow the sun penetrates like beams from heaven, bright and with crisply defined lines. Keep in mind that this is peak time, so expect to take your shot quickly before being herded along. If you don't like crowds, your best bet is to take one of the early morning or evening tours.

Logistically, each tour group gets into the back of an open-air truck that has been retrofitted to carry people. The driver heads into a sandy wash at a decent speed until the entrance of the canyon is reached. One tour driver pretended to be stuck in the sand, presumably to invoke

the thrill of adventure. Keep your hats in your lap or tightly on your head, there is no stopping. Once out of the vehicle, the tour guide does his or her genuine best to make the trip as intimate as possible for his group. The biggest advice is stay with your tour lead. Getting left behind has happened, but more typically, your late return to the vehicle will be met with glib looks from the fellow tour group members. Some tours feature a hoop dance back at the tour guide headquarters.

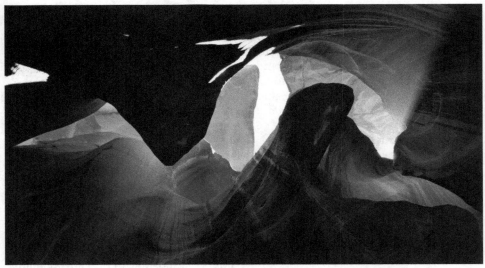

Looking up within the slot canyon

Antelope Slot Canyon Tours

Adventurous Antelope Canyon Photo Tours

Highway 98, Page, AZ 86040, Phone: (928) 380-1874, www.navajoantelopecanyon.com

Antelope Slot Canyon Tours by Chief Tsosie

55 S Lake Powell Blvd, Page AZ 86040, Phone: (928) 645-5594, www.antelopeslotcanyon.com

Ken's Guided Tour of Lower Antelope Canyon

Indian Route 222, Page, AZ 86040, Phone: (928) 606-2168, lowerantelope.com

Dixie Ellis' Lower Antelope Canyon Tours

Indian Route 222, Page, AZ 86040, Phone: (928) 640-1761, antelopelowercanyon.com

Quick Facts

Official Park Website:

* http://www.blm.gov/az/st/en/prog/blm_special_areas/natmon/vermilion.html

Visitor Center:

None in park, for a ranger contact:

* BLM St. George Field Office: 345 E. Riverside Drive, St. George, UT 84790-6714, Phone: (435) 688-3200

* Hours: 7:45 a.m.-5:00 p.m. Monday through Friday, 10:00 a.m.-3:00 p.m. Saturday, Closed Sunday

Park Accessibility:

* No paved roads, high clearance/4WD vehicles required for most of the park

* Primarily Overnight Use

Experience Level:

* Experienced Hiker – Backcountry Hiker

Camping in Park:

* Stateline: 4 T, no water, no trash, restrooms, first come/first served, open year round

* White House: 5 T, no water, no trash, restrooms, first come/first served, open year round

Lodging and Dining in Park:

* None

Nearest Town with Amenities:

* Page, AZ, 40 mi / 64 km to Marble Canyon entrance

Getting There:

* Southern Section: From Flagstaff: head north on US 89 to 89A at the Bitter Springs off ramp. From US I-15: take AZ 389 East to US 89A South

* Northern Section: From Kanab, Utah: take US 89 to the east or US 89A to the south. From US I-15: take UT 9 East to US 89 South

VERMILION CLIFFS NATIONAL MONUMENT

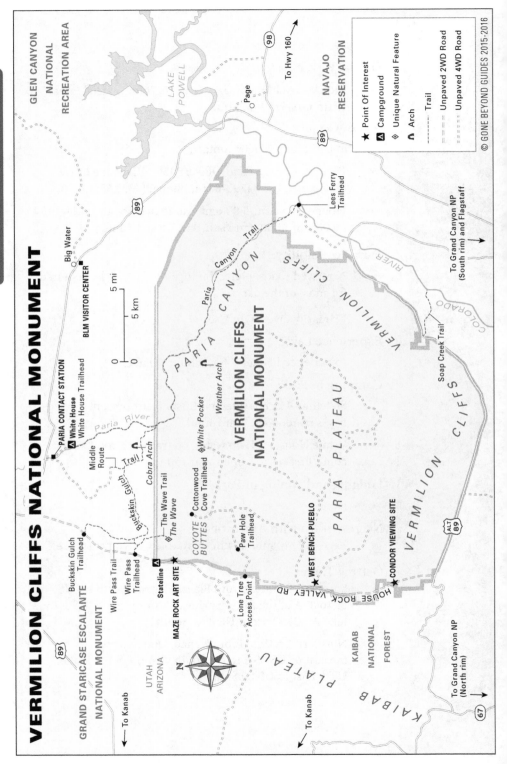

GLEN CANYON NATIONAL RECREATION AREA

LAKE POWELL

Page

To Hwy 160

NAVAJO RESERVATION

Point Of Interest ★
Campground ▲
Unique Natural Feature ◈
Arch ∩
Trail
Unpaved 2WD Road
Unpaved 4WD Road

© GONE BEYOND GUIDES 2015-2016

89

98

Big Water

89

PARIA CONTACT STATION
BLM VISITOR CENTER

White House
White House Trailhead

Paria River

Middle Route Trail

Cobra Arch

Buckskin Gulch

Buckskin Gulch Trailhead

Wire Pass Trail
Wire Pass Trailhead

Stateline
MAZE ROCK ART SITE

The Wave Trail
The Wave

COYOTE BUTTES

Cottonwood Cove Trailhead

White Pocket

Wrather Arch

Paria Canyon Trail

PARIA CANYON

VERMILION CLIFFS NATIONAL MONUMENT

Lees Ferry Trailhead

VERMILION CLIFFS

COLORADO RIVER

To Grand Canyon NP (South rim) and Flagstaff

Soap Creek Trail

PARIA PLATEAU

Paw Hole Trailhead

WEST BENCH PUEBLO

HOUSE ROCK VALLEY RD

Lone Tree Access Point

CONDOR VIEWING SITE

VERMILION CLIFFS

ALT 89

KAIBAB NATIONAL FOREST

To Grand Canyon NP (North rim)

67

KAIBAB PLATEAU

To Kanab

UTAH
ARIZONA

N

GRAND STAIRCASE ESCALANTE NATIONAL MONUMENT

89

To Kanab

0   5 mi
0   5 km

56

What Makes Vermilion Cliffs National Monument Special

Vermilion Cliffs National Monument is certainly a candidate for one of the top park destinations within the Grand Circle. Nearly as large as all of the three sections of the Canyonlands and yet relatively new and unheard of, this is one of the most unspoiled parks to be found. It is also one of the most remote. The park is located north of Grand Canyon and east of the Navajo lands, touching the border of Utah, referred to as the Arizona Strip. There is no visitor center, few roads, little previous development, and only a scattered handful of trails.

Vermilion Cliffs is true desert wilderness. It is untouched, insufferable, rugged, and pure. There are places within it where it feels as if no person has ever stepped foot. For the most part, Vermilion Cliffs is pure virgin sandstone, quietly being shaped over millions of years.

It was only made into a national monument in 2000, though the land had been protected under other measures prior. Much of the 280,000 acres protects the Paria Plateau, a significant mesa that spans over 20 miles and is roughly square in shape. The plateau itself is a vast desert island oasis, invoking freedom and being on top of the world. However, it is the areas along the edges of the plateau that offers some of the most amazing sections in the park, such as The Wave, a striated

Before heading out:

Here are some tips to ensure a safe and successful trip:

- First, get a permit. Overnight access to Buckskin Gulch is limited to 20 folks per day. The online process is listed in the web URL above.

- Speak to the BLM rangers. The rangers are the best versed in current conditions, what to expect and general guidance on how to prepare and execute this hike. Kanab Field Office – 318 North 100 East, Kanab, UT 84741 – Phone: (435) 644-4600 Fax: (435) 644-4620 or by email: utknmail@blm.gov

- Use a shuttle or two cars. These are long distances, so if you are short on time, this is best way to do this hike. Try Paria Outfitters (www.paria.com) for shuttle services. At the very least, check out

their site for the cool pics of the areas they serve.

- Check the weather forecast. Backpacker Magazine puts this as one of the 10 most dangerous hikes, primarily due to flash flood risks. As they put it, "Should thunderstorm-bloated flood waters come charging down the tunnel, you're no better than a bug in a firehose."

- Bring water shoes, plenty of drinking water, and multiple layers of clothing. There are points where the watercourse is the trail so bring some decent water shoes. While there are seeps, pools and water, it can be downright murky, so best to bring in what you need. Finally, fires are not permitted in the area, so make sure you have layer coverage for the temperature range of the trip.

section of carved sandstone that has to be seen to be believed. Then there is Buckskin Gulch, a tributary of the Paria River and at a length of 20 miles is a contender for the longest slot canyon in the world.

It must be stated that not all of this wonder and remote beauty comes without some caution and regulations. Much of the land is accessed by permit only. While day use permits are more available, overnight permits are limited and can be obtained by going to the URL below and following the online instructions: www.blm.gov/az/st/en/arolrsmain.html. The caution is that this land can be extremely challenging. Flash floods, venomous reptiles and insects, sun exposure, and remoteness make this park much different than say, taking the shuttle from the Zion Lodge and taking a hike. This area is ideally suited for experienced hikers and desert backpackers.

A quick note on the permitting system. One consistent theme within all of these parks is finding a balance between preservation of the land and the ability to share it for the enjoyment and recreation of others. Vermilion Cliffs NM pushes this balance more on the preservation side. There is a capacity to the number of visitors allowed to use the park each day and while it may be frustrating if you are the unfortunate soul that didn't

get a permit, you have to respect the process. The desert is fragile and takes a very long time to recover. Some parks, especially the national parks, are pushing the balance more towards recreation and the wear on them does show. Having explored all of these parks since the 1980's, the impact over just 35 years is quite evident and not in a good way. Vermilion Cliffs NM continues to retain that pristine hallowed ground of desert experience because of the permit process. Not everyone will get to go, especially for those permitted areas only available by lottery, but those that do will experience the difference.

Hiking Vermilion Cliffs National Monument

Paria Canyon Trails

Buckskin Gulch Trail
Moderate – (5.7 mi / 9.2 km), one way to Wire Pass Trailhead, allow 3 hours

Strenuous – (23 mi / 37 km), one way, to White House Trailhead, full day hike or 2-day backpacking trip

Strenuous – (47 mi / 76 km), one way, to Lee's Ferry Trailhead, 3-5-day backpacking trip

Buckskin Gulch is the longest and deepest slot canyon in the Grand Circle. The narrows extend nearly 15 miles, with some sections being but 10 feet in width. The terrain and views are as inspiring as they are varied, making this a popular hike. The slot canyon leaves for very few exits during a flash flood and rain as far as Bryce Canyon 50 miles away can drain into Buckskin. The gulch is also known for muck pools, where in the middle of summer you may find yourself with no other choice but to wade through residual pools that become foul smelling mud pots. They are normally no more than 3 feet deep, but some folks have noted being chest deep in one pool. Additionally,

Vermilion Cliffs

expect to do a fair amount of scrambling and even rappelling. In many spots, there is a rope left behind as a gesture of courtesy to rappel down the 15 foot drops, but you'll want to bring rope just in case.

There are many entry points into Buckskin Gulch. There is the Buckskin Gulch Trailhead or Wire Pass Trailhead to the east, heading downstream to a juncture where you can either head north to White House Trailhead or southeast through Paria Canyon down to Lee's Ferry. The most popular hike is from Wire Pass Trailhead to White House Trailhead. This section describes the route starting from Buckskin Gulch Trailhead. Use this route if you want to say you hiked the full extent of Buckskin Gulch.

Take Highway 89 east from Kanab, UT 38 miles or west from Page, AZ for 34 miles and turn onto House Valley Road. This will be a right if coming from Kanab. The Buckskin Trailhead is 4.5 miles down a dirt road and is suitable for 2WD vehicles. That said, the clay-based soils are super sticky in some areas and like driving on ice in others when wet. It is not recommended, even in a 4WD vehicle, to drive this road when wet.

There is no established campground here, but camping is allowed at the trailhead. The trail is obvious and dry for most of the year to the junction to Wire Pass Trailhead, starting off fairly wide relative to the narrows later on. From the junction to Wire Pass, the canyon begins its journey as the longest narrows in the Southwest. The next big milestone is Buckskin Gulch Junction (1.8 miles, 1 hour). Here, (and beyond), the narrows are quite spectacular. Every turn is a different "wow!" moment. Along this section are The Cesspools, a stretch of murky, muddy, god-awful water that you have to wade through to continue.

The trek through this section of the narrows is 6.5 miles long, with the next milestone being Middle Route. Allow 4

hours for this part. Middle Route is yet another passage into Buckskin over a 4WD drive road and is described later in the book.

From Middle Route to Rock Fall (aka Rock Jam) is another 3 miles (allow 2 hours). This area has some rock problem areas that require scrambling. In spots, it can get quite dark, though not enough for a flashlight. Rock Fall presents the toughest of the areas where scrambling is needed. The scramble is easy enough, with some footholds into the rock for the down climb or hikers can opt for the Rabbit Hole, which is the easiest of methods to get through this scramble of rock (look for a way down through the rocks rather than up). From Rock Fall the campground and Paria River Confluence is in sight and is the spot for an overnight rest for most folks. The distance here is 1.3 miles to the campground and another quarter mile to the confluence. Allow 1 hour. It is not recommended to camp at the confluence due to potential risk of "going to Lee's Ferry prematurely" due to flooding. The campground sits higher up providing some protection from rising waters.

The hike to the confluence is dry for the most part, aside from the mud pots and stronger seeps and springs providing some run off. While it may be tempting to get the water from these sources, it is not recommended. You will need 1.5 to 2 gallons of water for this leg in the summer, more depending on distance traveled and time spent.

If you are continuing upstream to White House Trailhead, you have another 4 hours and 7.5 miles ahead of you. This route is possible to do as a day trip, but it is a full day.

Heading downstream will take you Lee's Ferry. The total distance to Lee's Ferry from Buckskin Gulch Trailhead is 47 miles. Plan on a 3 - 5-day backpacking trip and definitely use a shuttle. Along

with Paria Outpost listed above, Circle Tours, (888) 854-7862 and End of the Trail Shuttles, (928) 355-2252 offer shuttle services.

Wire Pass Trail

Moderate – (5.7 mi / 9.2 km), one way to Buckskin Gulch Trailhead, allow 3 hours

Strenuous – (21 mi / 34 km), one way, to White House Trailhead, full day hike or 2-day backpacking trip

Strenuous – (44 mi / 71 km), one way, to Lee's Ferry Trailhead, 3-5-day backpacking trip

Wire Pass Trail offers an alternate entrance into Buckskin Gulch through Wire Pass Gulch. Wire Pass Trailhead is often chosen over entering directly from the Buckskin Gulch Trailhead because it is shorter and the gulch is itself a very nice set of narrows. It only cuts off 2 miles from any destination but does offer help satisfy the "slot canyon" fix a little faster than starting from Buckskin Gulch Trailhead. This trailhead is also used as the starting destination for a popular sandstone formation known as The Wave, described later on.

To get here, just follow the directions above to Buckskin Gulch Trailhead and continue on House Rock Valley Road another 3.8 miles (8.3 miles from Highway 89). Again, permits are needed as is read-

ing all the tips provided in the Buckskin Gulch Trail description. Stateline Campground is one-mile south of the Wire Pass Trailhead and camping is allowed at the trailhead if campground is full. There are restrooms here, but no water.

Middle Route

Strenuous – (1.4 mi / 2.3 km), one way to Buckskin Gulch, allow 1 - 2 hours

The Middle Route is a good alternative if you are looking to bypass many of the cold stagnant pools of water as you wind through the narrows of Buckskin Gulch. It also saves a day of hiking. It is a short easy route to navigate into the gulch via a long, sandy, unsigned, and at times impassable 4WD road with multiple forks to consider.

About midway through Buckskin Gulch, the walls of the canyon lower down to about 100 feet. Here there is a very steep crack that is possible to scramble up if one needs an early exit out of the gulch or as a means to down climb into the slot canyon. This is Middle Route. This crack is definitely for the experienced canyoneer and bringing a 50-foot rope is highly recommended for lowering packs. The crack contains steep drop offs and climbing down slickrock. Exposure aside, this is a Class 3 - 4 scramble and doesn't require any technical climbing per se.

Coyote Buttes South

Getting to Middle Route is not straight-forward as hinted at above. It's best to consult with the Paria Contact Station for directions, road conditions and even a video of Middle Route.

White House Trail

Strenuous – (23 mi / 37 km), one way to Buckskin Gulch Trailhead, full day hike or 2-day backpacking trip

Strenuous – (21 mi / 34 km), one way, to Wire Pass Trailhead, full day hike or 2-day backpacking trip

Strenuous – (38 mi / 61 km), one way, to Lee's Ferry Trailhead, 3-5-day backpacking trip

Continuing in our long list of trails that lead to Buckskin Gulch, let's add White House Trail.

Following the directions in the Buckskin Gulch Trail description, take the dirt road towards the Paria Contact Station and turn onto the obvious dirt road just before it. Follow this 2WD road for 2 miles to the trailhead.

White House trail is a popular exit route for Buckskin because of the possibility to utilize a shuttle or second car. It is also adjacent to the White House Camp-ground. There is no water here but there are restrooms. The trail follows the Paria

River downstream as it heads towards Lee's Ferry and the Colorado River. It is 7.5 miles to Buckskin Gulch. This section does require some wading at times, with the occasional spot of quicksand. Wrap gear and wear water shoes for this section. See the Buckskin Gulch Trail for more information.

Lee's Ferry Trailhead
See Glen Canyon National Recreation Area

Coyote Buttes North

The Wave
Strenuous – (5.6 mi / 9.0 km), round trip, from Wire Pass Trailhead, allow 3 – 4 hours

If ever there was a destination that could compete with Buckskin Gulch, the longest slot canyon in the Southwest and perhaps even the world, it a little place called The Wave. In the Grand Circle there is a lot of red rock, so much in fact, that after a few weeks within it, one starts dreaming of fantastic mashups of slick-rock canyons and formations that don't actually exist. The Wave is a place that is so fantastic; it is as if it came from one of these dreams. Seeing an image of The Wave is to reset the art of the possible within the realm of red rock. To see it in person can be surreal, as if it shouldn't

The Wave

exist, yet it does. As an added bonus, the whole terrain getting to it and around it is cool to explore. This area is part of the Coyote Buttes North. This is a day use only area and requires a permit. Permits are limited to 20 people a day with 10 folks chosen through a walk in lottery process the day before and 10 folks obtaining the permit via an online process via (www.blm.gov/az/paria/obtainpermits.cfm?usearea=CB).

For the online process, the lottery opens up 4 months prior to the use date. Generally, online permits for the Coyote Buttes North are hard to obtain. The cost to apply is $5 per group and you can select up to three dates. See the lottery schedule below for exact dates, but in general, the

Coyote Buttes North Lottery Schedule

Apply between	for a permit during	Lottery Run at 1:05 p.m. MST for remaining permits available
January 1 - 31	May	February 1
February 1 - 28	June	March 1
March 1 - 31	July	April 1
April 1- 30	August	May 1
May 1 - 31	September	June 1
June 1 - 30	October	July 1
July 1 - 31	November	August 1
August 1 - 31	December	September 1
September 1 - 30	January	October 1
October 1 - 31	February	November 1
November 1 - 30	March	December 1
December 1 - 31	April	January 1

process works like this. For a permit in say the month of May, one would apply at any time four months earlier, from January 1-31, in this case. On February 1, at 1:05 PM MST, the permits holders are chosen. If you are successful, you will be notified via email and will then need to pay $7 per individual.

There is no established trail to The Wave. There are two routes, however. The most readily accessible method is to start from Wire Pass Trailhead. The drive is easy enough and more straightforward of a hike then the other method known as The Notch. The route from Wire Pass Trailhead will be described here.

Start by following the instructions to Wire Pass Trailhead listed above. Enter into Wire Pass Gulch across the road and travel down the wash for about half a mile. Take the juncture to the right, marked Coyote Buttes, where you will find an obvious trail. The trail climbs up a hill and across a desert field ending at a wash. Total distance of the trail is approximately 0.65 miles.

From here on out the trail becomes route and the area is by permit only. On the other side of the wash is a slickrock incline that is typically marked with cairns. Climb this saddle and head towards the BLM marker ahead of you. This saddle is a great point to mark if you have a GPS, as it will greatly aid in finding the trail on the return.

Continue to follow the BLM markers south, heading towards and staying to the left of a landmark known as Twin Buttes. Once you pass by this landmark, you are about 0.6 miles from the Utah – Arizona border and 1.0 mile from the Wave. The next landmark to aim for is a narrow crack like gully in the cliffs as you continue south. As you get closer to the gully look for a small sand dune left of the gully. Climb the sand dune, then the slickrock to arrive at The Wave. There are many other features to check out in the area, including The Second Wave,

The Alcove, and some petroglyphs and dinosaur tracks. See the below website for a list of all of them.

One exceptional site dedicated to The Wave feature is a site called "thewave". It covers everything outlined here and has a virtual tour of the hike itself, sunset/sunrise calculator, weather, and other details. Go here: www.thewave.info/CoyoteButtesNorthCode/Map.html

Maze Rock Art Site

Just beyond Wire Pass Trailhead and State Line Campground is a trailhead to a rich petroglyph site. There are numerous examples of Ancestral Puebloan art, including the namesake, a petroglyph that looks like a maze. Head south from State Line Campground on House Valley Road for about a mile to find the trailhead.

Coyote Buttes South

The Coyote Buttes South region of Vermilion Cliffs NM is, like its northern counterpart, accessed by permit only. The good news is the permits are much easier to obtain for this region. Just go online and follow the instructions.

https://www.blm.gov/az/paria/obtainpermits.cfm?usearea=CB

All of the hiking here is for the experienced. Beyond needing a permit, you'll need a 4WD vehicle and topo maps. Per the BLM, these are both mandatory. As the BLM site indicates these aren't really trailheads, they are access points. After driving through deep sands and rough terrain, after figuring out on numerous occasions which junction you should take at the many spur roads on the way, you find yourself parking at the beginning of your own adventure.

For all of the below access points listed below, there are no trails, no markers, direction signs, or navigational information once you leave the road that got you there. In places like these, there is this advice. You will find at least one piece of

A land of soulfulness and escape

trash, typically a Budweiser can and you will wonder how it got there. You will have the opportunity to step where no human has stepped, and see things that no one has seen in quite the same way. You will hopefully take solace in knowing that the closest Starbucks to your tent is a good 3 hours away and that when the sun sets, you will likely see one of the darkest skies you have ever seen. This is the middle of nowhere. It is desert nirvana, BFE, God's country. Whatever you call it, the place will leave its mark on the soul as days remembered for the rest of your life.

Cottonwood Cove Trailhead

This access point leads to the Cottonwood Teepees, a series of cone shaped sandstone formations. In general, the red rock is twisted and deformed, resembling something more reminiscent to a Salvador Dali landscape.

The rocks at times look like huge spine fossils of some large monster, eroded away by time until only the backbone remains curved out on a pedestal of rock. There is also one teepee formation called the Queen, looking like a typical cone shaped formation but with the smallest of capstones on top.

Getting to Cottonwood Cove Trailhead starts by taking House Rock Road, the same road taken for Buckskin Gulch and Wire Pass Trailheads. Head south past Wire Pass for 20.2 miles and turn left on BLM 1017, (Pine Tree Road). If coming from the south, the distance on House Rock Road will be 9.4 miles to this intersection.

Mark the trip meter and take Pine Tree Road for 3.1 miles and then turn left on Red Pockets Road and begin heading in a northwest bearing. At 6.0 miles, you should see a cattle gate (leave as you found it, whether open or closed). At 8.3 miles, bear to the right and at 8.7 miles turn left onto Upper Pawhole Road. This area, called Poverty Flat has several out buildings worth checking out. At 9.0 miles keep to the right until you reach a closed gate with a sign that says Coyote Buttes Fee Area. End of the road worth driving on is at 11.4 miles. Park on your left, the Cottonwood Teepees are to the west.

Paw Hole Trailhead

Paw Hole is close to Cottonwood Cove, offering slightly different topography. It is possible to do both in one trip. Paw Hole has some interesting, often delicate striations in the sandstone. Paw Hole is a small water hole that looks like, (wait for it), a paw. One recommended route is to stay at Cottonwood Cove the first night and then Paw Hole the next. This method allows for a loop back to House Valley Road.

Coming from Cottonwood Cove, double back to BLM 1079 and take it to the signs indicating Paw Hole. To head out, continue on BLM 1079 to connect back to House Valley Road. It is not recommended to take this road to Paw Hole directly from House Valley as it is uphill and is too steep for many vehicles.

Lone Tree Access Point
This is an access point to Paw Hole and the Coyote Buttes South for folks that have a 2WD vehicle only. Take House Valley Road south to BLM 1079 and turn left. Drive on 1079 for 0.2 miles and park the car near the obvious lone tree. Continue hiking east to Paw Hole along BLM 1079 from here. It is approximately 2.4 miles to Paw Hole from the tree.

Marble Canyon

Soap Creek Trail
Strenuous – (8.0 mi / 12.9 km), round trip, allow 2 - 3 hours

Soap Canyon is a feeder canyon to the Colorado River. The trail passes much of its time within the Grand Canyon National Park, which protects either side of the river north to Glen Canyon NRA. The trail is found by driving south on Highway 89A approximately 9 miles from Marble Canyon, AZ. Look for mile marker 548 and thereafter a latched gate. Turn left onto this dirt road, pass some abandoned buildings, and drive about 0.6 miles to the trailhead.

Soap Canyon allows for a quick access to the Colorado River and is popular with anglers as a result. It does have two dryfalls that must be navigated. If you find yourself wondering how you are going to get down the first 10-foot one, then you might want to turn back as the second one is 25 feet high. The gradient is easy going at first and the canyon becomes narrower and steeper on its way to the river. Both dryfalls have alternate routes to allow access around them. The tributary opens up shortly after the second dryfall at the inspiring Soap Creek Rapids. If you plan to stay overnight, you will need to obtain a permit from Grand Canyon NP.

Stone House
A woman by the name of Blanche Russell was driving through the area and her car broke down. She took it as fate and built a house where her car stopped in 1930. The ruins, called Stone House, as well as oddly eroded and balanced rocks can be found here. Stone House is 8.4 miles south of Marble Canyon, AZ and about 0.3 miles north of the Cliff Dwellers Lodge.

Sunrise at Cottonwood Cove

Pipe Spring National Monument

Official Park Website: http://www.nps.gov/pisp

Visitor Center:

- (928) 643-7105

Park Accessibility:

- Okay for 2WD and RVs
- Day Use Only

Experience Level:

- Family Friendly

Camping in Park:

- None

Lodging and Dining in Park:

- None

Nearest Town with Amenities:

- Fredonia, AZ is 14 mi / 23 km from the park

Getting There:

- From St. George, UT: take UT-59 South and AZ-389 East for 60 mi / 97 km to the park

Covered wagon at Pipe Spring National Monument

What Makes Pipe Spring National Monument Special

- Touring a remote 19th century Mormon fortified ranch house in Arizona
- Learning about a period when your greatest fears were getting raided by the Navajo
- Checking out one of the best museums and visitor centers in the Grand Circle

Pipe Spring was first discovered in 1858 by Jacob Hamblin, a Mormon missionary on an expedition to the Hopi mesas. Two years later, James M. Whitmore and a group of fellow pioneers created a homestead and cattle operation. Building a group of homes in Navajo territory was one thing, keeping it was another. Once the Apache, Navajo, Utes, and Paiutes joined forces to start the Black Hawk War in 1866, primarily aimed at the Mormons, things came to a boiling point. After a raid of the Pipe Springs homesteads, it was decided to build a fort over the main spring.

This fortified ranch house was purchased by Brigham Young in 1872 for the Church of the Latter Day Saints (LDS). Brigham sent Mormon Bishop Anson Perry Winsor to run the ranch and he renamed it Winsor Castle. The ranch became a safe haven for travelers passing through and even acted as a refuge for polygamist wives during the late 1800's. In the end, the ranch's ties to polygamy would be its downfall and the LDS lost ownership of the property in 1887.

Today the monument is a cultural preserve, offering a 30-minute ranger led tour of the ranch house and an extensive museum and visitor center. It is also possible to take a self-guided walk amongst the out buildings, corral, and garden areas. Pipe Spring National Monument offers an informative and interesting step back in time; especially if the ranger led tour is taken. Definitely worth the drive.

The historic Winsor Castle

Grand Canyon - Parashant National Monument

Quick Facts

Official Park Website:

- http://www.nps.gov/para

Visitor Center:

- None in park, contact: Public Lands Information Center (NPS, BLM, Forest Service), 345 East Riverside Drive, St. George, UT 84790, Phone: (435) 688-3200

- Note: it is strongly recommended visitors pick up a copy of the BLM Arizona Strip Visitor Map before entering. This map shows all roads along the Arizona Strip. Maps can be purchased at 345 E. Riverside Dr., St. George, UT 84790, or by calling (435) 688-3275.

Park Accessibility:

- 2WD, 4WD recommended, no paved roads in park

- Primarily Overnight Use

Experience Level:

- Experienced Hiker – Backcountry Hiker

Camping in Park:

- No developed campgrounds, backcountry camping with permit

Lodging and Dining in Park:

- None

Nearest Town with Amenities:

- Bullfrog, Antelope Point, and Halls Crossing are the closest areas within the park with amenities. Page, AZ is closest town to the southern section of the park

Getting There:

- From St. George, UT: Take I-15 South to Southern Pkwy to Mount Trumbull Loop for 62 mi / 100 to park entrance

One of the stunning views of Grand Canyon - Parashant National Monument

What Makes Grand Canyon-Parashant National Monument Special

- A rugged and isolated million-acre park with no paved roads

- Exceptional solitude in a Grand Canyon NP like setting

- Two forested peaks that give a very different perspective to the area

If isolation and solitude are what you are looking for, Parashant is the answer. This is a very large monument at just over one million acres, yet the park has no paved roads, lodges, or visitor center. This is a land where two sets of spares are the norm and the extra tanks of gas clinging to the side or your rig aren't just for show. It is a land that continues the story of the greatness of the Grand Canyon and covers the high plateau forests and desert grasslands that surround the canyon. The park holds three large wilderness areas, multiple plateaus, deep canyons and numerous washes.

Hiking Grand Canyon-Parashant NM

For all of these hikes, bring a topo map of the area to be hiked (and surrounding area), a good high clearance vehicle and the ability to self-sustain in the desert. Most of the hikes described below are remote and some are not maintained. Check with the BLM monument manager before any trip in this area to sync on local conditions. The BLM St. George office phone is (435) 688-3202.

Grand Wash Bench Trail
Strenuous – (20.0 mi / 32.2 km), round trip, full day trip or 2-day backpacking trip

The Grand Wash Bench Trail travels along a bench north to south within the 36,300-acre Grand Wash Cliffs Wilderness. Area scenery includes narrow canyons, two sets of towering cliffs and sandstone buttes. Ecologically, this hike travels through a transition zone and holds varied wildlife including bighorn sheep, the Gila monster, and the desert tortoise. Flora includes pinyon juniper forests and desert grasslands.

NORTHERN ARIZONA

GRAND CANYON–PARASHANT NATIONAL MONUMENT

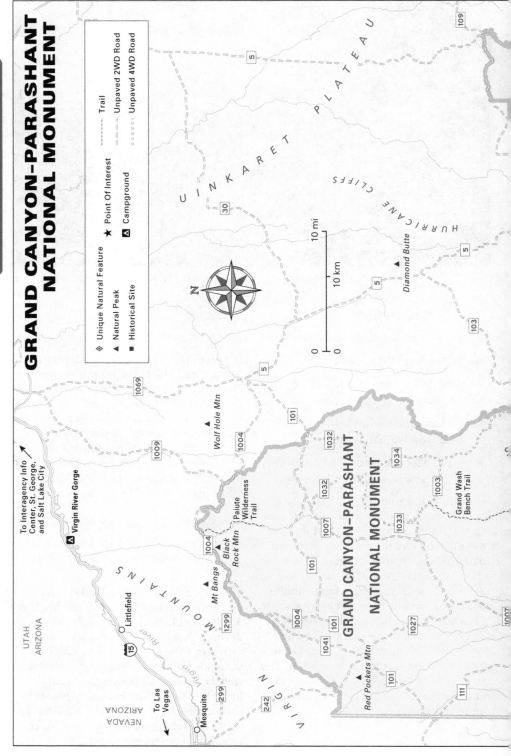

◈ Unique Natural Feature   ★ Point Of Interest
▲ Natural Peak   ◭ Campground
■ Historical Site

- - - - - Trail
═ ═ ═ Unpaved 2WD Road
═ ═ ═ Unpaved 4WD Road

N

10 mi
10 km
0   0

UINKARET PLATEAU

HURRICANE CLIFFS

▲ Diamond Butte

109
5
30
5
103
5
101
1069
1009
▲ Wolf Hole Mtn
1004
5

1032
1032
1007
1003
1034
Grand Wash Bench Trail

GRAND CANYON–PARASHANT NATIONAL MONUMENT

1033
101
1004
101
1027
1041
101
▲ Red Pockets Mtn
111
1007

To Interagency Info Center, St. George, and Salt Lake City →
◭ Virgin River Gorge

UTAH
ARIZONA

Virgin River
Littlefield
15
299
To Las Vegas →
Mesquite
NEVADA
ARIZONA
242

VIRGIN MOUNTAINS

1299
▲ Mt Bangs
1004
Black Rock Mtn
Paiute Wilderness Trail

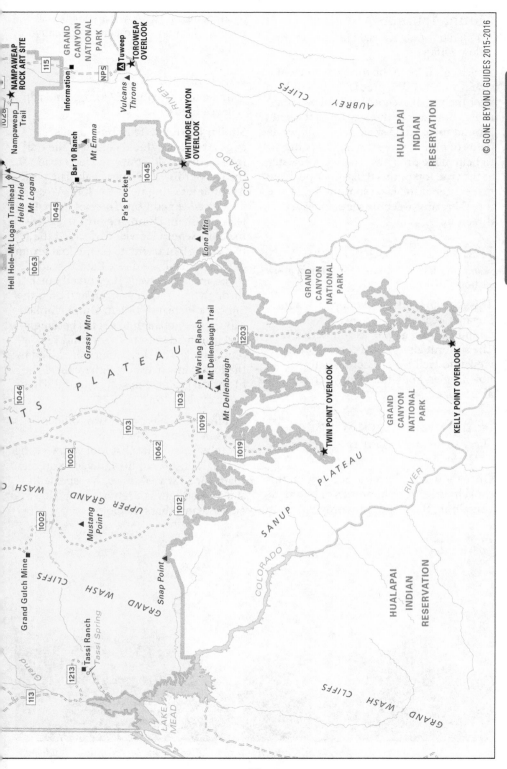

NAMPAWEAP ROCK ART SITE

GRAND CANYON NATIONAL PARK

115

NPS

Information

Nampaweap Trail

1028

△ Tuweep

TOROWEAP OVERLOOK

Vulcans Throne

Mt Emma

Bar 10 Ranch

Mt Logan

Hell Hole–Mt Logan Trailhead

Hells Hole

1045

WHITMORE CANYON OVERLOOK

COLORADO RIVER

1063

Pa's Pocket

1045

Lone Mtn

Grassy Mtn

1046

ITS

PLATEAU

GRAND CANYON NATIONAL PARK

1203

Waring Ranch

Mt Dellenbaugh Trail

Mt Dellenbaugh

103

1019

103

103

1019

TWIN POINT OVERLOOK

1062

1002

KELLY POINT OVERLOOK

GRAND CANYON NATIONAL PARK

PLATEAU

AUBREY CLIFFS

HUALAPAI INDIAN RESERVATION

1012

Mustang Point

UPPER GRAND

WASH C

WASH

1002

Grand Gulch Mine

CLIFFS

GRAND WASH

WASH

Snap Point

SANUP

COLORADO

COLORADO RIVER

113

1213

Tassi Ranch

Tassi Spring

Grand

LAKE MEAD

HUALAPAI INDIAN RESERVATION

GRAND WASH CLIFFS

GRAND WASH

© GONE BEYOND GUIDES 2015-2016

NORTHERN ARIZONA

Grand Canyon - Parashant

Mount Trumbull Trail
Moderate – (5.0 mi / 8.0 km), round trip, allow 4 hours

A pleasant hike to the top of an ancient shield volcano. The gradient up is mild after the initial ascent. The trail becomes route about 2/3 of the way up as the solid ground turns to deep cinders. Follow the paths of others and use a zigzag pattern to help make progress. There is a register at the true top of this 8,028-foot peak and no register at the false summit. From the top, there are sweeping views in every direction.

Hell Hole – Mount Logan Trail
Easy – (1.0 mi / 1.6 km), round trip, allow 1 hour

This is a short hike to the top of Mount Logan. Great majestic views into western Grand Canyon as well as southern Utah. The summit also gives a commanding view into Hell Hole, essentially the northern end of Grand Canyon's erosional artwork.

Nampaweap Rock Art Site
Easy – (1.0 mi / 1.6km), round trip, allow 30 minutes

Once thought to be a travel corridor, this short hike leads to hundreds of boulders containing thousands of petroglyphs left by ancient travelers over a 10,000-year period. Nampaweap means "foot canyon" in Paiute.

Mt. Dellenbaugh
Strenuous – (6.0 mi / 9.7 km), round trip, allow 4 hours

Similar to Mount Trumbull, this is another ancient shield volcano. The trail follows up an old converted jeep road to the top of this 7,012-foot peak. The peak has an interesting tie to the John Wesley Powell expedition. Three of Powell's team, William Dunn and brothers Oramel and Seneca Howland, decided they had enough of trying to be the first group of men to navigate down the Colorado River and left Powell. They hiked north through Separation Canyon and onto the Shivwits Plateau. William Dunn climbed Mount Dellenbaugh to get his bearings and inscribed both his name and year onto a rock. The three men were killed by the local Shivwits shortly thereafter. The historical graffiti can still be found with some exploration.

While this hike is one of two "official" hikes in the park (the other is Mount Trumbull), don't let that fool you. Getting to the trailhead requires traveling on dirt roads for nearly 90 miles. As repeatedly stated, Prashant is a remote land. However, for many, that's the point.

Looking south towards Grand Canyon from Mt Trumbull Wilderness

Lake Mead National Recreation Area

Quick Facts

Official Park Website:

- http://www.nps.gov/lake

Visitor Center:

- (702) 293-8990

Park Accessibility:

- Okay for 2WD and RVs
- Day and Overnight Use

Experience Level:

- Family Friendly – Experienced Hiker

Camping in Park:

- There are numerous campgrounds in the park, information can be found here: http://www.nps.gov/lake/planyourvisit/campgrounds.htm

Lodging in Park:

- There is a multitude of lodging options within the park, details can be found here: http://www.nps.gov/lake/planyourvisit/lodging.htm

Dining in Park:

- Lots of dining opportunities, details here: http://www.nps.gov/lake/planyourvisit/wheretoeat.htm

Nearest Town with Amenities:

- There are multiple areas within the park that offer full amenities, including Echo Bay. Outside the park, Boulder City, NV is close to the southwest section of the park

Getting There:

- From Las Vegas, NV: take I-515 South to US-93 South 26 mi / 42 km to the southwestern park entrance

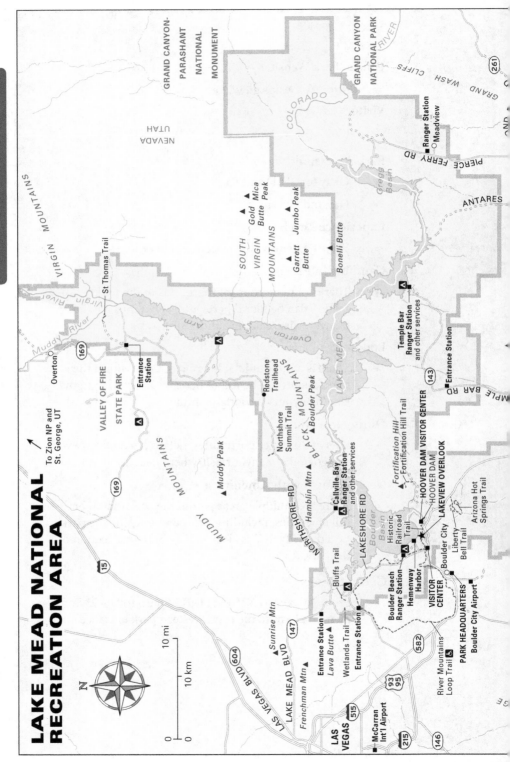

Lake Mead

NORTHERN ARIZONA

LAKE MEAD NATIONAL RECREATION AREA

74

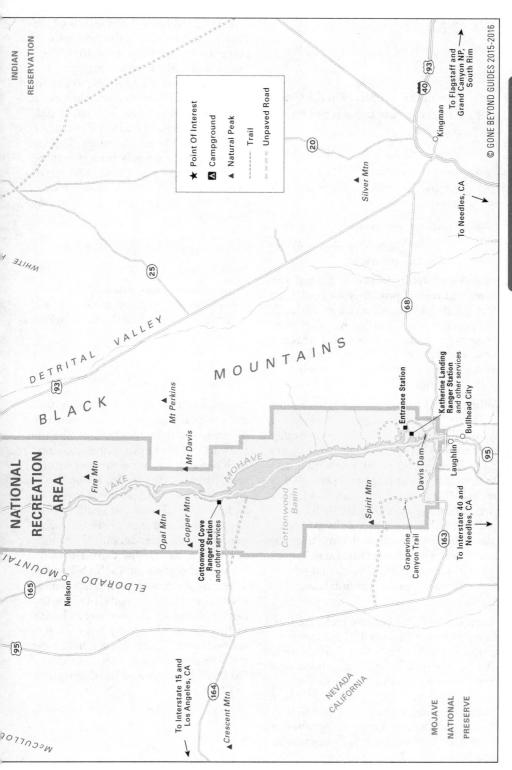

Legend:
★ Point Of Interest
◼ Campground
▲ Natural Peak
----- Trail
=== Unpaved Road

INDIAN RESERVATION

© GONE BEYOND GUIDES 2015-2016

Kingman

To Flagstaff and Grand Canyon NP, South Rim

To Needles, CA

Silver Mtn

WHITE H

DETRITAL VALLEY

BLACK MOUNTAINS

Mt Perkins

Mt Davis

Fire Mtn

LAKE

MOHAVE

Cottonwood Basin

Spirit Mtn

Entrance Station

Katherine Landing Ranger Station and other services

Bullhead City

Davis Dam

Laughlin

NATIONAL RECREATION AREA

Opal Mtn

Copper Mtn

Cottonwood Cove Ranger Station and other services

Grapevine Canyon Trail

To Interstate 40 and Needles, CA

ELDORADO MOUNTAINS

Nelson

To Interstate 15 and Los Angeles, CA

Crescent Mtn

NEVADA
CALIFORNIA

MOJAVE NATIONAL PRESERVE

McCULLOC

What Makes Lake Mead National Recreation Area Special

- One of the few places in the Grand Circle where you can rent a house boat

- When full, Lake Mead is the largest reservoir in the United States, serving 20 million people across 3 states

- Knowing that even if you lose it all in Las Vegas, you can always go hiking at Lake Mead

Lake Mead NRA covers over 1.3 million acres and is used primarily for boating, water skiing and other water activities. It is a popular place, getting over 6 million visitors per year. The land covers three desert ecosystems, including the Mojave, Sonoran and Great Basin, plus their transition zones.

While the lake is the primary destination for most folks, the varied ecosystems allows for hiking that is unique in both scenery and surrounding flora. There are a few standout hikes, with destinations that include hot springs and petroglyphs as well as an old railway path that is now a maintained trail, complete with the old railroad tunnels one walks through along the way. The park also includes the ambitious River Mountains Loop Trail, a 35-mile "mini Grand Circle", that passes through Las Vegas and Henderson, Nevada.

Some of the NPS's favorite picks are listed here, but given this is a 1.3-million-acre park, there are many other trails as well. For an extensive list of all area hikes go here: www.birdandhike.com. The site's author, PhD Ecologist, Jim Boone, has put a lot of passion into his effort to document just about everything when it comes to the hikes in the Las Vegas area and beyond.

The lake itself hasn't been full since the 1980's, as demand and drought have taken a toll on supply. As of 2010, the lake was at a bleak 39% capacity and fears that it would be too low to run the hydroelectric facilities come closer to reality with each year. As far back as 2002, boat launches have had to be relocated or have been closed altogether. This story is playing out currently throughout the entire western United States and all who live under the shadow of drought look each winter for a return to more average rainfall levels.

Hiking in Lake Mead National Recreation Area

Note: Some of these hikes can be extremely hot in the summer and can be hazardous to one's health due to dehydration and heat stroke.

River Mountains Loop Trail
Strenuous – (35.0 mi / 56.3 km), one-way

River Mountains is the Cadillac of trails. Professionally designed and constructed, covering multiple jurisdictions, the trail does a great job of providing residents with recreational opportunities within an urban area. The trail is a loop that effectively "starts" near the Hoover Dam and heads clockwise first south to Boulder City, NV and then north through the outskirts of Henderson, NV before connecting back to the dam. The trail is paved and great for a solid bike ride. There are restrooms, picnic tables and even an air stand for bicyclists. The trail can be picked up at a number of locations including the Historic Railroad Trail described below. The trail even has its own website: http://rivermountainstrail.org/. Go there for maps and full description.

Historic Railroad Trail

Moderate – (4.4 mi / 7.1 km), round trip, allow 3 – 4 hours

This is a fun hike that follows along an old railroad track from Hoover Dam. The railway was once used to haul the massive turbines and at five points of construction, the railroad carved tunnels through solid rock. The tunnels are 25 feet high. The easygoing wide dirt path allows for a pleasant stroll, with views of Lake Mead in the near distance.

Historic Railroad Trail

Arizona Hot Spring

Moderate – (6.5 mi / 10.5 km), round trip, allow 5 hours, including soak time

Within Lake Mead NRA is an area of minor active volcanism. While it may be awhile before one will have to dodge a lava flow, it is possible to warm one's bones in a natural hot spring. The majority of the hike is through a volcanic slot canyon, providing a different geological context from the usual sandstone slick rock.

Take the Hot Springs Canyon Route, starting in a clockwise direction from the trailhead. One can choose either the lower or the upper route. While the lower route does contain a class three scramble up a rock wall, there are some good handholds allowing most to navigate this dryfall. If climbing rocks isn't your thing, the upper route bypasses the scramble but is a bit longer.

As you draw up the route, the canyon becomes much narrower and you will need to walk in the stream itself. The warmth of the water is evident from the start. It's best to wear hiking boots that you can get wet, as the rock is a bit rough. There is a sturdy 20-foot ladder to climb at the end just before the hot springs.

The hot springs run at an average temperature of 111 degrees. The water is clear and inviting, though it is advised on the trail not to ingest the water or get it up your nose due to amoebas that are native to the hot springs. The amoeba, Naegleria fowleri, is rare, but lethal. Over the course of 9 years, from 2002 to 2011, the Center of Disease Control noted just 33 cases nationwide, but with a 98% death rate. With those statistics, odds of being affected by this amoeba are rare, but if you do, the only upside is you will finally get around to creating a will and choosing a cool epitaph. All in all, just don't ingest the water, either consciously or accidentally through the nose.

Once you've had a nice soak, continue clockwise; now onto White Rock Canyon Route for more stunning volcanic scenery as you walk back to your car. Note that it's common to see various items that were forgotten at the spring, don't forget your stuff before you leave.

Bluffs Trail

Moderate – (1.8 mi / 2.9 km), round trip, allow 1 hour

Bluff's Trail is there and back hike up a dry desert ridge to a minor summit. There are views of Lake Mead and the surrounding territory from the top.

Grapevine Canyon Trail

Moderate – (3.0 mi / 4.8 km), round trip, allow 1 – 2 hours

This is a pleasant hike with a small stream and other water features, as well as some unusual sandstone features along the way. The trail lands at a series of well-defined and easily found petroglyphs at a quarter mile in. There is a small but lush desert oasis further upstream with a waterfall at 1.5 miles.

Northshore Summit Trail

Easy – (0.6 mi / 1.0 km), round trip, allow 30 minutes

While this does have about 200 feet in elevation gain, the short distance makes this an easy hike to see some of the desert surrounding Lake Mead. No view of the lake itself, but the scenery is spectacular. The trail does have two routes to the top, allowing for a loop hike.

Redstone Trail

Easy – (0.5 mi / 0.8 km), round trip, allow 30 minutes

Near the Redstone Picnic area is an eroded layer of red sandstone that can be explored. This is a nice easy stroll and the tilted layers of sandstone are worth seeing up close. Plenty of opportunities to scramble up red rock islands. The picnic area has a lot of nice scenery as well. Great place for a lunch and hike during the cooler months.

St. Thomas Trail

Easy – (3.0 mi / 4.8 km), round trip, allow 90 minutes

One of the upsides to a drought is the re-surfacing of St. Thomas, a Mormon ghost town. The town was created in 1865 and had a population of 274 residents in 1930 before the townsfolk were asked to relocate. The small agricultural community moved to Logandale-Overton. Though most of the ghost town is made up of foundation structures only, it's still easy to piece together the layout of the settlement. Pick up a brochure from the ranger station to guide you. If you are looking for a scary hike, this is a good pick. Even in the daytime, many find it to be a spooky experience.

Redstone

Wetlands Trail

Easy – (1.3 mi / 2.1 km), round trip, allow 30 minutes

A short loop trail to Las Vegas Wash, a Lake Mead tributary. The trail travels within a riparian ecosystem along the water's edges, which is in contrast to the dry surroundings. Opportunity for wildlife viewing and late afternoon photo opportunities.

Liberty Bell Arch

Strenuous – (2.8 mi / 4.5 km), round trip, allow 2 hours

Liberty Bell Arch Trail is in the same vicinity as the Arizona Hot Spring Trail but is vastly different. The trail is exposed for nearly the entire length, providing some unique features on the way up to an overlook. This is typically a hot and dry dusty hike, so hot that the NPS has closed it to hiking during the summer months. There are two highlights beyond the views, a misshapen arch whose silhouette at the proper angle looks like the Liberty Bell and an old mine, complete with a dangerous, but inviting shaft and slowly decaying equipment. At the top, the views are commanding in every direction.

Fortification Hill

Strenuous – (4.0 mi / 6.4 km), round trip, allow 2 - 3 hours

This is a strenuous but otherwise straightforward there and back hike up to the top of Fortification Hill. Via the Ridge Route, the trail starts out climbing a sandy ridge, taking the hiker to a class 3 scramble up a rocky hill. From there, the trail dog legs to the left for the final approach to the summit. Along with the great views of Lake Mead, there is a summit register and marker. If bagging a peak is on your bucket list, this is an easy way to mark it off and get some good scenery along the way.

Lake Mead Muddy Mountains Wilderness

Central Arizona

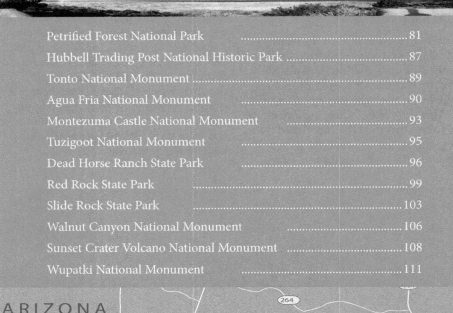

80

Petrified Forest National Park

Quick Facts

Official Park Website:

- http://www.nps.gov/pefo

Visitor Center:

- (928) 524-6228

Park Accessibility:

- Okay for 2WD and RVs
- Primarily day use, overnight use in backcountry allowed with permit

Experience Level:

- Family Friendly – Backcountry Hiker

Camping in Park:

- None

Lodging and Dining in Park:

- Painted Desert Diner

Nearest Town with Amenities:

- Holbrook, AZ is 26 mi / 42 km from park

Getting There:

- From Flagstaff, AZ: take I-40 East 116 mi / 187 km to park entrance

Petrified wood is a mashup of timelessness and beauty

Petrified Forest

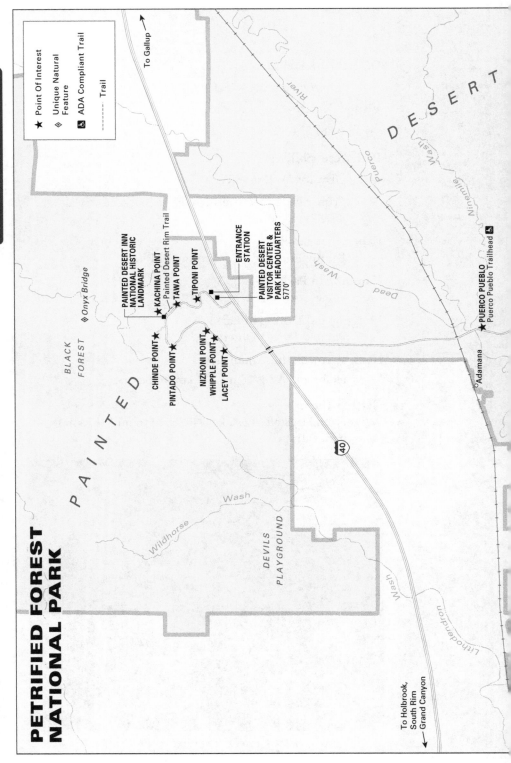

CENTRAL ARIZONA

PETRIFIED FOREST NATIONAL PARK

To Gallup →

LEGEND
- ★ Point Of Interest
- ◈ Unique Natural Feature
- ♿ ADA Compliant Trail
- ----- Trail

DESERT

Puerco River

BLACK FOREST

◈ *Onyx Bridge*

PAINTED DESERT INN NATIONAL HISTORIC LANDMARK

★ KACHINA POINT

Painted Desert Rim Trail

★ TAWA POINT

★ TIPONI POINT

★ CHINDE POINT

★ PINTADO POINT

★ NIZHONI POINT

★ WHIPPLE POINT

★ LACEY POINT

ENTRANCE STATION

PAINTED DESERT VISITOR CENTER & PARK HEADQUARTERS
5770'

P A I N T E D

Dead Wash

Ninemile Wash

PUERCO PUEBLO
Puerco Pueblo Trailhead ♿

○ Adamana

40

Wildhorse Wash

DEVILS PLAYGROUND

Lithodendron Wash

To Holbrook, South Rim Grand Canyon →

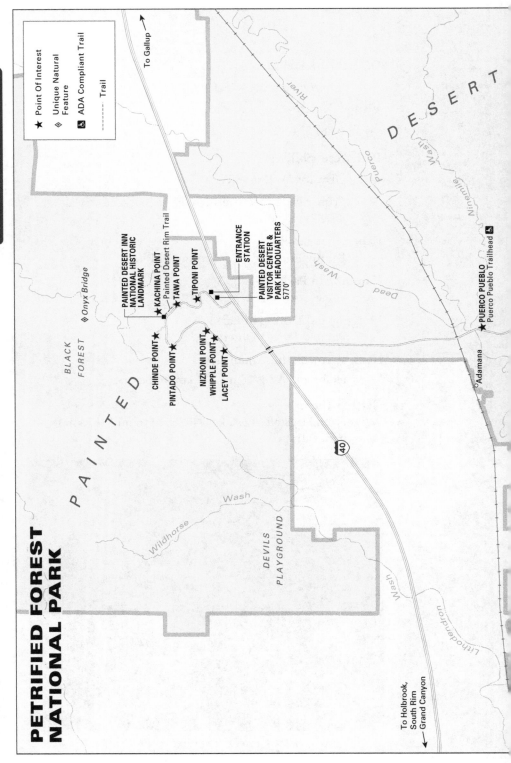

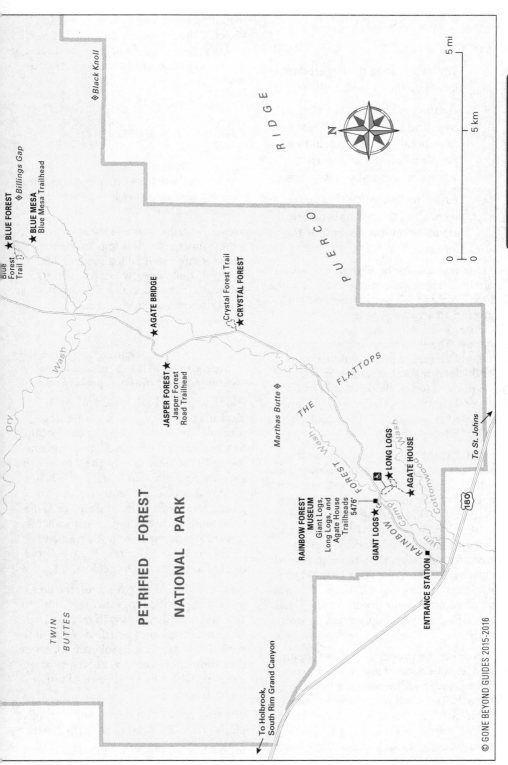

© GONE BEYOND GUIDES 2015-2016

Petrified Forest CENTRAL ARIZONA

83

What Makes Petrified Forest Special

- Walking among the largest deposits of petrified wood in the world.

- Getting up close to the petrified trees and seeing that they are full of mineralized color, including purple amethyst, clear quartz, smoky quartz and yellow citrine.

- Knowing that when these trees were alive, the ground you are standing on was down near the equator.

There was a forest here, that much is obvious. There are entire trees that somehow became rock lying strewn on the ground all around you, in a dry badland environment. How they got here is fascinating. There was once a supercontinent called Pangaea, which contained most of the land mass that makes up Earth as we know it today. Before it split into the several continents, the area now known as Arizona sat closer to the equator some 225 million years ago.

During this time, the land was a robust forest of plants, trees and shrubs, most of which are now extinct, including every species of tree found in Petrified Forest National Park. Standing in the park is to stand in an ancient river channel that not only acted as a collection mechanism for the fallen trees but also helped slow their decay. The river channel likely meandered, forming a U shape that was pinched off at some point. Alternatively, perhaps the river simply dried up over time.

Whatever the process, the river channel and its collection of logs were slowly covered with sediment such as volcanic ash. The silica within the ash slowly permeated the wood cells and replaced it with minerals. Once silica is allowed to crystallize, it can take on many forms, including agate, opal, chalcedony, and jasper. Other minerals such as iron oxide and manganese oxide help to produce the variety of color within the petrified wood.

Hiking in the Petrified Forest National Park

Giant Logs

Easy – (0.4 mi / 0.6 km), round trip, allow 30 minutes, elev. Δ: 41 ft / 12 m, trailhead behind Rainbow Forest Museum

This trail walks amongst some of the largest most accessible logs in the park. There is one petrified log named "Old Faithful" that is nearly ten feet wide at the base. There is a trail guide available at the Rainbow Forest Museum.

Long Logs

Easy – (1.6 mi / 2.6 km), round trip, allow 1 hour, elev. Δ:50 ft / 15 m, trailhead at Rainbow Forest Museum parking area

Along with the Blue Mesa and Agate House, Long Logs Trail is something more of a true trail. Don't let the fact the first half of it is well paved, it allows one the ability to fully take in the views of the surrounding grasslands. This area is hard to fully describe, the land carries a forgotten loneliness to it, while at the same time sends an invitation to just walk off towards the horizon in just about any direction. It is a place that is easy to lose oneself and yet hard to get lost.

As the trail loses its pavement, the collection of petrified logs increase, both in size and quantity. This is in fact the largest concentration of petrified wood in the park. There are wonderful examples here that allow the hiker to get up close and personal with some ancient and rather larger trees.

The trail can be combined with the Agate House trail. The total round trip distance for both is 2.6 miles (4.2 km).

Blue Meas badlands

Agate House

Easy – (2.0 mi / 3.2 km), round trip, allow 1 – 2 hours, elev. Δ: 41 ft / 12 m, trailhead at Rainbow Forest Museum parking area

As the name suggests this is a very cool eight-room pueblo made entirely out of agate blocks. It is believed to have been built some 700 years ago. The ruins of this pueblo were actually rebuilt in 1933-34 by the Civilian Conservation Corps (CCC). They rebuilt parts of the pueblo and completely rebuilt "room 7", including a roof.

The inhabitants entered in through the ceiling. The Agate House today is for viewing only. Please don't climb or sit on what is now a piece of history.

Agate House

Crystal Forest

Easy – (0.75 mi / 1.2 km), round trip, allow 30 minutes, elev. Δ: 121 ft / 37 m, trailhead at Crystal Forest parking area

One of the trails that contain the petrified wood you came for, the trail is named for the many amazing crystals that are found within the logs.

This is a chance to take a close look at the colorful crystal formations within the petrified logs. Please refrain from the temptation to take even small pieces. It's for everyone to enjoy

Jasper Forest Road

Easy – (2.5 mi / 4.0 km), round trip, allow 2 hours, elev. Δ: negligible, trailhead at Jasper Forest Road parking area

There is an eroded forgotten road built in the 1930's by the CCC that makes for a wonderful hike today. Originally, a wagon path for rock hounds coming in by train, it was later transformed into a proper road with the advent of the automobile. The path allows for a great hike today amongst a large display of petrified wood that has rolled down with erosion from the bluffs above the road. Given this isn't one of the main trails; it's a great find for those that want to feel they have the park to themselves.

85

Blue Mesa

Easy with short steep incline– (1.0 mi / 1.6 km), round trip, allow 30 -45 minutes, elev. Δ: 97 ft / 30 m, trailhead at Blue Mesa parking area

The Blue Mesa is one of the most unique areas within the Grand Circle. First off, it's not expected. You came for the petrified wood and anticipate seeing a red rock or two. The Blue Mesa Trail takes one into a bentonite badland hills that have alternate stripes of white and blue clay. It really must be seen to be believed and is certainly a photographer's paradise. As an added bonus, there are several fossils, including the famous namesake petrified trees.

Puerco Pueblo

Easy – (0.3 mi / 0.5 km), round trip, allow 30 minutes, elev. Δ: 41 ft / 12 m, trailhead at Puerco Pueblo parking area

A paved and accessible trail with petroglyphs near the southern segment. This trail passes by the foundational remains of a hundred ancestral Puebloan site, dating back some 600 years. Aside from the ruins, there are some good views of the grasslands that are the signature of the grasslands in this part of Arizona.

The silence of light and sky

Painted Desert Rim Trail

Easy – (1.0 mi / 1.6 km), round trip, allow 30 minutes, elev. Δ: 14 ft / 4 m, trailhead at Tawa Point and Kachina Point

The Painted Desert Rim Trail sits near the park visitor center and gives expansive views of the Painted Desert badlands. This area is comprised mainly of bentonite clay formed from volcanic ash and silt deposits. The entire area is a multicolored palette of red, pink, and white hillsides that are all the more striking due the lack of vegetation due to the poor soils. While this isn't the trail for petrified wood, it is worth seeing.

Jasper Forest

Hubbell Trading Post National Historic Park

Official Park Website:

- http://www.nps.gov/hutr

Visitor Center:

- (928) 755-3475

Park Accessibility:

- Okay for 2WD and RVs
- Day Use Only

Experience Level:

- Family Friendly

Camping in Park:

- None

Lodging and Dining in Park:

- None

Nearest Town with Amenities:

- Ganado, AZ is 1 mi / 1.6 km from park

Getting There:

- From Flagstaff, AZ: take I-40 East to AZ-87 North to Indian Route 15 to US-191 South for 156 mi / 251 km to park entrance

Step into the living history of Hubbell Trading Post

What Makes Hubbell Trading Post National Historic Site Special

- Oldest continuously operated trading post within the Navajo Nation

- An amazing step back in time coupled with being a present day active trading post

- Very cool place to browse and see the artistry designs of handcrafted rugs, kachinas, baskets and jewelry

Talk about a unique place, Hubbell Trading Post was created as a center for the Navajo to trade their wares into the non-Navajo world. At the center of it all was John Lorenzo Hubbell, who in 1878, purchased the trading post and became a focal point of trade. Ten years earlier in 1868, the Navajo were decimated as a people and in a depression economically. After the Long Walk of the Navajo, a torturous journey where the Navajo were forced to walk 13 miles a day under poor conditions, they returned to their lands to find their fields and cattle stripped. They rebuilt from what they had left and to obtain goods they didn't have, they traded. The Hubbell Trading Post became a major aspect in this part of their history.

Today, the 160-acre Hubbell homestead is protected as a National Historic Park. It includes the trading post, Hubbell's family home and some out buildings. Tours of Hubbell's home are given for $2. What is especially amazing is that the park is a living cultural preserve. The ranch and the trading post are still active. One can see not only Navajo Churro Sheep, horses and chickens, but also the trading post itself. The look and feel of this place is as if it is a museum where the items are available for purchase. All of the items are authentic. Auctions of items are also held twice a year. Hubbell's is truly a gem within the Grand Circle.

Original basket art

Rug making

Tonto National Monument

Official Park Website:

- http://www.nps.gov/tont

Visitor Center:

- (928) 467-2241

Park Accessibility:

- Okay for 2WD and RVs
- Day Use Only

Experience Level:

- Family Friendly

Camping in Park:

- None

Lodging and Dining in Park:

- None

Nearest Town with Amenities:

- Roosevelt, AZ is 2.4 mi / 4 km from the park

Getting There:

- From Phoenix, AZ: take AZ-87 North and AZ-188 South for 110 mi / 177 km to the park

Tonto National Monument embodies the soul of Arizona, with Saguaro cacti, the call of the Canyon wren, and a desert that at first glance seems sparse but on further pause uncovers a fascinating and rich ecosystem. The surroundings of Tonto are almost as incredible as the well-preserved cliff dwellings overlooking the man-made Theodore Roosevelt Lake.

There are two cliff dwellings, created by the Salado People, identified by their unique blend of styles borrowed from other pueblos within the surrounding region. This is especially evident in the pottery, which is vibrant and colorful. The lower cliff dwelling is accessible to all via a 0.5 mile (0.8 km) paved trail. The hike is easy to moderate and takes about an hour. The park closes at 5pm, so hikes must start by 4pm.

The second cliff dwelling can be observed by guided tour only. These tours are limited and are given about three times a week from November through April. The tour starts at 10 AM, is 3 miles (4.8 km) long, and lasts 3 to 4 hours. Tours are limited to 15 people and are given as staff availability allows. The trail is considered moderate to strenuous, climbing 600 feet in elevation along a rocky trail. Call (928)467-2241 for reservations.

Tonto cliff dwelling

CENTRAL ARIZONA

Tonto

Agua Fria National Monument

Official Park Website:

*   http://www.blm.gov/az/st/en/prog/blm_special_areas/
    natmon/afria.html

Visitor Center:

*   None in park, contact: Agua Fria National Monument,
    Monument Manager: Amanda James, 21605 N. 7th
    Avenue, Phoenix, AZ 85027-2929, Phone: (623) 580-
    5500

Park Accessibility:

*   2WD, 4WD recommended for most roads

*   Day and Overnight Use

Experience Level:

*   Primarily Casual Hiker – Backcountry Hiker

Camping in Park:
*   No developed campground, backcountry camping
    okay with permit

Lodging and Dining in Park:
*   None

Nearest Town with Amenities:
*   Cordes Lake, AZ is 24 mi / 39 km from park

Getting There:
*   From Phoenix, AZ: Take I-17 North for 79 mi / 127
    km to park

A beautiful and often overlooked park

AGUA FRIA NATIONAL MONUMENT

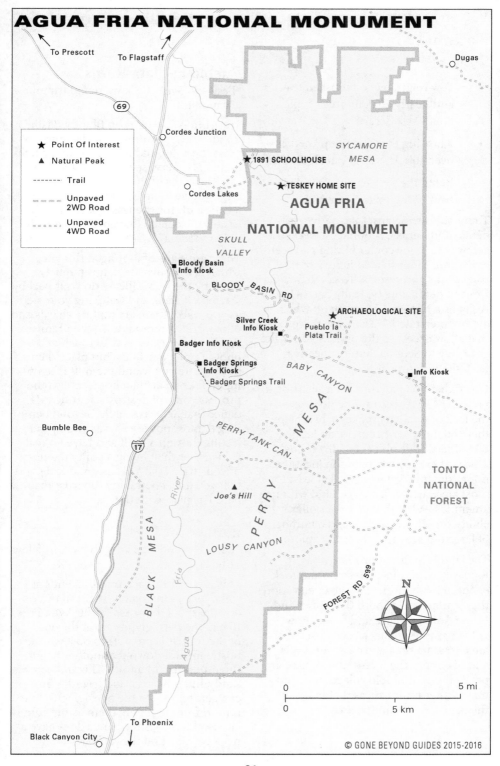

To Prescott

To Flagstaff

Dugas

69

Cordes Junction

Legend:
- ★ Point Of Interest
- ▲ Natural Peak
- ------- Trail
- ═ ═ ═ Unpaved 2WD Road
- ═ ═ ═ Unpaved 4WD Road

SYCAMORE MESA

★ 1891 SCHOOLHOUSE

★ TESKEY HOME SITE

Cordes Lakes

AGUA FRIA

NATIONAL MONUMENT

SKULL VALLEY

■ Bloody Basin Info Kiosk

BLOODY BASIN RD

ARCHAEOLOGICAL SITE ★

■ Silver Creek Info Kiosk

Pueblo la Plata Trail

■ Badger Info Kiosk

■ Badger Springs Info Kiosk

BABY CANYON

Info Kiosk ■

Badger Springs Trail

Bumble Bee ○

17

PERRY TANK CAN.

MESA

TONTO

NATIONAL

FOREST

Joe's Hill ▲

River

PERRY

BLACK MESA

LOUSY CANYON

Fria

FOREST RD 599

N

Agua

0   5 mi

0   5 km

To Phoenix

Black Canyon City ○

© GONE BEYOND GUIDES 2015-2016

91

What Makes Agua Fria National Monument Special

- Few roads, one established trail and nearly 70,000 acres of epic Southwest desert
- Knowing that this site preserves over 400 Ancestral Puebloan sites
- Being the journey less traveled from Phoenix to Sedona

To most Phoenicians, (aka native residents of Phoenix), Sedona is a weekend getaway to enjoy cooler hiking and scenery within the insulated luxury of fine restaurants and resorts. To get to Sedona from Phoenix, one typically passes by Agua Fria National Monument, which is cut by Interstate 17. There are three exits that allow access to the park as you make your way to Sedona, but for the most part, the monument is ignored.

Given that this park has been set aside to preserve 450 Ancestral Puebloan sites, the lack of publicity makes sense. Here there are no visitor centers, no lodges, one official trail, and three dirt roads. This isn't exactly a babymoon location nor a romantic getaway, well at least for most anyway. It is a rugged land with no amenities. What the park does offer is the ability for off trail hiking and a number of large unexcavated ruins to explore.

The land is inviting, primarily basalt top layers with older Precambrian rock exposed by the Agua Fria at an elevation that at times holds both the Upper and Lower Sonoran flora and fauna. Low golden grasses in black rock, lush riparian corridors set against canyon walls and of course, the many ruins. There are petroglyphs, multiple village sites, and many other minor ruins that make up the near 400 sites in the area.

Hiking Agua Fria National Monument

Pueblo la Plata Ruins
Easy – (0.5 mi / 0.8 km), round trip, allow 30 minutes

This ruin is 8.3 miles on Bloody Basin Road, which requires high clearance to cross the creek and in some rough patches, but is otherwise suitable for a 2WD car. The ruins of Pueblo la Plata was a large village of up to 100 rooms. The location of this site was by design as it sits on the defendable northwestern rim of Perry Mesa.

There are signs of looting at this site, which is the only site that is publicly listed by the BLM. Please do your part by staying off walls and watching your step as you walk. There are pottery shards and other artifact remnants on the premises. BLM's stance is its okay to touch and photograph your finds, but place them back where you found them. It is tempting to take an artifact home, but in the process you will destroy scientific evidence that helps research. Beyond being illegal, most pottery shards end up collecting dust on a shelf and have no real value other than being a guilty memory of your trip. Take a picture and feel good that you aren't betraying the trust that the park has placed on the visitor.

Badger Springs Trail
Easy – (1.5 mi / 2.4 km), round trip, allow 1 hour

This is a there a back trail that ends at some nice petroglyphs. The trail travels down a small dry wash to the Agua Fria River. The petroglyphs are at the end of the trail. It is possible to bushwhack upstream and down for another half to three-quarters of a mile. This trail is a bit sandy, but otherwise kid friendly. You can get right up to the petroglyphs, but refrain from touching them as the cumulative oil from visitor hands does have a negative effect on the rock art.

Montezuma Castle National Monument

Official Park Website:

- http://www.nps.gov/moca

Visitor Center:

- (928) 567-3322

Park Accessibility:

- Okay for 2WD and RVs
- Day Use Only

Experience Level:

- Family Friendly

Camping in Park:

- None

Lodging and Dining in Park:

- None

Nearest Town with Amenities:

- Camp Verde, AZ is 7 mi / 11 km from the park

Getting There:

- From Phoenix, AZ: take I-17 for 93 mi / 150 km to the park

Montezuma Castle

What Makes Montezuma Castle Special

- Makes for a pleasant side trip on the way to Sedona
- A well preserved cliff dwelling of the Sinagua People
- Seeing nearby Montezuma Well

Montezuma Castle is one in a long list of misnamed parks within the Grand Circle. It has nothing to do with Montezuma, the Aztec ruler killed by the Spanish conquests of Cortés. Nor is it a castle. It is actually one of the best-preserved cliff dwellings of the Sinagua People.

The ruins sit 90 feet up a sheer cliff within an alcove. Some of the walls have been reconstructed, complete with exterior plaster, which gives the visitor a great view into what the cliff dwelling would have looked like some 800 years ago.

The ruins are accessible to the eye only from a short one-third mile paved walkway amongst the fanning sounds of the surrounding Sycamore trees. This is what makes this park fun. There are no tours and no real hikes. Montezuma Castle is a quick side treat within one's journey from here to there. If you are traveling to Sedona from Phoenix, the park makes a nice respite to stretch the legs and experience a bit of history.

Another side trip is to Montezuma Well, which is eleven miles away. This spot is amazing, though on the surface it just looks like a big hole with water in it. In reality, this is a limestone sinkhole with an underground spring. What is impressive is the spring itself, which pumps a consistent 1.5 million gallons of water out each day. There are some remnants of early Sinagua usage, including some cliff dwellings tightly integrated into the walls of the sinkhole. The area is considered by the Yavapai to be where their people emerged into this world.

Strolling through the Montezuma Castle grounds

Tuzigoot National Monument

Official Park Website:

- http://www.nps.gov/tuzi

Visitor Center:

- (928) 634-5564

Park Accessibility:

- Okay for 2WD and RVs
- Day Use Only

Experience Level:

- Family Friendly

Camping in Park:

- None

Lodging and Dining in Park:

- None

Tuzigoot

Nearest Town with Amenities:

- Cottonwood, AZ is 4.4 mi / 7 km from the park

Getting There:

- From Phoenix, AZ: take I-17 N to AZ-260 W/Finnie Flat Rd. Continue on AZ-260 to Cottonwood, taking South Main Street to Tuzigoot Road for 107 mi / 172 km to the park

Tuzigoot National Monument is a local treasure of the towns of Cottonwood and Clarkdale, Arizona. The park's small site sits on a small hilltop at the base of the Woodchute Wilderness and Mingus Mountain Wilderness. Within sight of the ruins, one can see the old mining town of Jerome, AZ, as well as the red rocks of Sedona in the far distance to the east.

The ruins themselves are 2-3 story ruins laid out in an elongated rectangle. There are some 110 rooms within the complex. The rooms towards the center of the ruins stand higher than the other rooms and are thought to have been used for public activities.

Tuzigoot is a great way to spend an afternoon if you are visiting the area and makes a great side trip if you are visiting Jerome. It takes no more than 30 – 45 minutes to explore the site. Camping is at the nearby Dead Horse Ranch State Park or in nearby Sedona. Call (928) 467-2241 for reservations.

Dead Horse Ranch State Park

Official Park Website:

- http://az-stateparks.com/Parks/DEHO/

Visitor Center:

- (928) 634-5283

Park Accessibility:

- Okay for 2WD and RVs

- Day and Overnight Use

Great birding opportunities

Experience Level:

- Family Friendly – Casual Hiker

Camping in Park:

- Camping in Park: 106 RV/T sites plus 17 tent only sites and 1 group site (holds 23 people), ADA accessible restrooms, drinking water, showers, hookups, dump station

Lodging and Dining in Park:

- 8 camping cabins, shared shower, heating and cooling, beds, must provide own linens

Nearest Town with Amenities:

- Cottonwood, AZ is 2 mi / 3 km from park

Getting There:

- From Flagstaff, AZ: Take I-17 South to County Rd 30/County Rd 77 in Lake Montezuma. Take exit 293 from I-17 South to park entrance. Total distance is 64 mi / 103 km to park.

- From Phoenix, AZ: take I-17 North to AZ-260 West/Finnie Flat Rd in Camp Verde to Dead Horse Ranch Road in Cottonwood. Total distance is 105 mi / 169 km to park.

What Makes Dead Horse Special

- Short and serene riparian hikes in a peaceful setting

- Great base camp for visiting nearby Tuzigoot National Monument, Jerome, Sedona or the Verde River

- Perfect place for camping, fishing and relaxing

Boy, if you ever want a place to become a state park, give it the name Dead Horse. This is one of two parks within the Grand Circle that have "dead horse" as part of its name (the other being Dead Horse Point State Park in Utah). The name aside, this is a fun park. Dead Horse Ranch State Park is a small park just outside the city center of Cottonwood that is a favorite of campers and anglers. There are stocked lagoons, picnic ramadas, cabins for rent, as well as numerous campsites to pitch a tent or park an RV.

There is also a system of mountain bike trails that extent outside of the park. For information on the mountain biking trails, go to http://azstateparks.com/Parks/DEHO/downloads/DEHO_Trails_Map.pdf

Most of the hikes within the park are gentle walks. Dead Horse is often used as an alternate camping destination for the Verde Valley Area. The park is centrally located near the red rocks of Sedona as well as the living ghost town and artist community of Jerome, Arizona. Dead Horse is also within walking distance of Tuzigoot National Monument, which holds one of the largest and best-preserved pueblo ruins of the Sinagua people.

Hiking Dead Horse Ranch State Park

Canopy Trail

Easy – (0.25 mi / 0.4 km), round trip, allow 15 -30 minutes

This is a spur trail off Forest Loop and simply goes into the center of the loop. It is ADA accessible and once on the trail gives a good feeling of remoteness and nature under the blanket of Fremont's cottonwoods. The trail is a favorite of bird watchers.

Forest Loop

Easy – (0.5 mi / 0.8 km), round trip, allow 30 minutes

A short loop from the river day use area and nearby picnic area. Great for walking off a BBQ feast or simply exploring just for the fun of it. The trail is used for river access and as the name implies, runs through of a forest of Fremont's cottonwoods. This is a nice tranquil hike.

Mesa Trail

Easy – (1.0 mi / 1.6 km), one way, allow 30 minutes to 1 hour

The Mesa Trail is an interpretive loop that climbs to the top of a hill overlooking the Red Hawk Campground. From the top are good views of the Verde Valley, the towering Mingus Mountain and even the distant red rocks of Sedona. Along the way are kiosks pointing out various educational tidbits.

Tavasci Marsh Trail

Easy – (2.0 mi / 3.2 km), round trip, allow 1 hour for the hike, more if visiting the ruins

Located at the end of Flycatcher Road at the north end of the park, Tavasci Marsh Trail is a very pleasant hike that ambles along a robust and healthy marshland ending at the entrance to Tuzigoot

National Monument. This trail is like stepping back in time as you go from a campground type setting into one of the best-preserved pueblo ruins of the Sinagua people. This is a great hike, but make sure you plan for time to explore the ruins. The marsh provides excellent birding opportunities.

Quail Wash Trail
Easy – (0.25 mi / 0.4 km), round trip, allow 15 - 30 minutes

This is a short and popular riparian trail near the River Day Use Area and intersects with the Hickey Ditch Trail. The trail is located at the south end of the West Lagoon parking lot.

Hickey Ditch Trail
Easy – (0.5 mi / 0.8 km), round trip, allow 30 minutes

This trail walks under a canopy of Arizona Black Walnut and Willow trees along a historic irrigation ditch. A pleasant little hike that can be combined with Quail Wash.

Creosote Trail
Easy – (0.5 mi / 0.8 km), round trip, allow 30 minutes

This trail is a spur from Hickey Ditch and Quail Wash that connects to the Lime Kiln Trail.

Lime Kiln Trail
Moderate – (4.2 mi / 6.8 km), round trip, allow 2 – 3 hours

The described stretch of the Lime Kiln Trail is a 2.1-mile segment that is part of a larger 15-mile trail that connects Dead Horse Ranch State Park to Red Rock State Park in Sedona. The trail began as a road in the 1800's to transport lime from Cottonwood to Sedona. It was then forgotten until 2006 when it was reinstated as an official trail connecting the two parks.

The initial 2.1 miles of this trail heads outside of the park towards Sedona before intersecting with Thumper Trail. Lime kiln ruins can be seen along the way. Once at the Thumper Trail, you can either head back the 2.1 miles or make a 5.2-mile extension by taking Thumper Trail (2.3 miles) to Lower Raptor Trail (2.9 miles), which returns Blackhawk Loop campsite at the northern end of the park. (See the mountain biking trail website listed above for more information on Thumper and Lower Raptor Trails).

Verde River Greenway
Easy – (2.0 mi / 3.2 km), round trip, allow 1 -2 hours

The Verde River Greenway winds through a forested canopy along the Verde River. This is a great place for seeing wildlife, especially for birds. Go for an early morning or dusk hike for optimal wildlife viewing. Can be made into a loop that follows along the lagoons.

The gentle grounds of Dead Horse Ranch

Red Rock State Park

Official Park Website:

- http://azstateparks.com/Parks/RERO/

Visitor Center:

- (928) 282-6907

Park Accessibility:

- Okay for 2WD and RVs
- Day Use Only

Experience Level:

- Family Friendly – Casual Hiker

Camping in Park:

- None within park, multiple seasonal campgrounds along Oak Creek Canyon (AZ-89A)

Lodging and Dining in Park:

- None

Nearest Town with Amenities:

- Sedona, AZ is 9 mi / 15 km from park.

Getting There:

- From Flagstaff, AZ: take AZ-89A South to Red Rock Loop Road, turn left at either end of Red Rock Loop Road to park entrance
- From Phoenix, AZ: take I-17 North to AZ-260 W/ Finnie Flat Rd in Camp Verde to AZ-89A North, then right on Red Rock Loop Road to park entrance

Cathedral Rock

What Makes Red Rock State Park Special

- That special feeling of hiking amongst the Sedona red rocks and fragrant pinyon juniper woodlands

- Knowing that the entire town of Sedona is one of the most hiker friendly places in Arizona

- Becoming a bit light headed and wondering if it's because of a vortex

Sedona contains the soft strength of red rock monoliths that in the subtlety of dawn and dusk radiate the sun's glow as art. The area has become one of the most photographed areas in Arizona to the point that even if you aren't aware of the town, you have most likely seen a photo of it. It is of no wonder then that the town is a center for artists of all mediums, from painters to sculptures to ceramists.

It sits at the very edge of the Mogollon Rim, putting it at the intersection of three ecosystems. This translates to the viewer as lush pinyon juniper forests cut by a riparian thread of Oak Creek, with conifers at higher elevations. For its ability to balance three ecosystems, the area supports a large variety of birds and is a favorite for bird lovers.

Sedona's beauty is nearly magical at times and the very rock is said to hold energy, which is why so many have tried to call it home after seeing it for the first time. They come to Sedona and are transfixed. There are many stories of folks who come to visit and decide this is where they want to live, as if the red rocks were a calling.

For hikers, it is a paradise. The number of day hikes here are in the dozens and there are trails for every experience level. After the hike is done, one can eat at decent restaurants and sleep in resort class settings. It is the best of both the world of nature and the world of comfort.

Red Rock State Park is tucked outside of the city bustle and was created rather late in the history of the town, coming to bear in 1986. The trails throughout all of Sedona are remarkable and the ones inside this park are no exception. The trails within Red Rock State Park are

Hiking in red rock country

listed here. If you are interested in local hiking trails outside of the park, please visit http://www.redrockcountry.org/.

Hiking Red Rock State Park

Note: There was some flooding in the park in March of 2014. This has washed out bridges, making access to some of the trails more challenging and certainly wetter. Ask about current trail conditions at the visitor center.

Rattlesnake Ridge Trail

Easy – (1.3 mi / 2.1 km), round trip from visitor center, allow 1 hour

This is an easy trail giving great views of the park and Sedona. The trail connects to the Smoke Trail or the visitor center from the front picnic armadas.

Smoke Trail

Easy – (0.4 mi / 0.6 km), round trip from visitor center, allow 30 minutes

Typically done as a part of a number of loops within the park, the Smoke Trail ambles peacefully along Oak Creek. It is accessible for all users. Lots of riparian flora here along with ample bird watching possibilities. The great egret and blue heron have both been spotted on occasion along with woodpeckers and ravens.

Bunkhouse Trail

Easy – (0.5 mi / 0.8 km), round trip from visitor center, allow 30 minutes

This is a level and accessible loop trail that also allows connection to other trails. The trail gives easy viewing of the surrounding red rocks, including Cathedral Rock, one of the most photographed monoliths in the world.

Kisva Trail

Easy – (1.7 mi / 2.7 km), round trip from visitor center, allow 1 - 2 hours

This is a connector trail to Eagle's Nest Loop, Smoke and Yavapai Ridge Trail and the Apache Fire Loop. The trail follows along a branch of Oak Creek for the most part, climbing 112 feet as it connects with the other trails. Kisva is a Hopi word meaning "shady water", which describes this tranquil hike with near perfection.

Eagle's Nest Loop

Moderate – (1.9 mi / 3.1 km), round trip from visitor center, allow 1 – 2 hours

The Eagle's Nest Loop is a great way to take in Sedona. It starts along Oak Creek before climbing to the top of a ridge, giving great views of Cathedral Rock, Seven Warriors, House Mountain, and West Sedona. The view also shows the ribbon of the Oak Creek riparian corridor as it weaves through the surrounding pinyon juniper forests. The deciduous trees along Oak Creek are quite dramatic in the fall as the changing color of the leaves meander through the desert. Eagle's Nest can be combined with other trails and is accessed via the Smoke, Kisva, or Sentinel trails.

House of Apache Fire Loop

Moderate – (1.7 mi / 2.7 km), round trip from visitor center, allow 1 - 2 hours

Also shown as "Apache Fire Loop", this trail climbs about 100 feet to encircle the House of Apache Fire, a retreat home of Jack Frye, the president of Trans World Airlines. Jack and his wife Helen owned several hundred acres as a retreat from their east coast lives and built this house in 1947. The house was named from the campfires Yavapai Apache workers would make while building the house. The house was never completed.

The trail loops around the house giving signature views of the park and Sedona. Like most of the trails in this park, it can be combined with other trails for extended hiking.

Yavapai Ridge Trail

Moderate – (1.5 mi / 2.4 km), round trip from visitor center, allow 1 - 2 hours

This trail can be accessed by either the Apache Fire Loop or the Javelina Trail. The trail loops through pinyon juniper forest giving views of the surrounding area. The trail is also the entry point into Turkey Valley and beyond up into House Mountain. The area of Turkey Valley is used extensively by students of the nearby Verde Valley High School.

Javelina Trail

Moderate – (1.8 mi / 2.9 km), round trip from visitor center, allow 1 - 2 hours

This trail is an add on to the Apache Fire Loop and Yavapai Ridge Trail. The trail has scenic overlooks of the southern portion of Sedona, giving views of Cathedral Rock and the distant Seven Warriors. This "Javelina Trail" should not be confused with a new mountain bike trail in the Soldier Pass area that was also given the same name.

The Red Rock Perimeter Loop

Moderate – (5.8 mi / 9.3 km), round trip from visitor center, allow 2 - 3 hours

All told, the Red Rock State Park holds a trail system of about 6 miles. If you want to walk the perimeter of the park and take in a longer hike, this is the trail for you. This loop, which is made up of a number of trails, takes the hiker in a counter-clockwise direction from the visitor center over the Kingfisher Bridge to the Javelina Trail. From there it connects to the Coyote Ridge Trail, then to Eagle's Nest before taking the Kisva Trail back to the visitor's center via a very short stint on the Sentinel Trail.

There are other variants you can add to make the hike longer or shorter. This loop was selected over one that is shorter via the Smoke Trail for the sole reason that the Black Hawk Crossing is damaged, making it a wetter hike once you get to Oak Creek. This loop is a great way to take in the entire park, giving a sample of creek side environments to scenic vistas. There are plenty of benches along the trail to just sit and take it all in as you make your way.

Slide Rock State Park

Official Park Website:

- http://azstateparks.com/Parks/SLRO/

Visitor Center:

- (928) 282-3034

Park Accessibility:

- Okay for 2WD and RVs

- Day Use Only

Experience Level:

- Family Friendly

Camping in Park:

- None within park, multiple seasonal campgrounds along Oak Creek Canyon (AZ-89A)

Lodging and Dining in Park:

- None

Nearest Town with Amenities:

- Sedona, AZ is 7 mi / 11 km from park.

Getting There:

- From Flagstaff, AZ: take AZ-89A South to park entrance

- From Phoenix, AZ: take I-17 North to AZ-179 N to AZ-89A North to park entrance

"The slide" at Slide Rock SP

What Makes Slide Rock State Park Special

- Being up in the tremendous beauty of Oak Creek Canyon

- Siding down a natural water slide formation in Oak Creek

- Coming in the off season when you have the park to yourself

Slide Rock State Park is one of the most beloved outdoor spots in all of Arizona. The lure is simple, a clear flowing creek that is so smooth and slick in one spot that it creates a natural water slide. For this reason, the place is a zoo during peak season, with all manner of tourists looking for the choice sunny spots during the morning and the choice shady spots during the afternoon.

Beyond the water slide attraction, there are a handful of small trails. If you have kids, you have to go to Slide Rock State Park. It is for them one of the coolest places on earth. When you are done for the day, the Dairy Queen just below the park is another highlight for folks providing ice cream and snacks.

Notes:

The Slide Rock area was recently hit by a wildfire. The entire area was closed for a year to minimize erosion. Please help the area recover by staying on the trails in this area.

There are times when Oak Creek receives too much use resulting in high concentrations of E. coli bacteria. This can happen at any time, but is especially prevalent during the summer when the population of visitors is up and the water levels are down. The park does close as a result. Call the Oak Creek Water Quality Hotline at (602) 542-0202 prior to going. E. coli is definitely a thing at Slide Rock State Park. Despite multiple nonprofit agencies working to protect the Oak Creek watershed, the park and the creek are a victim of being "loved to death".

The varied colors of Oak Creek Canyon

Hiking Slide Rock State Park

Pendley Homestead Trail

Easy – (0.5 mi / 0.8 km), round trip, allow 30 minutes

This is a paved trail that takes the visitor through a portion of the Pendley Homestead. The historical remnants seen along the trail includes the Pendley apple orchards and apple-packing barn along with magnificent views of the Oak Creek Canyon walls and watershed. This level trail is great for everyone and is still quite peaceful despite the crowds.

Slide Rock Route

Moderate – (0.6 mi / 1.0 km), round trip, allow 30 minutes

This trail is listed as moderate by the park, but will seem easy to navigate for most. This is the primitive route you take to get to the swimming area. Simply find parking and follow the hordes of people in front of you. Towards the creek, you'll need to step over sunbathers as the route becomes more like a public beach area with folks claiming base camp territories wherever they can. Look for a historic cabin on the west side of the creek that was used along with a Pelton wheel to generate electricity. Unless the creek is running high, there is a footbridge to get to the other side.

Despite being crowded, the park is good fun. The water slide is capable of accommodating all, from kids to adults. It is very refreshing and if you do it once, you will want to do it again, despite the line. Then there is the setting, which is arguably magical. Filtered canyon sun against red and white cliff walls that bring forth emotions of a gentle strength. This is one of the top parks in the United States and for good reason. During peak season, get there early to avoid the crowds.

Clifftop Nature Trail

Easy – (0.5 mi / 0.8 km), round trip, allow 30 minutes

Like the name says, this trail sits on the cliff banks above the creek and overlooks the sunbathers of the Slide Rock Swim Area below. There are picnic tables along the trail to enjoy a lunch while people watching along with great views of Oak Creek Canyon.

Outside the park is Broken Arrow, one of the many amazing trails in Sedona, Arizona

Walnut Canyon National Monument

Official Park Website:

- http://www.nps.gov/waca

Visitor Center:

- (928) 526-3367

Park Accessibility:

- Okay for 2WD and RVs
- Day Use Only

Experience Level:

- Family Friendly

Camping in Park:

- None

Lodging and Dining in Park:

- None

Nearest Town with Amenities:

- Flagstaff, AZ is 12 mi / 19 km from the park

Getting There:

- From Flagstaff, AZ: take I-40 East to Walnut Canyon Road. Total distance is 12 mi / 19 km to the park

Cliff dwellings

What Makes Walnut Canyon Special

- 300 cliff dwellings close to Flagstaff
- Easily covered as a day trip
- Some of the best maintained trails in the Grand Circle

Though relatively close to Wupatki NM and Flagstaff, the terrain is much different here. The cliff dwellings are found within Kaibab limestone, which also forms the rim of the Grand Canyon. Here the land is dry with some high desert scrub fauna and the limestone is a mud white, which provides a unique contrast to the usual red sandstones. The limestone also allows for the creation of alcoves, which offered protected building locations for the ancestral people.

The park is very small, about 3,500 acres, but don't let that fool you, there are over 300 cliff dwellings here. There is also a visitor center and two trails. The ruins are situated along the cliff walls of Walnut Canyon, at a deeply striated gooseneck that has formed within the canyon. The ruins share a similarity to those at Mesa Verde in that they both make use of the naturally formed limestone alcoves in their architecture.

Hiking Walnut Canyon National Monument

Rim Trail
Easy – (0.7 mi / 1.1 km), round trip, allow 45 - 60 minutes

This trail offers a paved and wheelchair accessible self-guided tour of the ruins and surrounding canyon. There are two overlooks with benches and a number of ruins to see, with descriptions along the way. It is possible to see ruins off in the canyon from the overlooks as well as several sites right along the path.

Island Trail
Strenuous – (1.0 mi / 1.6 km), round trip, allow 1 hour

This is a paved trail that travels along the rim of the park's main gooseneck and down into the canyon to observe some cliff dwellings first hand. The trail is steep in sections, with many steps as well. There are a number of sites to see along the way, including a number of rooms built into the alcove that are intact enough for shelter today. The trail brings the visitor remarkably close to the sites, which allows for an up close and personal view of these rooms.

The landscape of Walnut Canyon NM

Sunset Crater Volcano National Monument

Official Park Website:

- http://www.nps.gov/sucr

Visitor Center:

- (928) 526-0502

Park Accessibility:

- Okay for 2WD and RVs
- Day Use within park, overnight use just outside of park

Experience Level:

- Family Friendly – Casual Hiker

Camping in Park:
None in park, however Bonito Campground, run by the Forest Service, is just outside the western boundary of the park

- Bonito Campground: 44 T/RV, drinking water, flush toilets, no hookups, first come-first served

Lodging and Dining in Park:

- None

Nearest Town with Amenities:

- Flagstaff, AZ is 20 mi / 32 km from the park

Getting There:

- From Flagstaff, AZ: take US-89 North to FR 545 for 20 mi / 32 km to the park

Sunset Crater

What Makes Sunset Crater National Monument Special

- Explore a series of cinder cones and view the recently erupted Sunset Crater
- Close to Flagstaff, Arizona
- Twisted and tortured volcanic landscape with little vegetation and sweeping views.

Sunset Crater itself is a 900-year young cinder cone created as the result of volcanic activity. The area has undergone a smattering of such activity, but Sunset Crater is unique in that it occurred very recently from a geologic perspective. There are lava caves to explore, cinder cones to climb and lava fields to one can walk within. The red and yellow color of the cinders creates a wonderful offset to the tortured blacks and greys of the surrounding lava and is a favorite spot for photographers. Typically, the snow-capped San Francisco Peaks frame the background of these shots.

Sunset Crater sits at 7,000 feet and the altitude does have an effect on hiking if you aren't acclimated. The crater itself is closed to climbing but there are other hikes in the area.

Volcanic basalt terrain of Sunset Crater

Hiking Sunset Crater National Monument

Lava Flow Trail
Easy – (1.0 mi / 1.6 km), round trip, allow 30 minutes

Be sure to pick up a brochure for this self-guided interpretive trail. The trail covers a small loop at the base of the crater. One-quarter mile of the trail is paved and accessible. Great views of Sunset Crater and the San Francisco Peaks.

Lenox Crater Trail
Strenuous – (1.0 mi / 1.6 km), round trip, allow 30 – 45 minutes

This trail allows access to a lava field that was once an ancient volcano. Though the trail is but one mile round trip, it is steep with loose cinders that make for laborious walking.

O'Leary Peak Trail
Strenuous – (10.0 mi / 16.1 km), round trip, allow 3 – 4 hours

This is a there and back trail that climbs a lava dome volcano. The trail is an old roadbed and is very evident from a distance. The old forest service road climbs six switchbacks to obtain the top. Great views and a radio tower are at the top to greet you.

This trail doesn't get too much traffic, but offers some really commanding views. From the top, you get an amazing shot of the San Francisco Peaks as well as into Sunset Crater. The Painted Desert is to the north. As ho hum as hiking an old forest service road to a radio tower might sound, this is a cool hike from the perspective of the views. They are spectacular, making this a hidden gem within the Grand Circle catalog of trails.

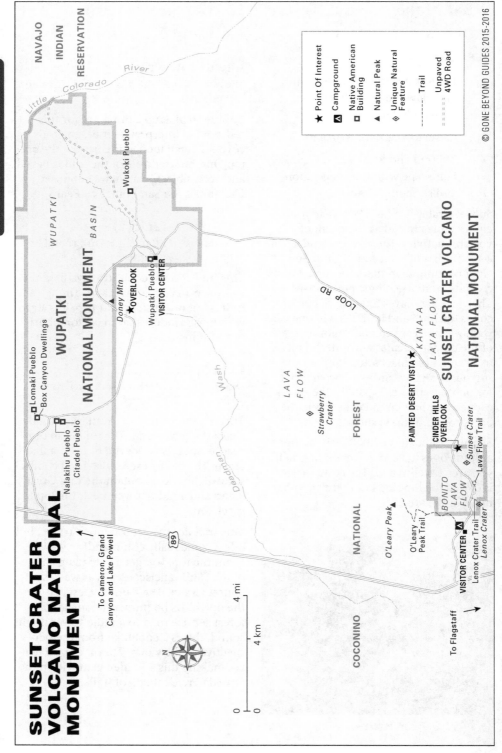

Sunset Crater Volcano

CENTRAL ARIZONA

SUNSET CRATER VOLCANO NATIONAL MONUMENT

To Cameron, Grand Canyon and Lake Powell

NAVAJO INDIAN RESERVATION

Little Colorado River

WUPATKI NATIONAL MONUMENT

Lomaki Pueblo
Box Canyon Dwellings

Nalakihu Pueblo
Citadel Pueblo

Wukoki Pueblo

WUPATKI BASIN

Doney Mtn
OVERLOOK

Wupatki Pueblo
VISITOR CENTER

Strawberry Crater

LAVA FLOW

LAVA FOREST

Wash

Deadman

PAINTED DESERT VISTA

KANA-A LAVA FLOW

LOOP RD

CINDER HILLS OVERLOOK

SUNSET CRATER VOLCANO NATIONAL MONUMENT

Sunset Crater Lava Flow Trail

BONITO LAVA FLOW

O'Leary Peak

O'Leary Peak Trail

NATIONAL

COCONINO

Lenox Crater Trail
Lenox Crater

VISITOR CENTER

89

To Flagstaff

N

0 — 4 mi
0 — 4 km

Legend

★ Point Of Interest
◭ Campground
□ Native American Building
▲ Natural Peak
◈ Unique Natural Feature
------- Trail
===== Unpaved 4WD Road

© GONE BEYOND GUIDES 2015-2016

110

Wupatki National Monument

Official Park Website:

- http://www.nps.gov/wupa

Visitor Center:

- (928) 679-2365

Park Accessibility:

- Okay for 2WD and RV's
- Day Use Only

Experience Level:

- Family Friendly – Casual Hiker

Camping in Park:

- None

Lodging and Dining in Park:

- None

Nearest Town with Amenities:

- Flagstaff, AZ is 44 mi / 71 km from the park

Getting There:

- From Flagstaff, AZ: take US-89 North to Loop Rd for 44 mi / 71 km to the park

Clouds over Crack in the Rocks

What Makes Wupatki Special

- The austere beauty of the landscape these ruins are set in

- The impressive San Francisco Peaks on one side, the soulful Hopi Reservation on the other

- Being close to Sunset Crater National Monument

In writing about these different Ancestral Puebloan sites, it's very easy to start to wonder if the reader will feel that in seeing one, they have seen them all. Nothing could be farther from the truth at Wupatki. It is the landscape that these ruins reside in that really makes this a special place. The land encapsulates the raw austerity of the high desert. The sagebrush covers the red land as a dotted green tapestry of nature. Typically, the skies are a deep blue and the clouds are above in an explosion of pure white, massive, giant things, beautiful and magical to the eye. The sapphire blue color of the sky is due to the altitude and in the late afternoon, the land comes alive in colors that are rich and simply beyond description.

The ruins themselves are also special, with ball courts and multi-storied structures. The park is small enough to feel that you can explore it completely, yet spread out to allow one to experience it fully. There is a scenic drive leading to many different interpretive sites, where one can learn about the lifeways of these people, such as how they grew corn by planting a single seed about six inches into a hole. This brought the roots closer to water and protected the young seedling from harm.

The real gem of this park is a very limited two-day, 16 mile backpacking trip that is led by a park ranger. One can only get on this trip via lottery and there is a fee, as of this writing it is $75 per person. If you are lucky enough to be selected, be prepared for an amazing trek. With a maximum group of 12, the ranger travels 8 miles each day, taking folks to special areas not normally open to the public, where one will find a vast amount of petroglyphs, pottery shards, arrowheads, and of course, ruins. The hikes travel through open country; there are no trails on this journey. The tour is about as robust in coverage as one can get and the rangers do an incredible job of describing the lifeway of these people. The trek is called Crack in Rock hike and information can be found here: http://www.nps.gov/wupa/planyourvisit/crack-in-rock.htm.

Wupatki landscape and ruins

Southern Utah

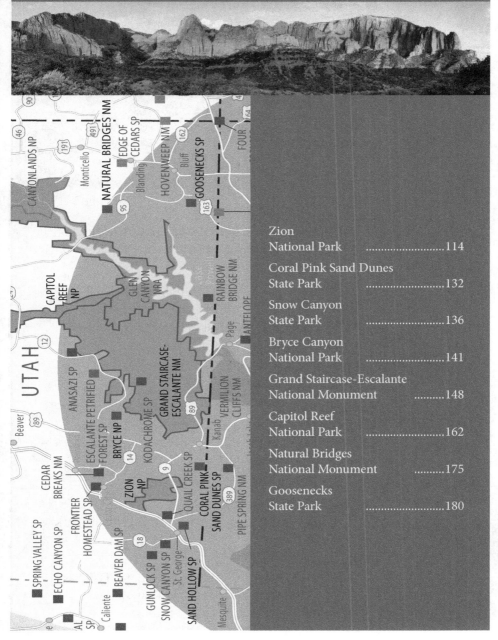

Zion National Park

Official Park Website: www.nps.gov/zion

Visitor Center:
(435) 772-3256

Park Accessibility:
- Okay for 2WD and RVs
- Day and Overnight Use

Experience Level:
- Family Friendly to Experienced Hiker

Within The Narrows

Camping in Park:
- Watchman: 176 T/RV, 2 ADA, 6 group sites, host on site, water, hookups, reservations at www.recreation.gov or by calling (877) 444-6777
- South: 127 T/RV, 3 ADA, host on site, water, no hookups, first come/first served, open seasonally
- Lava Point: 6T, Pit Toilets, no water, first come/first served, open seasonally

Lodging in Park:
- Zion Lodge: (888) 297-2757

Dining in Park:
There are two options, both at Zion Lodge
- Red Rock Grill Dining Room, open year round, reservations recommended, (435) 772-3213
- Castle Dome Café, open seasonally

Nearest Town with Amenities:
- Springdale, Utah is within 1 mi / 2 km of main park entrance

Getting There:
- From St George, UT: Take I-15 North to UT-9 East. Total distance is 41 mi / 66 km to park

What Makes Zion Special

- The afternoon light striking wall after wall of massive 2,000-foot red rock cliffs extending into a deep river canyon

- The Narrows, a hike whose trail is the Virgin River itself in a slot canyon over fifteen hundred feet tall

- Hiking Angels Landing, a hike hewn into cliff walls to the top of the canyon for stunning views

Zion National Park has a lot of "Wow" factor and for good reason. The entire Colorado Plateau was once a massive sand dune in line with the current Sarah Desert. As with any set of sand dunes, there is one area where the winds are just right and the dunes are at their highest. For the Colorado Plateau, those highest dunes were where Zion sits today and as a result, when the mechanics of geology turned those dunes into sandstone, it left the area with some really big chunks of rock to play with. Enter water and wind, which cut into the stone over millions of years, leaving sheer cliffs of epic rock in hues of reds, oranges and tans. There are many singular words to describe Zion, stunning, humbling, majestic, and even heavenly. Whatever one word that comes to mind, there are really no words that give this place a proper description. You just have to go and see it.

Angels Landing

Hiking in the Main Park

Pa'rus Trail

Easy – (3.5 mi / 5.6 km), round trip, allow 2 hours, elev. Δ: 50 ft / 15 m, trailheads at South Campground and Canyon Junction

Pa'rus, which is from the Paiute language, means bubbling, tumbling water. The name describes this trail well as it meanders along the Virgin River. The trail is paved and thus accessible for those with wheelchairs. Pa'rus starts at the visitor center and heads upstream at a very slight incline. The surrounding cliffs and valley open up throughout the journey.

There are several places along the way that provide beach access to the river and it is not uncommon to see families enjoying the heat of the day by cooling off in the water. Pa'rus trail crosses six bridges as it makes its way to trail's end at Canyon Junction. From here you can hike back (downhill all the way) or pick up the shuttle to your next destination. Dogs and bikes are welcome on this trail.

Watchman Trail

Moderate – (3.3 mi / 5.3 km), round trip, allow 2 hours, elev. Δ: 368 ft / 112 m, trailhead near visitor center

If you are looking to get higher up for better views but don't want to climb the 2,000 feet or so to the top of the rim, the Watchman Trail is a good alternative. The trail starts at the Zion Canyon Visitor Center and ends at a mesa top that gives some commanding views of Zion NP and even a glimpse of the Towers of the Virgin and the town of Springdale.

The trail begins by following along the banks of the North Fork of the Virgin River and then juts away from the water to connect to a series of moderate switchbacks that wind their way to the top of the mesa. There is a nominal 368 feet elevation gain, but the views are worth every step. Once at the mesa top there is a half-

ZION NATIONAL PARK

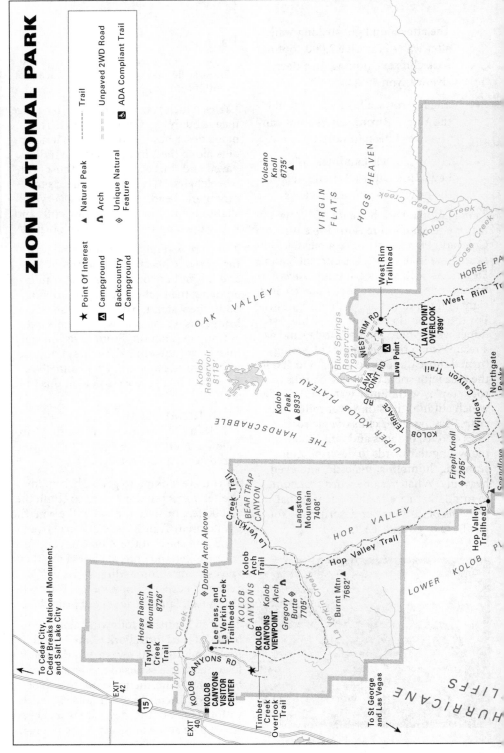

★ Point Of Interest	▲ Natural Peak	----- Trail	
◭ Campground	∩ Arch	==== Unpaved 2WD Road	
▲ Backcountry Campground	◈ Unique Natural Feature	♿ ADA Compliant Trail	

To Cedar City, Cedar Breaks National Monument, and Salt Lake City

EXIT 42

EXIT 40

15

To St George and Las Vegas

KOLOB CANYONS VISITOR CENTER

KOLOB CANYONS RD

Timber Creek Overlook Trail

KOLOB CANYONS VIEWPOINT

Lee Pass, and La Verkin Creek Trailheads

Horse Ranch Mountain 8726' ▲

Taylor Creek Trail

Taylor Creek

◈ Double Arch Alcove

La Verkin Creek Trail

BEAR TRAP CANYON

Langston Mountain 7408' ▲

KOLOB CANYONS

Kolob Arch Trail

Kolob Arch ∩

Gregory Butte 7705' ◈

Burnt Mtn 7682' ▲

La Verkin Creek

HOP VALLEY

Hop Valley Trail

Hop Valley Trailhead

LOWER KOLOB

THE HARDSCRABBLE

Kolob Reservoir 8118'

Kolob Peak 8933' ▲

UPPER KOLOB PLATEAU

KOLOB TERRACE RD

Blue Springs Reservoir 7921'

LAVA POINT RD

Lava Point ◭

WEST RIM RD

LAVA POINT OVERLOOK 7890'

West Rim Trailhead ★

West Rim Trail

OAK VALLEY

VIRGIN FLATS

HOGS HEAVEN

Deep Creek

Kolob Creek

Goose Creek

HORSE PA

Volcano Knoll 6735' ▲

Northgate Peaks

Wildcat Canyon Trail

Firepit Knoll ◈ 7265'

HURRICANE CLIFFS

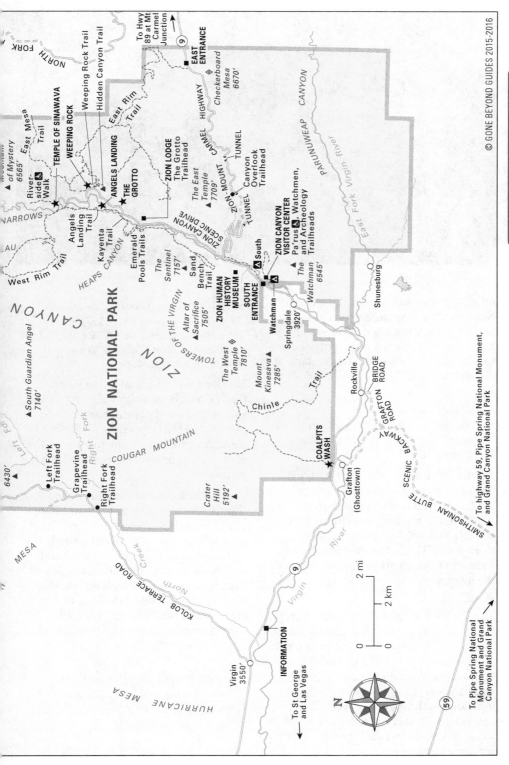

© GONE BEYOND GUIDES 2015-2016

NORTH FORK

Weeping Rock Trail

Hidden Canyon Trail

To Hwy
89 at Mt
Carmel
Junction

EAST
ENTRANCE

9

East Mesa
Trail

TEMPLE OF SINAWAVA

WEEPING ROCK

Checkerboard
Mesa
6670'

East Mesa
6565'

Monument
of Mystery
6565'

East Rim
Trail

ANGELS LANDING

Riverside Walk

THE GROTTO

ZION LODGE
The Grotto
Trailhead

CARMEL HIGHWAY

TUNNEL

NARROWS

Angels
Landing
Trail

Kayenta
Trail

The East
Temple
7709'

ZION-MOUNT

Canyon
Overlook
Trailhead

PARUNUWEAP CANYON

PLATEAU

West Rim Trail

HEAPS CANYON

Emerald
Pools Trails

ZION CANYON SCENIC DRIVE

TUNNEL

TUNNEL

ZION CANYON
VISITOR CENTER

Pa'rus, Watchmen,
and Archeology
Trailheads

South

East Fork Virgin River

Shunesburg

CANYON

South Guardian Angel
7140'

TOWERS OF THE VIRGIN

The
Sentinel
7157'

Sand
Bench
Trail

ZION HUMAN
HISTORY MUSEUM

SOUTH
ENTRANCE

Watchman
3920'

The
Watchman
6545'

ZION NATIONAL PARK

ZION

Altar of
Sacrifice
7505'

Springdale
3920'

Left Fork

6430'

Left Fork
Trailhead

Grapevine
Trailhead

Right Fork

Right Fork
Trailhead

COUGAR MOUNTAIN

The West
Temple
7810'

Mount
Kinesava
7285'

Chinle

Trail

Rockville

GRAFTON ROAD

BRIDGE
ROAD

To highway 59, Pipe Spring National Monument,
and Grand Canyon National Park

MESA

North Creek

Crater
Hill
5192'

COALPITS
WASH

Grafton
(Ghosttown)

Virgin
River

SMITHSONIAN BUTTE SCENIC BACKWAY

KOLOB TERRACE ROAD

9

Virgin
3550'

INFORMATION

To St George
and Las Vegas

Virgin River

HURRICANE MESA

2 mi

2 km

0

0

N

59

To Pipe Spring National
Monument and Grand
Canyon National Park

117

Sunrise in Zion Canyon

mile loop that walks around the edge. Note that the loop mileage isn't listed as part of the distance noted in the NPS hiking guide. This is a popular trail due to both the views and the fact it starts at the visitor center.

Archeology Trail

Easy – (0.4 mi / 0.6 km), round trip, allow 0.5 hour, elev. Δ: 80 ft / 24 m, trailhead near visitor center

The Archeology Trail is a great hike if you are looking for an early evening stroll. The trail is short, less than half a mile (0.6 kilometers), but climbs fairly steadily to a 1000-year-old prehistoric storage site. While the site requires a fair amount of imagination to piece together the history, this is not the only reason for going.

The site is close to the Watchman campground and rises to a nice vantage point in a very short distance. One can take in phenomenal views both up and down the canyon. You will notice the green riparian corridor of the Virgin River as it meanders through an ever-widening canyon. In all, this is a short but worthwhile trek you can take if you are looking for something near camp.

Sand Bench Trail

Moderate – (7.6 mi / 12.2 km), round trip, allow 5 hours, elev. Δ: 466 ft / 142 m, trailhead at Zion Lodge or Court of the Patriarchs shuttle stops

This long ambling trail follows along Birch Creek before climbing up to a long and decent sized plateau named Sand Bench. The trail does have a 466-foot elevation gain but for the most part, the gain is felt primarily as you ascend to the plateau.

Start at the Court of the Patriarchs shuttle stop and pick up the Sand Bench Trail as it follows from the Virgin River up Birch Creek. The trail then heads up to and runs the length of the Sand Bench plateau. As the hike unfolds, the Patriarchs, East Temple, Streaked Wall, Sentinel, Mountain of the Sun, and many other peaks can be seen. This trail is shared with horse riders, so be mindful as you take in the views.

Lower Emerald Pool Trail

Easy – (1.2 mi / 1.9 km), round trip, allow 1 hour,, elev. Δ: 69 ft / 21 m, trailhead at Zion Lodge shuttle stop

There are two trails described in the Zion hiking guide that make up the Emerald Pools, the lower pools and upper pools. Lower Emerald Pools is flat, is paved much of the way, is short in distance and provides incredible views of waterfalls and shallow pools. You do climb a bit on the lower trail, which allows for some nice views of the valley.

The two pools on the lower trail are nice enough, but as is almost always the case, the best pool is at the top. As the canyon is surrounded on both sides by steep cliffs, it will be well into morning before the sun hits the western side of the canyon. By mid-afternoon, the sun will have passed over the other side, providing more shade. In warm weather, plan on hitting the trail either in early morning or late afternoon to stay cool.

Upper Emerald Pool Trail

Moderate – (1.0 mi / 1.6 km), round trip from lower pools, allow 1 hour, elev. Δ: 200 ft / 61 m, trailhead at Zion Lodge shuttle stop

Here the trail continues from the Lower Emerald Pool Trail for the final mile. The paved trail is now dirt and the trail climbs more steeply. If you are doing this trail in the morning, the sun may have passed over the monolith walls and is now part of the climb up. The views do get better as you gain elevation, and the pool at the top is by far the biggest, sitting at the base of the western cliff faces. It is well worth the effort for the views. These pools are not intended for swimming.

Kayenta Trail

Moderate – (2.0 mi / 3.2 km), round trip, allow 2 hours, elev. Δ: 150 ft / 46 m, trailhead at Grotto shuttle stop

Kayenta Trail is often done along with the Grotto Trail and the Emerald Pools Trail to create a loop. The trail is great

in its own right, giving some great views deeper into the canyon near the Zion Lodge. The trail has a small 150-foot elevation gain.

Waterfall at Emerald Pools

The trail can be picked up easily from The Grotto shuttle stop. From the shuttle stop cross the Virgin River via a bridge and follow along its upper banks for a short distance. The trail then enters into Behunin Canyon from the North side before meeting up with the Emerald Pools Trail. To make a loop of it, continue along and down the Emerald Pools Trail until it ends at the Zion Lodge and then pick up the Grotto Trail back to where you started.

The Grotto Trail

Easy – (1.0 mi / 1.6 km), round trip, allow 30 minutes, elev. Δ: 35 ft / 11 m, trailhead at Grotto shuttle stop

The Grotto Trail is a simple little flat jaunt that connects the Zion Lodge with the Grotto Picnic Area. It is used by

119

many to connect the Emerald and Kayenta Trails to make a 2 ½ mile loop. The Grotto area itself contains picnic tables and grates for grilling. It also contains the Grotto Museum, which is the oldest building in Zion. If you are a fan of the historical stonework of the Zion Lodge, be sure to include the Grotto Trail to the mix to see both the museum and the artist in residence house.

Angels Landing via West Rim Trail

Strenuous – (5.4 mi / 8.7 km), round trip, allow 4-5 hours, elev. Δ: 1,488 ft / 453 m, trailhead at Grotto shuttle stop

The views are unparalleled from the unique Angels Landing trail. Built during the wake of the Great Depression by the CCC, it comprises a series of switchbacks cut into solid rock. The final half mile is along a narrow knife-edged ridge that uses chains and carved footholds to assist you to the final destination. It is strenuous, but the end result is well worth it. You will have climbed from the bottom of the canyon to close to the top, giving you a view that will most certainly become a life moment. It is a world famous hike and one of the most popular in Zion.

The trail's name was coined by Frederick Fisher in 1916 when he looked up at the monolith and exclaimed, "only and angel could land on it." With the help of the CCC, (Frederick Fisher) forged a trail to the top.

The trail is composed of six distinct parts. The first follows a paved path along the river before dog legging west from the river toward a cliff wall. If you look carefully at this point in the trail, you will see the second portion of the journey, a series of switchbacks up this cliff wall. Even from a distance, the switchbacks are impressive if not audacious. The trail builders carved a fairly wide paved trail into solid rock and while you are indeed

climbing up a cliff face, this portion is merely strenuous and no more dangerous than any well-established trail with exposure.

There is a reprieve at the third portion. At the top of the switchbacks, the trail goes between two massive monolithic columns through what is aptly named Refrigerator Canyon. The monoliths climb high enough to block out the sun and there is a cool breeze that greets visitors as soon as they reach the top of the switchbacks. This lasts for only a short half mile before you arrive at the fourth portion, called Walter's Wiggles. The Wiggles are a series of 21 short but consistently steep switchbacks that wind back and forth until you get to the next respite, called Scout's Lookout.

The lookout is the fifth portion of the journey and a great place to take a rest. The Wiggles are below you and from the lookout, you can see the final half mile pitch ahead of you to Angels Landing. The area offers incredible views. There is also a pit toilet and plenty of places to relax before your final leg. Up to this point you have been on the West Rim Trail, so make sure you follow the signs to the top of Angels Landing, as the West Rim Trail does continue onward.

The final pitch is a bit exciting as it has the adventure of chains that you can grab onto to ensure you get up the last leg. This portion is a razor back ridge. It is fairly narrow with steep drop offs on either side. The trail is well marked by the chains and crosses the back of the ridge several times as you climb. Many hikers have made this journey and in the end, it is not as scary as it sounds. That said, this is not a place to test yourself; a handful of people have fallen to their deaths on this trail. I've seen teenagers on this trail but only two children who were in the single digit age bracket. Use caution, for both yourself and your fellow hikers.

Once at the top, there is a somewhat narrow but flat area to take in the lofty vista. To the north is a grand view of the end of Zion Canyon. You will find yourself gazing at an enormous cul-de-sac of towering rock. As the eye travels from the edge of Angels Landing down the canyon, the citadel of rock stands as one complete sentry extending to the horizon. The red cliff walls meet the green of the desert, culminating in a dense riparian snake of vegetation that surrounds the Virgin River. At times swallows soaring at incredible speeds up to 40 miles per hour (64 km/hour) can be seen. They will soar seemingly straight into the cliff walls only to stop at the last second and land in their nests.

Weeping Rock Trail

Easy – (0.4 mi / 0.6 km), round trip, allow 30 minutes, elev. Δ: 98 ft / 30 m, trailhead at Weeping Rock shuttle stop

This is a short paved trail that ends at an alcove called Weeping Rock. True to its name, water seeps through the sandstone and then falls gently like a soft rain once it reaches the overhang. It is possible to stand underneath and watch the magic of water and stone, even on a sunny day. The trail is great for kids and casual hikers looking for a great view of the Great White Throne. There is about 100 feet of elevation gain and some trailside exhibits.

Hidden Canyon Trail

Strenuous – (2.4 mi / 3.9 km), round trip, allow 2-3 hours, elev. Δ: 850 ft / 259 m, trailhead at Weeping Rock shuttle stop

If you don't mind exposure to steep drop offs, this is a really cool hike. Mind you, there are long drops and chains are put in places to assist in some areas, so if you do have a fear of heights, this trail may not be for you. Hidden Canyon starts from the Weeping Rock shuttle and follows a paved trail steeply upwards along a set of well-constructed switchbacks. At the trail junction for Hidden Canyon, East Rim Trail and Observation Point, keep to the right and head up a series of short and steep switchbacks not unlike Walters Wiggles found over at Angels Landing.

Climbing up Angels Landing

After the switchbacks, the trail clings at various times to the edge of a steeply sloping rock face. In some areas there are chains to assist the hiker, in others, the trail looks a little intimidating but is wide and safe enough. In one part, steps have been carved directly into the sandstone. This whole part of the hike is akin to being Indiana Jones looking for some ancient treasure. This is truly a fun and exhilarating hike. That said, if you aren't a fan of heights, this might not be the best trail.

The hike ends at the mouth of Hidden Canyon. With some basic scrambling, it is possible to continue up the canyon a bit to a small 10-foot arch along a sandy stream-bed section of the trip. Hidden Canyon throws off a lot of the visitors due to its exposure and while it can be dangerous under wet conditions, is quite fine for those who have figured out how far to trust the grip of sandstone un-der one's feet. The other plus is the hike is typically in the shade for most of the day, which helps in the heat of the summer. Elevation gain for this trail is 800 feet.

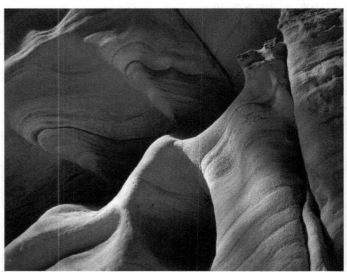

The magic of color at Zion

destination due to the numerous spur trails, including Deertrap Mountain and Cable Mountain Trails.

Starting from the East Entrance, views of Checkboard Mesa and the head of Jolly Gulch can be seen. This initial portion of the trail does have some elevation gain as the trail navigates the contour of the pla-teau. There are some very dramatic views along this portion. At 6 miles in there is a trail to the left that leads to Cable Mountain and Deertrap Trails as well as a

trail junction farther on for Observation Point. The trail then comes to the top of Echo Canyon, where it heads swiftly downwards 1,000 feet (see Observation Point for more details here).

East Rim Trail

Strenuous – (10.6 mi / 17.1 km), one way, allow 6 – 7 hours, elev. Δ: 1,365 ft / 415 m, two trailheads, described below

Like the West Rim Trail, most hikers start at the upper end with the descent in front of them. For this trail, that is done by starting at the East Rim Trailhead, located at the Zion East Entrance Ranger Station and heading to the Weeping Rock shuttle stop. This is a great backpacking

Observation Point via East Rim Trail

Strenuous – (8.0 mi / 12.9 km), round trip, allow 6 hours, elev. Δ: 2,148 ft / 655 m, trailhead at Weeping Rock shuttle stop

Okay, if you found yourself wanting to get to the top of Zion Canyon from the moment you arrived, this is one of the trails that will get you there. The trail climbs some 2,148 feet over four miles with some serious drop offs along the way and is all done in full sun. While strenuous, this is a hike to remember.

Start at the Weeping Rock shuttle stop and proceed up the shared trail to Hidden Canyon, East Rim Trail, and Observation Point following a series of well-built switchbacks. At the junction, stay left and continue through Echo Canyon, a narrow and steep canyon with little pools of running water carved into the sandstone. As the climb continues, the trail starts to bring the white Temple Cap formation closer into view. Zion Canyon, Angels Landing, Cathedral Mountain, and Three Patriarchs are in full view. The views from the top as well as the trip through Echo Canyon make this steep hike well worth the effort.

Cable Mountain Trail
Strenuous – (17.5 mi / 28.2 km from East Entrance), round trip, allow 8-10 hours, elev. Δ: up 1,000 ft, down 2,000 ft

Strenuous (15.5 mi / 25.0 km from Weeping Rock shuttle stop), round trip, allow 7-9 hours, elev. Δ: 2,100 ft / 640 m

Moderate (7.5 mi / 12.1 km from Zion Ponderosa Ranch, round trip, allow 5 hours, elev. Δ: 300 ft / 91 m

There are three ways to get to Cable Mountain Trail. See the trail descriptions for Observation Point and East Rim Trail for additional information on the routes to Cable Mountain Trail. For the Zion Ponderosa Ranch route, head out to the East Entrance and make a left to North Fork Road. Follow the signs to Zion Ponderosa and once at the resort, look for signs to Cable Mountain Trail, making a left at the main entrance, and then going straight past the resort buildings. The trailhead connects with the East Rim Trail and onwards to Cable Mountain Trail.

In 1901, there was a tram that carried lumber from the top of Zion Canyon to the valley floor. This engineering marvel, built by pioneer David Flanigan contained 3,300 feet of cable and could supply lumber to the valley floor in several minutes, which was a massive improvement over the 3-day journey by wagon that it took prior. Many of the original buildings in Zion were built with this lumber. The frameworks were destroyed twice by fire and in 1930; the park service removed the cables. The draw works still sits at the top of Cable Mountain at the end of the trail.

Deertrap Trail
Strenuous – (19.5 mi / 31.4 km from East Entrance), round trip, allow 11-12 hours,, elev. Δ: up 1,000 ft, down 2,000 ft

Strenuous (17.5 mi / 28.2 km from Weeping Rock shuttle stop), round trip, allow 8-10 hours, elev. Δ: 2,100 ft / 640 m

Moderate (9.5 mi / 15.3 km from Zion Ponderosa Ranch, round trip, allow 6 hours, elev. Δ: 300 ft / 91 m

This is certainly a long day hike or as an add on within the East Rim Trail. Use the East Rim, Observation Point and Cable Mountain Trail descriptions to initiate the three routes, as appropriate.

Once on the side trail from East Rim Trail, continue past Cable Mountain Trail for another two miles to a series of overlooks collectively referred to as a sky island. Each view is slightly different, offering expansive views into the north and south portions of Zion Canyon as well as the outer peaks and terrain.

Canyon Overlook Trail
Moderate – (1.0 mi / 1.6 km), round trip, allow 1 hour, elev. Δ: 163 ft / 50 m, trailhead near east Zion Tunnel entrance

This is another in the list of "great views without too much effort" category. The trail starts right before the Zion Tunnel as you head into the park. There are parking lots on either side of the Zion-Mount Carmel Highway. The trail gets a fair amount of "impulse hiking" as folks wait for the directed traffic of the tunnel to open up. After all, hiking in Zion does beat out being stuck in traffic in Zion. The hike has a modest 163-foot elevation gain and climbs some steps cut into the sandstone. At the end of the trail is an overlook with a railing at the cliff's edge giving great views of the lower portions of Zion Canyon and Pine Creek immediately below, as well as an interesting perspective of the Zion Tunnel.

Riverside Walk

Easy – (2.2 mi / 3.5 km), round trip, allow 90 minutes, elev. Δ: 57 ft / 17 m, trailhead at Temple of Sinawava shuttle stop

Riverside Walk starts at roads end of the wide main portion of the Zion box canyon. From here, the canyon begins to narrow but is still wide enough for the paved Riverside Walk trail that meanders until it reaches The Narrows proper. The trail is fairly flat, with several rolling ups and downs as it contours to the land. There are also a few spots with watery grottoes as well as multiple spots for river beach access. The trail ends at a stonework terrace where you can gaze at the mouth of The Narrows and the various hikers beginning or ending their hike of this landmark trek.

The Narrows

Imagine walking up a river flowing clearly and gently around your feet. At times there is no shore, only river and massive sandstone walls that run from the edge of the water and rise swiftly straight up 2000 feet into the sky. There are places where the canyon is wide enough to permit a view of distant sandstone monoliths and other places where the canyon is delightfully slender, only 20-30 feet wide. Each turn gives a different view, all wondrous and grand. For a bit, the river stretches out, allowing a chance to walk on soft sand. You see deer grazing on the banks. Waterfalls come sliding down

curved walls from unreachable heights. There is no trail but the river. If you think about it, each step up and down is a step no one has ever taken before in exactly the same way.

Be warned, it is possible that you won't be able to hike the Narrows. If the Virgin River is running too high, either due to winter/spring runoff or to summer flash floods, you will not be able to go on this hike. That said, if the river is running favorably, then make it a point to add this to your itinerary. The park service actively controls access to the Narrows, which does take the guesswork out of the safety of hiking this trail.

Going Upstream from the Bottom of the Canyon

Easy to Strenuous – (9.4 mi / 15.1 km), round trip, allow up to 8 hours depending on distance traveled, elev. Δ: 334 ft / 102 m, trailhead at Temple of Sinawava shuttle stop

Into the Narrows

The Narrows is found by taking the shuttle to the very end of the canyon via the Riverside Walk Trail. It will take about 40–45 minutes from the campground to the end of the canyon via the shuttle. It will take another hour to 90 minutes to walk the 2.2 miles (3.5 km) needed to complete the Riverside Walk Trail. Make sure you add in this time when you plan your hike.

The Riverside Walk Trail is flat, easy and paved. The trail follows the Virgin River up along its banks, and there are plenty of places to drop off the trail to explore the river itself. At the end of the trail is a small set of steps down to the river where The Narrows begins and where the hike gets really interesting.

There are a few trails, but for the most part, you walk in the river itself. You will be walking upstream on uneven ground at times, so be prepared to get wet. Depending on how far up you decide to go, you will need to wade and even swim in some stretches. If you feel confident that the trail will be open, it's best to pick up

water shoes beforehand and bring them on the trip for this hike. It will make your hike more enjoyable.

Depending on the time of year, the water may be swift and cold. In the summer, usually by June, the river slows down to a steady but not terribly swift pace, and the temperature is more refreshing than cold.

There are restrictions to how far up you are allowed to travel upstream without a permit. There is a tributary creek called Orderville Junction, which is a common destination for most hikers and is the limit of how far up you can travel without a permit. Orderville Junction is about two hours from the trail. That said, it is possible to never make it this far and still have an amazing hike. Each bend offers a different experience and new view with another bend at the end that beckons you farther.

Returning will take slightly less time since you are going downstream with the flow of water. If you are doing the hike in late afternoon, make a note of when

If You Hike the Narrows

- Have a full understanding of the weather before you go. Flash floods can originate from storms that aren't close to where you are hiking.

- Carry a gallon of water per person and some food, sunscreen and a first aid kit.

- Bring a pullover if the weather is temperate. It is colder in the canyon.

- Bring waterproof bags for cameras and other items that you need to keep dry.

- The only restroom on the hike is at the beginning of the Riverside Walk. There are no other places

to go, even if you "have to." This is a popular destination and there are no discreet bushes. Make sure everyone goes prior to beginning the hike.

- Walking sticks are preferred by most folks for added stability, as are sturdy hiking boots. Water shoes and tennis shoes are okay for the casual hike up river. Sandals are not recommended though hiking sandals are okay.

- This is not a great hike for young children. My 9-year-old did fine, but keep in mind it is over two miles of walking just to get to the beginning of The Narrows. While the current is typically fine for adults, it may be too much for smaller ones.

you start the hike from the shuttle drop off and how much time you have left before sunset. If you have 3 hours, hike up for 90 minutes and turn around. The Narrows is not an easy hike in the dark especially if you don't have a flashlight.

Going Downstream from the Top of the Canyon

Strenuous – (16 mi / 25.7 km), one way, full day hike, elev. Δ: 1,400 ft / 427 m, trailhead at Zion Narrows parking area

Going downstream can be done with a National Park Service wilderness permit. Allow a full day for this 16-mile hike. You can find private jeep shuttles that regularly go up to the drop off spot. This is a strenuous day's hike. There are ample stories of folks that find themselves having to stick it out for the night because they thought it would be an easier hike. Hiking in streambeds is slow work and is more tiring than walking on even pavement. Underestimating this hike in the wrong conditions can be dangerous as well. Flash floods and exposure from the night's elements are serious matters.

West Temple and Altar of Sacrifice

Chinle Trail

Strenuous – (6.8 mi / 10.9 km), round trip to Huber Wash, allow 3 – 5 hours, elev. Δ: 650 ft / 198 m, two trailheads off SR-9

This is a very different hike than most of Zion, showing off the diversity of Lowland Desert Ecology as well as crossing through a petrified forest. The trail is well exposed and will be very hot in the full sun of summer. The trail is more wel-

coming in spring and fall, with wildflowers present in the spring.

The hike has two trailhead entrances, both from Highway 9. The entrance closest to the town of Springdale requires parking in the designated lot labeled "Trailhead Parking". Parking in the subdivision will get you towed. From the trailhead wind through the local neighborhood to the park's boundary and continue through a forested area with absolutely remarkable views. After 3.2 miles, the trail meets up with Huber Wash. Head back from here.

It is also possible to continue to make this somewhat of a loop trail; however, as some of the loop is Highway 9, it's best to have two cars. Taking the full loop to Coalpits Wash from Chinle Trailhead is a total of 15 miles.

Right Fork Trailhead

Strenuous – (10.6 mi / 17.1 km), round trip from bottom up, allow 8 – 12 hours, elev. Δ: 1,000 ft / 300 m, trailhead on Kolob Terrace Road

Like the Left Fork Trailhead, this is more route than maintained trail. The first couple of miles were hit by a fire in 2006 and the area is in a cycle of recovery. The hike within the streambed is pretty slow going, so allow extra time. That said, while the Right Fork is a bit more rugged to navigate, the scenery is quite peaceful and meandering with the route ending at a set of pretty incredible double waterfalls. Like the Left Fork, this trail can get hot in the summer despite the lure of water.

Start the hike at the Right Fork Trailhead on Kolob Terrace Road. The first quarter mile crosses the fire area to a bluff overlooking North Creek. From here head steeply down and into the creek bed. Do make note of this entrance, as it is easy to miss on the way out. Once at North Creek, start heading upstream passing the confluence of Left Fork. Cross the stream on the left side here and follow the path that crisscrosses the creek multiple times.

At about 2.5 miles into the hike, pass Trail Canyon on the right. A short spur trip up this canyon about one quarter of a mile will lead to a set of cascades. Back in North Creek, at close to 4 miles in, the hiker will encounter a very cool five-foot waterfall pouring through the slickrock into a nice pool. About a half mile further up, the canyon narrows and holds multiple waterfalls, pools, and hanging gardens. Further up another mile is Double Falls, another picturesque set of cascades.

From here, the end of the journey without ropes is Barrier Falls, about a third of a mile further upstream. The going here is tougher, requiring one to scramble up slick rock, bushwhack and otherwise navigate slowly to the falls. There is a set of falls in between, but you will know you are at Barrier Falls, its name holds true.

Unlike the Left Fork Trail, a permit is not required for Right Fork. Coming back, be glad you made note of the trail you came down as getting back up to the rim without the trail can be dangerous.

Left Fork Trailhead

Strenuous – (7.0 mi / 11.3 km), round trip, allow 5 - 8 hours, elev. Δ: 1,000 ft / 300 m, trailhead on Kolob Terrace Road

The Left Fork of North Creek is most popular for a stretch labeled The Subway, a short and rather amazing section of the creek that looks more like a worm tunnel than a streambed. This is one of the best hikes in the park and is more route than actual trail. The whole journey is alongside and often in the creek, which makes for slow going. Unlike The Narrows, which can be cooler in the summer heat, this hike is definitely a hot hike when temperatures are high. Start early if it looks to be a hot day.

The Subway

It is possible to enter from the top and make your way down stream, but this is longer and requires a bit of rappelling and swimming (and carrying your rappelling gear). A permit is required no matter which direction you travel. From bottom to top is described here.

From the bottom, the trail starts by picking ones way down a 400 foot gully starting from the Left Fork Trailhead on Kolob Terrace Road. Once in the creek, head upstream for about two to three hours. The Subway section is a tight section of the creek with several twists and turns right above a cascading set of falls called Red Waterfalls. The Subway itself is spectacular with clear pools and an almost subterranean feel.

It is possible to continue upwards but be mindful of time. Shortly after The Subway you will be met with large black pools that you must swim to get across to continue exploring the slot canyon. Further up is a soothing little waterfall with a secret natural room behind a watery curtain. Journeying from here requires bouldering and rappelling experience. Enjoy and head back down before dark.

Like The Narrows, this slot canyon does experience extreme changes in water volume due to flash floods. The permit process helps provide education along the way for this route, but do enter well informed as to the weather for the day.

Hiking in the Kolob Canyon Section

Hop Valley Trail

Strenuous – (15 mi / 24.1 km), round trip, allow 10 hours, elev. Δ: 1,050 ft / 320 m, trailhead off Kolob Terrace Road

The Hop Valley Trail, located in the Kolob Canyons section of Zion is typically done as part of the Trans Zion hike, a 48 mile, 5-day trek that crosses Zion from the Kolobs at Lee Pass to the East Rim. Lacking the fame of the main Zion and Kolob Canyons, the Hop Valley trail is a hidden gem. It is possible to use Hop Valley as a longer and more remote method to Kolob Arch. The route described here is from Kolob Terrace Road to Kolob Arch and back.

From the Hop Valley Trailhead on Kolob Terrace Road pick up the northern trailhead into Hop Valley. The trail starts out in a wide and open valley filled with deep sand and plenty of sagebrush. Walking in deep sand is a consistent trait of this trail. In areas, grazing has left its mark on the vegetation. As you continue, the valley narrows and travel is along a pleasant stream. The trail does have a fair amount of creek crossings; look for NPS trail markers to keep you on the trail. Campsites are about five miles in at an NPS boundary gate. The vegetation is more pristine once you cross into

the park. Take a series of switchbacks downhill to connect to La Verkin Creek and follow it downstream to the Kolob Arch Viewpoint.

Overall, this hike has about 1,000 feet elevation gain, mostly felt on the return. That said, the trail is more strenuous due to its length than the elevation.

Northgate Peaks Trail

Easy – (4.5 mi / 7.2 km), round trip, allow 3 hours, elev. Δ: 50 ft / 15 m, trailhead off Wildcat Canyon trail

If you wondered if you could find a hike that wasn't too hard but also wasn't shared with millions of other tourists, this trail is a good bet. Northgate Peaks Trail is off the beaten path and isn't in the popular NPS hiking brochures so it doesn't get as much traffic. The hike also shows a different view of Zion, ambling through large ponderosa pine forests found in the higher elevations. The hike is cooler and walks amongst the white Temple Cap monoliths dotting the landscape.

While the name of this there and back hike makes it sound like it climbs some massive Zion mountain, the elevation gain is only 250 feet. The trail ends at a craggy volcanic knob offering views that

Kolob Canyon

are distinctively different from the main portions of Zion and the Kolob Canyons. Access to Northgate Peaks Trail is from the Wildcat Canyon parking lot on Kolob Terrace Road.

Wildcat Canyon Trail

Moderate – (12.0 mi / 19.3 km), round trip, allow 4-7 hours, elev. Δ: 450 ft / 137 m, two trailheads off Kolob Terrace Road

Normally done as a connector trail, this is a great day hike in its own right. The hike is incredibly pleasant with only modest elevation gain/loss. The trail passes through groves of ponderosa pines and high meadows before dropping down into Wildcat Canyon. The trail offers a leisurely way to see the countryside, with plenty of opportunities to find wildflowers and wildlife along the way. This trail is not the standard Zion high red rock cliffs and there are no striking viewpoints to be found at trail's end, but the entire feel that the journey is the destination is what makes this hike so special.

West Rim Trailhead

Strenuous – (12.9 – 14.4 mi / 20.7 – 23.1 km), one way, allow 10 hours, elev. Δ: 3,600 ft / 1097 m, trailhead at Lava Point

This is a long day hike or a pleasant overnight backpacking trip. The hike is best if started from the West Rim Trailhead at Kolob Terrace Road and heading towards the other end at The Grotto shuttle stop. Since the shuttle doesn't go to both ends of the trail, you will need a means of transportation back to your car.

Starting near Lava Point on Kolob Terrace Road pick up the trail and keep straight to avoid the Wildcat Canyon Trail. The trail heads along the Horse Plateau through sparsely forested ponderosa pines. After 4.5 miles, the trail descends into a happy little meadow named Potato Hollow. Here there is a small pond and a spring that is usually running. This is a good place to relax and fill up canteens, (be sure to treat or filter). There are some great views into Imlay canyon by taking a short side spur to the east.

The trail then climbs about 500 feet out of the hollow and back onto Horse Plateau proper over a distance of 1.5 miles. At this point, the hike offers two routes. There is the primary West Rim Trail, which is 1.5 miles longer, and the Telephone Canyon Trail. The West Rim variation gives great views of Phantom Valley and the southern Zion canyons. The Telephone Canyon variation is named by settlers trying to establish a telephone line into Zion Canyon. The route here is shorter and sticks more to the interior of Horse Plateau.

Both variations meet up at Cabin Springs, a small seep that collects into a small pool. There are campsites nearby. This water is fine to drink given you filter or treat it and have a strong amount of patience. From Cabin Springs, the real fun begins as the trail heads steeply down into Zion Canyon. There are long drop-offs here, but this is a well-maintained trail. Take the path cut into the slick rock and head downwards until you reach a respite at Lookout Point. From here, the trail is an inverse of what is described for the Angels Landing Trail. Follow down Walters Wiggles, through Refrigerator Canyon and down until you end at The Grotto shuttle stop. It is completely possible and recommended to add the Angels Landing to the journey. If you do, be sure to allow another 45 minutes to the overall duration of the hike.

La Verkin Creek Trail (and Kolob Arch)

Strenuous – (14.0 mi / 22.5 km), round trip, allow 8 hours, elev. Δ: 1,037 ft / 316 m, trailhead at Kolob Canyon Road

La Verkin Creek Trail, in the Kolob Canyons section, is a fun trail all around, offering great views including Kolob Arch, one of the largest free-standing arches on earth. The hike itself does have some elevation gain, a little over 1,000 feet; however, the surroundings are amazing enough to help keep

Kolob Arch

your mind off the inclines. Most folks get a permit and camp overnight; however, it is possible to do this as a long day hike to Kolob Arch.

The trail starts at Lee Pass and crosses in front of the southern portion of the Kolob Canyon cliffs. The trail meets up quickly with Timber Creek and follows along its banks, giving some spectacular views in a pinyon juniper forest setting. After about two miles, the trail veers away from the creek into the woods as it heads towards La Verkin Creek. The trail then descends down into the creek's clear waters, with each step putting you into a more immersive Kolob Canyon experience. Cliffs are now towering around you on either side with the sound of water adding to the magic of this hike.

The end of the trail is Kolob Arch viewpoint where the arch can be seen by hiking up about 150 feet to a viewing area. While the official end of the trail listed here is 7 miles, La Verkin Creek Trail does continue up stream for another two miles. There are many side canyons to explore, some of which require canyoneering techniques that lead to triple waterfalls and other delights. If backpacking, it is possible to connect to the Hop Valley Trail, which leads southeast to the Lower Kolob Plateau.

Timber Creek Overlook Trail

Moderate – (1.0 mi / 1.6 km), round trip, allow 30 minutes, elev. Δ: 100 ft / 30 m, trailhead at end of Kolob Canyon Road

This is one of those trails that could labeled as "Easy" without much argument; however, the park lists it as moderate. It does have a 100-foot elevation gain, but is otherwise a straightforward trail. The trail is picked up at the very end of Kolob Canyon Road. From there the trail follows a small ridgeline to an overlook of Kolob Canyon, looking south. On a clear day, it is possible to see all the way to the north rim of the Grand Canyon.

This trail is located within the Kolob Canyon section. Groups are limited to a maximum size of 12 people at a time. Look for wildflowers in season, which can be abundant on this trail.

Taylor Creek Trail

Moderate – (5.0 mi / 8.0 km), round trip, allow 4 hours, elev. Δ: 470 ft / 143 m, trailhead at Kolob Canyon Road

This trail lies within the Kolob Canyons Wilderness and ambles up the Middle Fork of Taylor Creek. This entire area gets less visitation than the main Zion Canyon and this trail in particular has strict limits on prohibiting groups larger than 12 people. Taylor Creek Trail heads into a narrow box canyon of red Navajo Sandstone along a normally gently flowing creek. There is a welcome interplay of the green vegetation and the red hue of the rocks here and the hike overall is one of delight and wonder. Before the trail begins to fade as it nears the end of the box canyon, look for Double Arch Alcove, an impressive set of alcoves, one on top of the other.

Trans- Zion Hike

Strenuous – (47.3 mi / 76.1 km), one way, allow 3 - 5 days

This hike is a wondrous way to get an immersive multi-day experience that covers the broad spectrum that makes up Zion. The route typically starts from Lee Pass in the Kolobs and cuts down into La Verkin Creek before climbing up to the top of Zion Canyon via the West Rim Trail. From here, the trail heads steeply down, crosses the Zion Valley floor, and heads up the other side via the East Rim.

The trip can be done at a nice pace over five days, but one can hoof it in less. That said, the National Park Service allows camping only in designated areas, so plan your camping junctures carefully. The typical route and stops are given below.

The best part of this trek is there is a net elevation gain of just 325 feet! Don't let that fool you though, one ascends and descends over a whopping 6,000 feet getting to that net elevation number.

Trans-Zion Hike Route:

- La Verkin Trail via Lee Pass Trailhead
- La Verkin Trail to Hop Valley Trail
- Hop Valley Trail to Connector Trail
- Connector Trail to Wildcat Canyon Trail
- Wildcat Canyon Trail to West Rim Trail
- Short side trip to Angels Landing (a must for any Trans Zion hike)
- West Rim Trail down to The Grotto shuttle stop
- Hard core walk or shuttle bus ride to Weeping Rock shuttle stop
- East Rim Trail to East Entrance

Typical Itinerary:

Mileage is approximate, as it will depend on what campsites you get or where designated camping isn't a requirement such as on the East Rim and Echo Canyon, where you can find a campsite.

- Day 1 – 6.9 miles: Camp near Kolob Arch along La Verkin Creek Trail
- Day 2 – 16 miles: Camp at Lava Point Campgrounds or Sawmill Spring
- Day 3 - 8 miles: Camp at West Rim, (Potato Hollow or campsite #6)
- Day 4 – 10 miles: West Rim to Echo Canyon
- Day 5 – 6.5 miles: Exit to East Entrance

Coral Pink Sand Dunes State Park

Quick Facts

Official Park Website:

http://state-parks.utah.gov/parks/coral-pink/

Visitor Center:

(435) 648-2800

Mid Afternoon at Coral Pink Sand Dunes

Park Accessibility:

- Okay for 2WD and RVs
- ATVs, 4WD needed for some areas
- Day and Overnight Use

Experience Level:

- Family Friendly to Experienced Hiker

Camping in Park:

- Coral Pink Sand Dunes Campground: 16 T/RV plus 1 group site, drinking water, showers, restrooms, no hookups, many pull thru sites, reservable at www.reserveamerica.com/

Lodging and Dining in Park:

- None

Nearest Town with Amenities:

- Kanab, UT is 20 mi / 32 km from park

Getting There:

- From St George, UT: Take I-15 North to State Hwy 9 East/State St to UT-59 South to AZ-389 East to Co Hwy 237 to Co Rd 43. Note that final 4 miles is a dirt road. Typically, passable by 2WD and smaller RV's. Total distance is 62 mi / 100 km to park.

- From Page, AZ: Take US-89 West to Hancock Road to Coral Pink Sand Dunes Road. Note that final leg from Hancock Road to park is on an unpaved gravel road, suitable for all vehicles.

What Makes Coral Pink Sand Dunes Special

- The cool color of the sand dunes, especially at dawn and dusk

- The ability to hike in a Zion like world with all the wonder but with less fellow tourists

- Knowing you can put that ATV you brought to great use

The first thing to note about this park is while the color is distinctly different from other sand dunes; it may not be the pink color you envisioned when you first pull up. The color is more of a sandstone red much of the time and requires the right soft and low but direct lighting to bring out the picture perfect coral color.

The elusive pink color aside, the park is a great stay over spot within the typical route of the Grand Circle. Here there are nice campgrounds, good restroom facilities and a playground of sand nearby. Perhaps the only downside if you aren't riding an ATV is all the ATV's in the dunes area. One definitely needs to be mindful of these high-speed vehicles

in this multiuse area. That said, if you do have an ATV, the area allows exploration into canyons that are very much like Zion NP, but without all the people. For many locals, this is how they see Zion, by riding into the wilderness surrounding it.

There is one other minor but very cool feature of this park. It has an extensive collection of sand from all over the world. Each little jar is labeled with the sand's location. The collection, which takes up an entire wall in the visitor center, started as a ranger's hobby, but has grown considerably as tourists have sent in their local samples. It is quite possibly the largest collection of sand in the world and is worth checking out.

Hiking in Coral Pink Sand Dunes State Park

Coral Pink Sand Dunes Arch

Easy – (0.2 mi / 0.3 km), round trip, allow 15 minutes elev. Δ: 50 ft / 15 m, trailhead on Hancock Road

This is by no means the grandest arch you will see, but is a welcome surprise for a park whose primary feature is a set of

Coral Pink Sand Dunes after a rain shower

sand dunes. Getting to this arch is easy. At the turnoff from Hancock Road from Highway 89, mark your trip meter and drive 0.8 miles. Drive off the road on your right for about 150 yards, heading towards the sole obvious hoodoo. From here, get out and walk past this hoodoo using the ATV trail on the left and look for two rock outcroppings. Here you will find a small but definite arch.

Coral Pink Sand Dunes

Easy – (1.0 mi / 1.6 km), round trip, allow 1 - 2 hours, elev. Δ: a00 ft / 30 m, trailhead at campground

The dunes are in easy sight as you pull up and the trailhead is easy enough to find, however it is recommended to keep along the established route so as not to disturb the fragile flora. Like all dunes, walking in sand can be more tiring than the same distance on hard ground. Also, hiking to the tallest dune, at a 300 feet elevation gain from its base, will add to the time. Look for insect and animal tracks, as well as areas of "plant art", where tall grasses have left their marks in the sand by the prevailing winds.

The one caution with the dunes is that the area is shared with ATV's. Keep an eye out for fast moving visitors. The ATV's can be a bit loud, but they are also fun to watch from the tall dunes.

South Fork Indian Canyon

Easy – (1.0 mi / 1.6 km), round trip, allow 30 minutes, elev. Δ: 150 ft / 46 m, trailhead at end of South Fork Indian Canyon Road off Sand Spring Road

This trail leads to some truly amazing pictographs. Formed around 1200 BCE, this rock art was created using natural pigments versus a petroglyph, which are formed by actually carving into the rock. The pictographs are quite rare and sit behind a protective fence. Bring a zoom lens if you want great pictures. This trail requires a 4WD vehicle that can handle the aptly named Sand Spring Road.

Take Sand Spring Road from Hancock for about a mile through the edge of the dunes and then a little less than two miles up South Fork Indian Canyon to the obvious parking lot for the pictographs. In many ways, this is the gem of the park and not the only one of its kind (See Hell Dive Canyon below)

Hell Dive Canyon

Moderate – (6.6 mi / 10.6 km), round trip, allow 4 – 5 hours, elev. Δ: 580 ft / 177 m, trailhead on 4WD road west of Water Canyon

This is another set of pictographs that are farther to get to and not protected. Please do not touch these very fragile pieces of

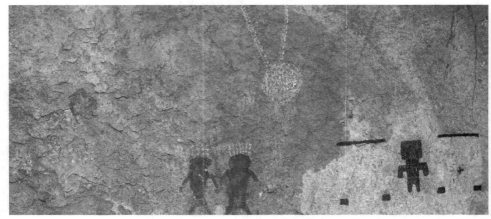

Pictographs at South Fork Indian Canyon

Still Life with Sand

history. Any contact with them can do permanent harm. To get here, head to the South Fork Indian Canyon road on Sand Spring Road and upon reaching it, stay right for about 0.8 miles, continuing on Sand Spring Road. At a fork in the road, head left and continue another 0.75 miles stopping when the road gets too rough for vehicles.

After parking, continue hiking down this road. The road becomes more trail and winds down to the bottom of Water Canyon and then climbs up a ridge to another intersection. Turn left here and continue in a southerly direction. Don't fret, as the trail veers to the northeast for a couple of miles, just make sure you don't take any right turns and you'll end up at Hell Dive Canyon. Continue into the alcove, where the pictographs can be found. Again, please be respectful in this area and don't touch the art.

Peek-a-Boo Slot Canyon
Easy – (0.7 mi / 1.1 km), round trip, allow 1 hour, trailhead described below

Peek-a-Boo or Red Canyon is not that long and is a very easy walk through a narrow red rock walled slot canyon with plenty of twists and turns (hence the nickname). While the trail itself isn't that long, the primary reason is the journey itself. It takes about 3 hours to get to the trailhead along deep sandy 4WD roads or optional ATV routes. The scenery along the way and the adventure getting there makes the slot canyon itself icing on the cake.

This canyon isn't in the park boundaries itself, but is very popular for ATV enthusiasts staying in Coral Pink Sand Dunes SP. From the park, head back to Highway 89 via Hancock Road and turn south. Look for the Best Friends Animal Society and make a left towards it. Total distance from the park to the sanctuary is 16 miles. Now on road 102M, make a left just before the animal sanctuary and continue on this deep sandy path for the canyon. Stay right at the first juncture where 102M splits for road 102. Continue on road 102 unless you can navigate very deep sand and want a bit more adventure, then take 102L, which is slightly shorter but has a nice steep hill to navigate. The slot canyon is at the end of the road.

135

Snow Canyon State Park

Quick Facts

Official Park Website: http://stateparks.utah.gov/parks/snow-canyon/

Visitor Center: (435) 628-2255

Park Accessibility:
- Okay for 2WD and RVs
- Day and Overnight Use

Experience Level:
- Family Friendly to Experienced Hiker

Camping in Park:
- Snow Canyon Campground: 31 T/RV, drinking water, flush toilets, showers, hookups, dump station, some pull thru sites, call visitor center for reservations

Lodging and Dining in Park:
- None

Nearest Town with Amenities:
- Ivins, UT is 4 mi / 6 km from park

Getting There:
- From St George, UT: Take UT-18 North to Snow Canyon Drive. Total distance is 13 mi / 21 km to park

Sweeping views and fantastic trails at Snow Canyon State Park

SNOW CANYON STATE PARK

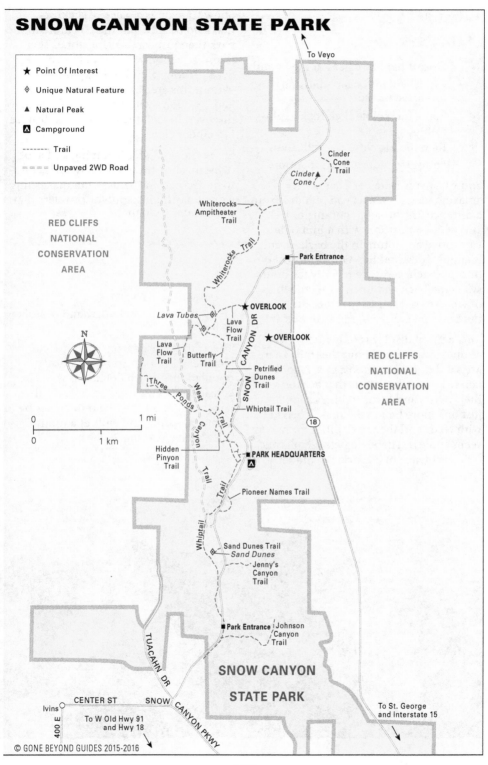

Legend:
- ★ Point Of Interest
- ◇ Unique Natural Feature
- ▲ Natural Peak
- Ⓐ Campground
- ----- Trail
- ==== Unpaved 2WD Road

To Veyo

Cinder Cone Trail

Cinder Cone ▲

Whiterocks Ampitheater Trail

Whiterocks Trail

RED CLIFFS NATIONAL CONSERVATION AREA

■ Park Entrance

Lava Tubes ◇

★ OVERLOOK

Lava Flow Trail

★ OVERLOOK

Lava Flow Trail

Butterfly Trail

SNOW CANYON DR

Petrified Dunes Trail

RED CLIFFS NATIONAL CONSERVATION AREA

N

Three Ponds

West Canyon Trail

Whiptail Trail

18

0 ——— 1 mi
0 ——— 1 km

Hidden Pinyon Trail

■ PARK HEADQUARTERS Ⓐ

Whiptail Trail

Pioneer Names Trail

Sand Dunes Trail
Sand Dunes ◇

Jenny's Canyon Trail

■ Park Entrance

Johnson Canyon Trail

SNOW CANYON STATE PARK

TUACAHN DR

Ivins ○

CENTER ST

SNOW CANYON PKWY

400 E

To W Old Hwy 91 and Hwy 18

To St. George and Interstate 15

© GONE BEYOND GUIDES 2015-2016

What Makes Snow Canyon State Park Special

- One of the few places in the Grand Circle where Navajo sandstone and lava have mixed
- Some incredible slick rock exploration
- Remarkably close to civilization and yet remote at the same time

Snow Canyon State Park has some amazing views, even as you pull up. From a distance, the broad panorama of red and white sandstone, with a hint of lava-capped adventure in the background, is simply breathtaking. One's eye, just on the approach, can gaze merrily for hours, sweeping back and forth along the lines of white to red sandstone. It is, even on the horizon, a place of sandstone as art.

This natural display is only intensified as one draws in and onto the trail. There are sand dunes, hoodoos, fins, razor thin labyrinths, and canyons that beckon with their twists and turns to hike around just one more bend. The rock is bright with color and the possibilities for hiking seem endless. There are petroglyphs and other evidence of use prior to modern times as well.

Snow Canyon is a place of slickrock magic to be sure, but there is more to the park than just carved sandstone. There is also a section where lava has covered over, creating a different exploration. Within this area are lava tubes, caves, and lava flows with some cool features to discover. In fact, the park's tallest feature is a cinder cone.

Snow Canyon offers camping and a lot of established trails. Given that it's close to St. George and Ivins, Utah makes this a great day hiking spot for travelers that don't want to camp.

Hiking Snow Canyon State Park

Johnson Canyon
Easy – (2.0 mi / 3.2 km), round trip, allow 1 hour

This trail is closed from March 15 to October 31 to protect nesting bird populations. When open, this is considered one of the top hikes in the park. Easy and level, the trail passes by a natural spring and ends at a monster thick arch spanning 200 feet.

Whiptail Trail

Easy – (6.0 mi / 9.7 km), round trip, allow 3 hours

Whiptail is a paved there and back route popular with the locals. There are plenty of bikers, joggers, and walkers on this trail. The trail sits at the base of Snow Canyon's red (and white) rocks, giving a nice backdrop for all users. There is a small elevation gain but the trail is wheelchair accessible. This is a popular hike, especially on weekends.

Jenny's Canyon

Easy – (0.5 mi / 0.8 km), round trip, allow 30 minutes

This trail is closed from March 15 to June 1 to protect nesting bird populations. A short level hike that ends at an interesting slot canyon. Jenny's Canyon Trail is great for kids.

Sand Dunes

Easy – (0.5 mi / 0.8 km), round trip, allow 30 minutes

A quick an easy jaunt to a small set of sand dunes. This is a great family hike with fabulous scenery from every angle. If you have small children, this is a perfect place for playing in the dunes.

Pioneer Names Trail

Easy – (0.5 mi / 0.8 km), round trip, allow 30 minutes

Pioneer Names Trail takes a somewhat sandy but otherwise ambling and quick path to a red rock alcove. Within it are the names of several Mormon pioneers from 1881. Getting to the alcove and up close to the pioneer graffiti requires a short but steep climb up slick rock at the end. The surroundings are a pleasing mix of red sandstone and the green of the desert pinyon juniper woodlands.

West Canyon Trail

Moderate – (8.0 mi / 12.9 km), round trip, allow 4 hours

This trail is an old dirt road that leads up into the main canyon in the park. The hike itself is level for the most part and offers great views into all of the side washes, sand stone hills, and cliff faces. This is a great place to go on an adventure, with plenty of slickrock to explore. The canyon is wide and inviting, traveling much of the time through grasslands. Stay on the trail whenever possible and avoid walking on undisturbed soil.

Snow Canyon

Hidden Pinyon

Moderate – (1.5 mi / 2.4 km), round trip, allow 1 hour

Stunning views are to be found on this hike. Great hike to capture the essence of the park in a short amount of time. This is an interpretative trail that describes the geologic features and native flora in the park.

Three Ponds

Moderate – (3.5 mi / 5.6 km), round trip, allow 2 hours

This is for the most part a hike through a sandy wash with some slick rock. The trail follows through a twisty wash with deep "slog worthy" sand to the mouth of a large canyon. The trail ends at the first of three potholes that seasonally fill with water. There are two other pools further on. While hiking to murky stagnant water may not be for everyone, the surroundings along the way are very nice and sure to please.

Petrified Dunes Trail

Moderate – (1.0 mi / 1.6 km), round trip, allow 45 minutes

Here is another trail taking the hiker to "sand dunes frozen in time". Geologically speaking, much of the Grand Circle was a vast sand dune, so in effect, all the redrock you see falls under this moniker. That said, this is one of the nicest hikes in the park. The sandstone here is unique, odd, and beautiful, all at the same time.

Butterfly Trail

Moderate – (2.0 mi / 3.2 km), round trip, allow 1 hour

This trail is a continuation of Petrified Dunes Trail giving similar awesome scenery. Connects with West Canyon Overlook and the Lava Flow Trail. Some steep sections.

Lava Flow Trail

Moderate – (2.5 mi / 4.0 km), round trip, allow 1 - 2 hours

This is an easy to follow trail with some caves near the trailhead. Bring your headlamps. The trail itself is uneven throughout as it heads up into an ancient lava field. This trail can be very hot in the summer, but does show a different side of the park.

Whiterocks Amphitheater

Moderate – (4.0 mi / 6.4 km), round trip, allow 2 hours

This is a straightforward trail into the main white sandstone area of Snow Canyon. The trail starts out in moderately deep sand, but quickly hits the slickrock for an ascent of about 100 feet. The trail officially ends at a bowl of white rock, surrounding the hiker in amphitheater fashion, on three sides. It is possible to continue on in scramble mode to the top for better views. Some parts require Class 3 level scrambling. At the top, the hiker is rewarded with some fantastic views of the park.

There is a shorter trail of about one mile in length located north of the junction of Snow Canyon Drive and SR18 (north of the junction 0.5 miles).

Cinder Cone Trail

Strenuous – (1.5 mi / 2.4 km), round trip, allow 1 - 2 hours

Hiking up cinder cones can feel like you are going nowhere fast, but the trail does reach the top. The trail corkscrews up with an elevation gain of 500 feet. Once at the top, you will be greeted with a view of the crater and the park's gorgeous views.

Bryce Canyon National Park

Sunrise at Bryce Canyon

Quick Facts

Official Park Website: www.nps.gov/brca

Visitor Center: (435) 834-5322

Park Accessibility:

- Okay for 2WD and RVs
- Day and Overnight Use

Experience Level:

- Family Friendly to Experienced Hiker

Camping in Park:

- North Campground: 102 T/RV, drinking water, vault toilets, some pull thru sites, no hookups, dump station in summer, some sites reservable. Reserve at http://www.recreation.gov/
- Sunset Campground: 101 T/RV, drinking water, showers, vault toilets, no hookups, closed in winter, some sites reservable. Reserve at http://www.recreation.gov/

Lodging in Park:

- Bryce Canyon Lodge, Phone: (435) 834-8700

Dining in Park:

- Bryce Canyon Lodge offers breakfast, lunch and dinner. There is also a general store.

Nearest Town with Amenities:

- Bryce, UT is 1.5 mi / 2.4 km from park

Getting There:

- From St. George, UT: Take I-15N to UT-9 East, US-89 North and UT-12 East to UT-63 South 125 mi / 201 km to park entrance

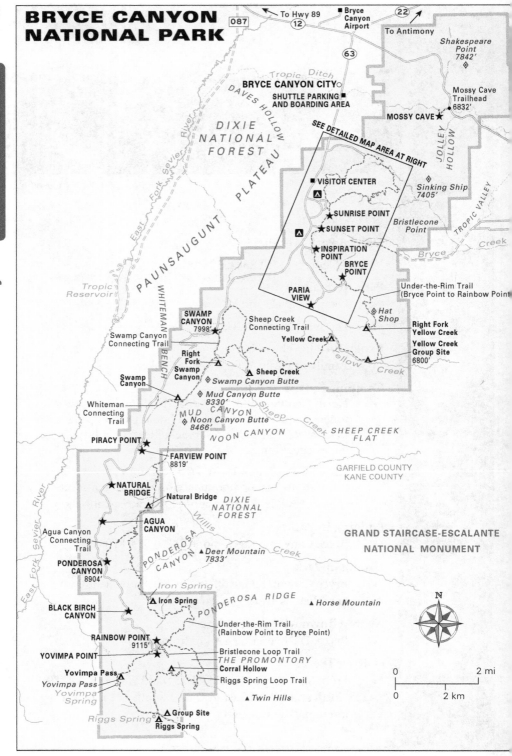

BRYCE CANYON NATIONAL PARK

087

To Hwy 89

12

Bryce Canyon Airport

22

To Antimony

Tropic Ditch

63

BRYCE CANYON CITY

SHUTTLE PARKING AND BOARDING AREA

Shakespeare Point 7842'

DAVES HOLLOW

Mossy Cave Trailhead 6832'

MOSSY CAVE ★

DIXIE NATIONAL FOREST

SEE DETAILED MAP AREA AT RIGHT

JOLLEY HOLLOW

East Fork Sevier River

PLATEAU

■ **VISITOR CENTER**

★ **SUNRISE POINT**

★ **SUNSET POINT**

★ **INSPIRATION POINT**

BRYCE POINT

Sinking Ship 7405'

Bristlecone Point

TROPIC VALLEY

Bryce *Creek*

PAUNSAUGUNT

PARIA VIEW

Under-the-Rim Trail (Bryce Point to Rainbow Point)

Tropic Reservoir

WHITEMAN BENCH

SWAMP CANYON 7998'

Sheep Creek Connecting Trail

Hat Shop △

Right Fork Yellow Creek

Swamp Canyon Connecting Trail

Right Fork Swamp Canyon △

Yellow Creek △

△

Yellow Creek Group Site 6800'

Swamp Canyon

△ **Sheep Creek**

Yellow *Creek*

Whiteman Connecting Trail

△

◇ *Swamp Canyon Butte*

◇ *Mud Canyon Butte 8330'*

MUD CANYON

◇ *Noon Canyon Butte 8466'*

Sheep *Creek*

SHEEP CREEK FLAT

PIRACY POINT ★
★

NOON CANYON

★ **FARVIEW POINT** 8819'

GARFIELD COUNTY
KANE COUNTY

★ **NATURAL BRIDGE**

★

Natural Bridge

DIXIE NATIONAL FOREST

East Fork Sevier River

★ **AGUA CANYON**

Agua Canyon Connecting Trail

PONDEROSA CANYON

Willis

▲ *Deer Mountain 7833'*

Creek

GRAND STAIRCASE-ESCALANTE

NATIONAL MONUMENT

PONDEROSA CANYON 8904'

★

Iron Spring

△ **Iron Spring**

PONDEROSA RIDGE

▲ *Horse Mountain*

N

BLACK BIRCH CANYON
★

Under-the-Rim Trail (Rainbow Point to Bryce Point)

RAINBOW POINT 9115'
★
★

YOVIMPA POINT

Bristlecone Loop Trail

THE PROMONTORY

Corral Hollow

0   2 mi

Yovimpa Pass

△

Yovimpa Pass

Riggs Spring Loop Trail

0   2 km

Yovimpa Spring

▲ *Twin Hills*

△ **Group Site**

Riggs Spring

Riggs Spring

142

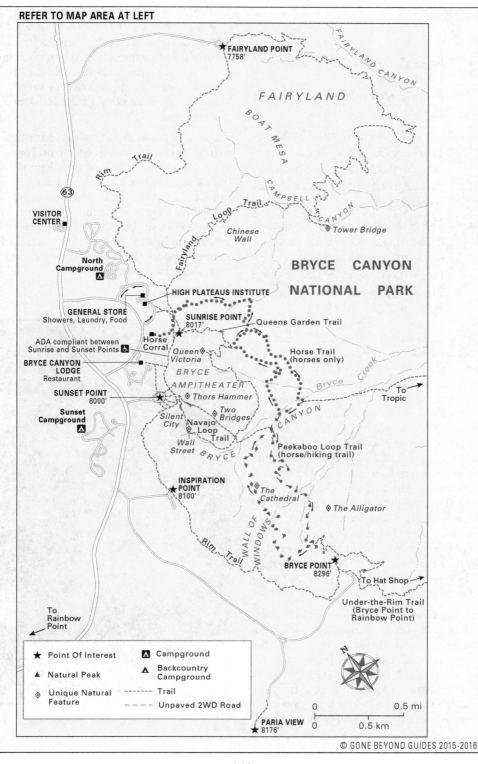

★ FAIRYLAND POINT
7758'

FAIRYLAND CANYON

FAIRYLAND

BOAT MESA

CAMPBELL CANYON

Rim Trail

63

VISITOR
CENTER ■

Loop Trail

Fairyland

Chinese
Wall

◇ Tower Bridge

North
Campground Ⓐ

BRYCE   CANYON

NATIONAL   PARK

HIGH PLATEAUS INSTITUTE

GENERAL STORE
Showers, Laundry, Food

★ SUNRISE POINT
8017'

Queens Garden Trail

ADA compliant between
Sunrise and Sunset Points ♿

Horse
Corral

Horse Trail
(horses only)

BRYCE CANYON
LODGE
Restaurant

◇ Queen
Victoria

BRYCE
AMPITHEATER

Bryce   Creek

To
Tropic

★ SUNSET POINT
8000'

◇ Thors Hammer

◇ Two
Bridges

C
A
N
Y
O
N

Sunset
Campground Ⓐ

Silent
City

Navajo
◇ Loop
Trail

Wall
Street

BRYCE

Peekaboo Loop Trail
(horse/hiking trail)

★ INSPIRATION
POINT
8100'

◇ The
Cathedral

◇ The Alligator

W
A
L
L

O
F

Rim Trail

W
I
N
D
O
W
S

★ BRYCE POINT
8296'

To Hat Shop ➔

Under-the-Rim Trail
(Bryce Point to
Rainbow Point)

To
Rainbow
Point

Legend

★ Point Of Interest
▲ Natural Peak
◇ Unique Natural
  Feature

Ⓐ Campground
Ⓐ Backcountry
  Campground
------- Trail
==== Unpaved 2WD Road

N

0   0.5 mi
0   0.5 km

★ PARIA VIEW
8176'

What Makes Bryce Canyon Special

- Bryce Canyon is the template for Southwest scenery, holding the entire spectrum of desert colors in one place.

- It is an amusement park for hikers. There are tunnels, spires, hoodoos, (aka fairy chimneys) and pinnacles, all in an amphitheater of fruit colored rock.

- The park is considered one of the darkest night skies in the contiguous United States and has some of the farthest-reaching views during the day, up to 150 miles to the horizon.

Bryce Canyon is a wonderland of fluted rock and hoodoo pinnacles; hoodoos being thin tall spires of rock. Bryce Canyon has been the inspiration of movies, amusement park rides, desert-themed musicals, and art to the point of being the template for Southwest scenery. It is full of grandness and color all wrapped within a succession of massive natural amphitheaters. Bryce Canyon holds the entire spectrum of the colors of the desert in one place. From the top of the mesa, the view is breathtaking, grand, and colorful in so many hundreds of tones that it defies description. Light seems to emit from the canyon walls rather than reflect off of them, radiating to a glow at the tips of each hoodoo.

Hiking down inside Bryce amphitheater is like going on an amusement park ride. All journeys wind steadily downward followed by a delightful tramp up and down knolls, through man-carved tunnels and past massive hoodoos that form fragile spires. Once down below, the canyon floor is more whimsy and wonder with

pines growing as tall as the spires, each turn worthy of another amazing shot. Hiking or horseback riding within Bryce is simply a fun experience. When you are done, you are a short shuttle ride back to Bryce Canyon Lodge, where they serve hearty meals in an atmosphere fashioned after the mid-1920s.

The other special quality of this national park is its elevation. Bryce Canyon NP sits at 9,000 feet (2,743 meters). From the mesa tops, one can see clear out 150 miles (241 km) to the horizon, an amazing view, and one of the farthest horizons visible in North America. The high elevation also brings snow in the winter and spring, capping the fruity-colored rocks with a sugary coating.

Douglas firs within the hoodoos

Hiking in Bryce Canyon NP

Mossy Cave

Easy – (0.8 mi / 1.3 km), round trip, allow 30 minutes, elev. Δ: 300 ft / 91 m, trailhead on Highway 12, 4 mi east of SR 63

A short hike that follows along a stream created by a man made diversion during the late 1800's by Mormon Pioneers. There are two spurs to this hike. The left spur ends at Mossy Cave, a large rocky overhang with a small waterfall that creates a nice mossy environment for plants. During the winter, look for icicle sheets created by the dripping waters, which are very cool and unusual. The right spur leads to a good-sized waterfall that also has been known to freeze completely during the winter.

Rim Trail

Easy – (0.9 mi / 1.5 km), one way, allow 1 hour, elev. Δ: 1,235 ft / 376 m, multiple trailheads along rim of Bryce Canyon

The Rim Trail from Sunrise Point to Sunset Point is flat and offers a leisurely way to take in the park. Pick up the trail from either point and follow the well-marked path. The Rim Trail does continue south from Sunset Point for a total of 5.5 miles (9.2km) one-way, but the trail from here has a lot of ups and downs and is considered strenuous.

Fairyland Loop

Strenuous – (8.0 mi /12.9 km), round trip, allow 5 hours, elev. Δ: 2,309 ft / 704 m, trailheads at Sunrise and Fairyland Points

Fairyland Loop is similar to Peekaboo but as it is a little longer, offers even more to the hiker. There is plenty to see on the trail, including China Wall, an impressively long wall of rock. You can also see a double arch with unique monolithic sentinels called Tower Bridge. Fairyland Loop is the least crowded trail of the popular trails at Bryce Canyon and is well worth it if you want to do a longer

hike. Pick up the trail at Fairyland Point. The trail uses the Rim Trail to create a full loop.

Tower Bridge

Moderate – (3.0 mi / 4.8 km), round trip, allow 2 – 3 hours, elev. Δ: 950 ft / 290 m, trailhead at Sunrise Point

See Fairyland Loop for additional details. The trail starts at Sunrise Point and follows Fairyland Loop partially down until a juncture to a short spur trail to view Tower Bridge. Tower Bridge is a formation of two colorful hoodoos connected by a fragile layer of rock midway down the "towers". There is another natural bridge that can be seen in the same view. Head back up the same way you came down or continue onwards on the longer Fairyland Loop.

Queen's Garden Trail

Easy – (1.8 mi / 2.9 km), round trip, allow 2 hours, elev. Δ: 320 ft / 98 m, trailhead at Sunrise Point

Queen's Garden is 0.9 miles (1.4 km) down and the same distance back up. The trail is the least strenuous in terms of steepness compared to the other trails that head into the canyon, but it is by no means a flat trail. Picking up the Queen's Garden trail from Sunrise Point, hike down and wind your way through tunnels to the hoodoo called Queen Victoria and the surrounding rock formations that make up her garden. You can follow the trail back to the top, though many folks opt to combine this trail with the Navajo Trail to create a loop.

Peekaboo Trail

Strenuous – (5.5 mi / 8.8 km), round trip, allow 3 – 4 hours, elev. Δ: 1,555 ft / 473 m, trailhead at Bryce Point

Peekaboo is one of the best trails in Bryce Canyon. The loop is picked up from either Bryce Point or Sunset via the Navajo Trail. The trail gives the hiker a sense of

remoteness and a personal experience as you walk up and down gullies and past goblins, fins and rows of hoodoos. Every bend rewards the hiker with a different view of often-unimaginable rock shapes. You will find yourself a ways from the rim, in the heart of the amphitheater, which gives a better sense of grandness of Bryce Canyon. The loop can be done on its own or combined with Navajo or Queen's Garden Trails. Peekaboo is not terribly crowded, though it does get a fair amount of horse traffic.

Hat Shop Trail

Moderate – (4.0 mi /6.4 km), round trip, allow 2 - 3 hours, elev. Δ: 1,436 ft / 438 m, trailhead at Bryce Point

From the trailhead, descend via the Under the Rim Trail for 2 miles to a set of thin spired hoodoos with delicately balanced capstones defying gravity. The hike is a down and up, there and back hike. There are ample other Bryce Canyon type features along the way to the final destination.

Swamp Canyon

Moderate – (4.3 mi / 7.2 km), round trip, allow 2 - 3 hours, elev. Δ: 800 ft / 244 m, trailhead at Swamp Canyon Overlook

Swamp Canyon Trail starts at about the mid-point in the park, further south of the main amphitheaters. This loop trail offers a mixture of denser forest and the famous hoodoos. Unlike the endless stream of hikers coming down Navajo Trail, Swamp Canyon is definitely more intimate and may be a better option on crowded days.

Bristlecone Loop

Easy – (1.0 mi / 1.6 km), round trip, allow 30 minutes, elev. Δ: 195 ft / 59 m, trailhead at Rainbow Point, southern end of park

While most of the attention in Bryce is near the entrance of the park, the southern section of the park receives lets attention. Here the area contains more of a pleasant evergreen forest offering. Bristlecone Loop is a short hike in the southern section, displaying expansive views from 9,100 feet across a forested and green part of the state. As the trail name suggests, there are examples of the bristlecone pine, a gnarled and aged tree that can grow to 1,800 years here. The

Bryce Canyon in early spring

hike is pleasant and as the highest trail in the park, can be a little breathtaking for many reasons.

Riggs Spring Loop
Strenuous – (8.5 mi / 13.7 km), round trip, allow 4 – 5 hours, elev. Δ: 2,248 ft / 685 m, trailhead at Yovimpa Point

A very different side of Bryce, Riggs Spring is an ambling pleasant hike through fir, spruce, quaking aspens, and even ancient bristlecone pines. The hike is the southernmost trail in the park. As the trail's title suggests, there is a little spring in a shady setting. Do treat the water before using. This is a popular trail for overnight campers.

Along the floor of Bryce Canyon

Grand Staircase-Escalante National Monument

Quick Facts

Official Park Website: www.blm.gov/ut/st/en/fo/grand_stair-case-escalante.html

Visitor Center:

None in park, contact: BLM Kanab Headquarters, 669 South Highway 89A, Kanab, Utah 84741, Phone: (435) 644-1200

Park Accessibility:

- 2WD, 4WD recommended for most roads

- Day and Overnight Use

Experience Level:

- Primarily Experienced Hiker – Backcountry Hiker,

- Some trails Family Friendly - Casual Hiker

Camping in Park:

- No developed campground, backcountry camping okay with permit

Lodging and Dining in Park:

- None

Nearest Town with Amenities:

- Tropic, UT is 5 mi / 8 km from park

Getting There:

- From St. George, UT: Take UT-59 South and AZ-389 East 81 mi / 130 km to park entrance

- From Page, AZ: Take US-89 North 17 mi / 27 km to park entrance

Wahweap Hoodoo

What Makes Grand Staircase-Escalante Special

- Being nearly 1.9 million acres of pristine, diverse and multifaceted Utah desert, knowing you are hiking in the heart of the Colorado Plateau

- A remarkable and vast array of all manner of rarely seen arches, petroglyphs, hoodoos, canyons, slot canyons, lush riparian folds cut deep into rock walls and well, anything and everything that can be found in the Utah desert

- Roughly the size of three Rhode Islands and only two paved roads

A connection can be made with Glen Canyon National Recreation Area and the Grand Staircase-Escalante National Monument. The most obvious is that they are two very large parks siting right next to each other. Glen Canyon NRA protects a substantial portion of the Escalante River and its watershed, so they both share the last river to be named in the continental US. They both cover land that has been little disturbed, primarily because it is so rugged a country as to make it hard for the toils of man to penetrate. This is in fact why nearby Glen Canyon was filled with water, because there were no roads or towns to move. From the lens of the Bureau of Reclamation, there was nothing there.

It was only after the deed was done that folks realized there was something there after all, that this was a land worth protecting. Perhaps then, this is the deepest connection between the two parks. Within the profound disappointment by many of burying Glen Canyon with water, there was an acknowledgment that more must be done for those lands around it that are similar in spirit. To that, using the Antiq-

uities Act, President Bill Clinton created Grand Staircase-Escalante National Monument in 1996. It is the largest land area of all the US National Monuments.

While this act was applauded by environmentalists and can be seen as a sentiment in the right direction over what was done with Glen Canyon, it was not seen as positive by many of the residents of Utah. Clinton barely gave 24-hour notice to the Utah governor and state congress, giving them no time to react. The designation was attacked from many different angles and remains a sore subject with Utah residents.

Politics aside, Grand Staircase-Escalante is a massive, rugged, and pristine world. Entering it requires preparation, topo maps, and backcountry skills and for all of this preparation, its rewards are many. It is in many ways, the last frontier within the contiguous United States, where the meter of a person is on equal ground with the land.

Hiking Grand Staircase-Escalante NM

All of these hikes have dozens of variants. The routes described below are the most commonly traveled routes.

Lower Calf Creek Falls

Moderate – (5.9 mi / 9.5 km), round trip, allow 3 hours, elev. Δ: 250 ft / 76 m, trailhead at Calf Creek Campground

The trail starts by acknowledging the soft sand underneath your feet on a trail that seems nearly surreal in its beauty. The line of the trail cuts into a tree-lined oasis as the canyon floor meets with massive blocks of darkly streaked walls of Navajo Sandstone that tower above on each side. The hike up has to be seen to be believed. Look for numerous cliff dwelling ruins tucked into alcoves as well as alien looking humanoid petroglyphs.

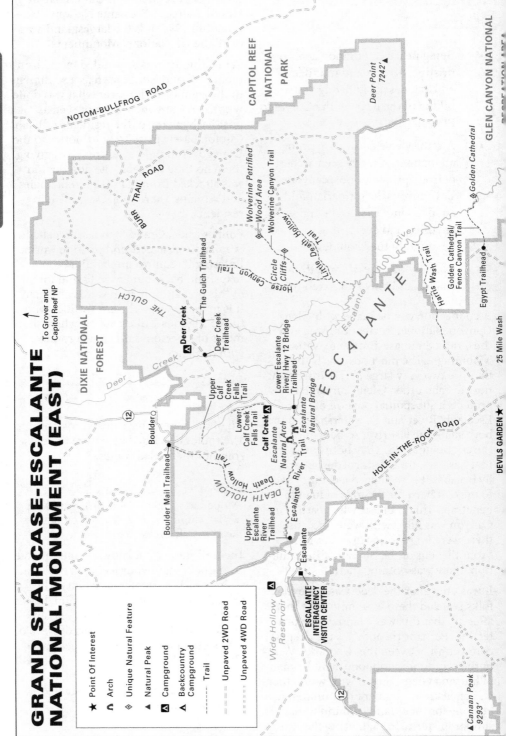

GRAND STAIRCASE-ESCALANTE NATIONAL MONUMENT (EAST)

Legend:

★ Point Of Interest
∩ Arch
◈ Unique Natural Feature
▲ Natural Peak
🅰 Campground
▲ Backcountry Campground
------ Trail
=== Unpaved 2WD Road
===== Unpaved 4WD Road

To Grover and Capitol Reef NP

NOTOM-BULLFROG ROAD

CAPITOL REEF NATIONAL PARK

BURR TRAIL ROAD

THE GULCH

DIXIE NATIONAL FOREST

Deer Creek

Deer Point 7242'

Wolverine Petrified Wood Area

Wolverine Canyon Trail

Little Death Hollow Trail

Horse Canyon Trail

Circle Cliffs

The Gulch Trailhead

Deer Creek Trailhead

Boulder

12

Boulder Mail Trailhead

Upper Calf Creek Falls Trail

Lower Calf Creek Falls Trail

Calf Creek

Escalante Natural Arch

Escalante Natural Bridge

Lower Escalante River/Hwy 12 Bridge Trailhead

DEATH HOLLOW

Death Hollow Trail

Escalante River Trail

Upper Escalante River Trailhead

Escalante

ESCALANTE

Escalante River

Golden Cathedral

Golden Cathedral/Fence Canyon Trail

Harris Wash Trail

Egypt Trailhead

GLEN CANYON NATIONAL RECREATION AREA

HOLE-IN-THE-ROCK ROAD

25 Mile Wash

DEVILS GARDEN ★

Wide Hollow Reservoir

ESCALANTE INTERAGENCY VISITOR CENTER

12

▲ Canaan Peak 9293'

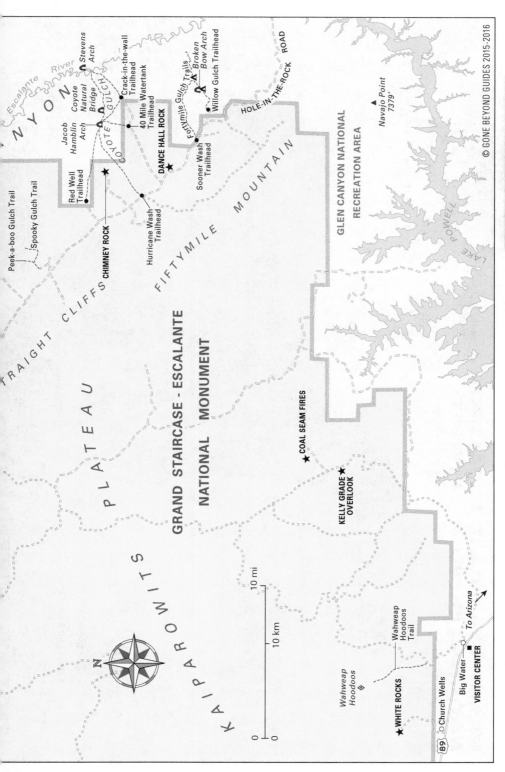

Peek-a-boo Gulch Trail

Spooky Gulch Trail

STRAIGHT CLIFFS **CHIMNEY ROCK**

Red Well Trailhead

Hurricane Wash Trailhead

Jacob Hamblin Arch

Coyote Natural Bridge

COYOTE GULCH

River

Escalante

CANYON

Stevens Arch

Crack-in-the-wall Trailhead

40 Mile Watertank

Fortymile Gulch Trails

Broken Bow Arch

Willow Gulch Trailhead

Sooner Wash Trailhead

DANCE HALL ROCK

HOLE-IN-THE-ROCK ROAD

FIFTYMILE MOUNTAIN

PLATEAU

GRAND STAIRCASE - ESCALANTE NATIONAL MONUMENT

GLEN CANYON NATIONAL RECREATION AREA

Navajo Point 7379'

LAKE POWELL

★ **COAL SEAM FIRES**

★ **KELLY GRADE OVERLOOK**

KAIPAROWITS

N

0

10 mi

10 km

Wahweap Hoodoos

Wahweap Hoodoos Trail

★ **WHITE ROCKS**

○ Church Wells

Big Water

VISITOR CENTER

To Arizona

89

© GONE BEYOND GUIDES 2015-2016

Grand Staircase - Escalante SOUTHERN UTAH

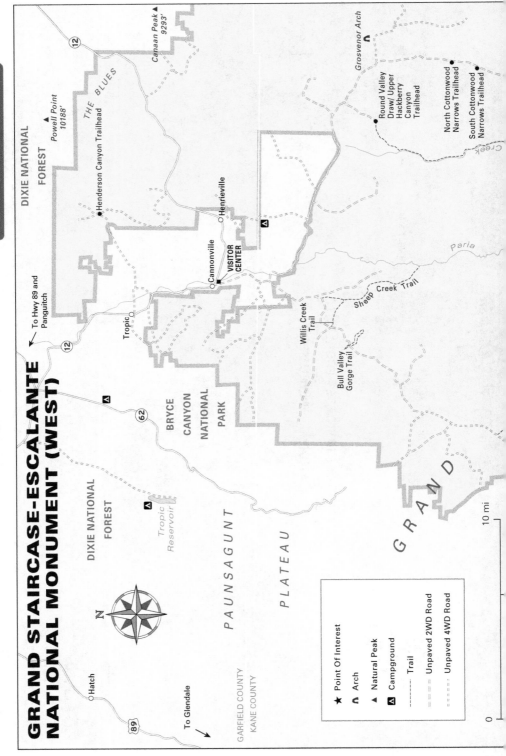

GRAND STAIRCASE-ESCALANTE NATIONAL MONUMENT (WEST)

DIXIE NATIONAL FOREST

Canaan Peak ▲ 9293'

THE BLUES

Powell Point ▲ 10188'

Henderson Canyon Trailhead

Grosvenor Arch

Round Valley Draw/ Upper Hackberry Canyon Trailhead

North Cottonwood Narrows Trailhead

South Cottonwood Narrows Trailhead

Creek

Henrieville

Paria

To Hwy 89 and Panguitch

Cannonville

VISITOR CENTER

Tropic

Sheep Creek Trail

Willis Creek Trail

Bull Valley Gorge Trail

BRYCE CANYON NATIONAL PARK

G R A N D

DIXIE NATIONAL FOREST

Tropic Reservoir

PAUNSAGUNT

PLATEAU

N

Hatch

To Glendale

GARFIELD COUNTY
KANE COUNTY

★ Point Of Interest
∩ Arch
▲ Natural Peak
◰ Campground
------- Trail
== Unpaved 2WD Road
===== Unpaved 4WD Road

10 mi

0

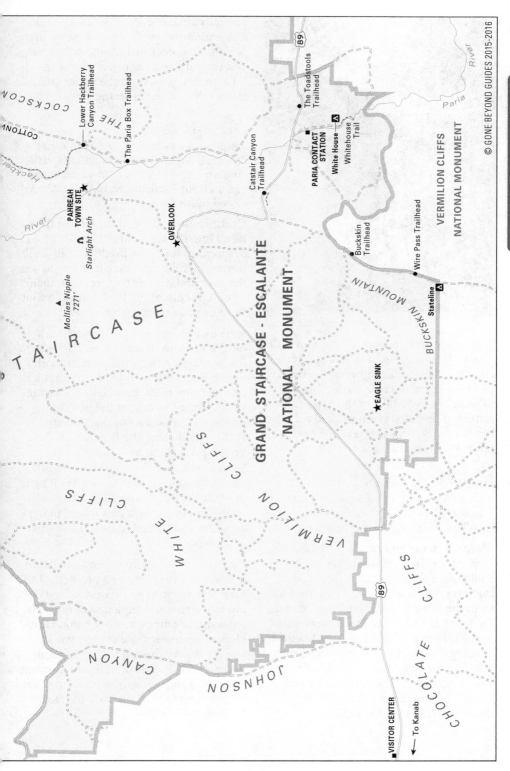

SOUTHERN UTAH

Grand Staircase - Escalante

Lower Calf Creek Falls

The trail leads to one of two falls on Calf Creek. The lower set of falls is spectacular and in fact is the higher of the two at 130 feet. There is a nice swimming hole to relax in as you take in the grotto like setting of the falls, greenery, and colored layers of rock. This is one of the best-known trails in the park.

Upper Calf Creek Falls

Strenuous – (2.2 mi / 3.5 km), round trip, allow 1 – 2 hours, elev. Δ: 505 ft / 154 m, trailhead on SR 12, east of milepost 81

More strenuous but no less beautiful, the Upper Calf Creek Falls may be the better choice during peak season. The trail starts on the west side UT 12 further up from the more popular parking area for the lower falls. The trailhead, near milepost 81, does not have a signpost. Start by heading downslope steeply on slickrock, using cairns as guides. The route descends 600 feet to the rim overlooking the falls. From there, follow the route down to the base of the falls.

The falls are more of a free fall of water and are shorter at 88 feet in height. There is a nice and deep swimming hole here and typically less people. As far as the hike quality goes, both the upper and lower falls are worth seeing.

Death Hollow

Strenuous – (14.0 mi / 22.5 km), round trip, full day trip or overnight backpacking trip, elev. Δ: 600 ft / 183 m, trailhead 24 mi from Escalante on Hell's Backbone Road north

Death Hollow is one of the largest tributaries into the Escalante River. This hike description takes the Boulder Mail Trail route. The hike is an excellent way to see the park and doesn't require more than minimal scrambling. Best done as a shuttle with two cars at each trailhead.

Start by driving about 3.8 miles south on UT 12 from Anasazi State Park to the Boulder Landing Strip on McGath Bench Road, which is your very first left after turning right onto Hells Backbone Road. Begin the hike at the junction on the northeast side of the McGath Point Bench along the Boulder Mail Trail. Travel along McGrath Bench, Sand Creek, and then Slickrock Saddle Bench for about 3.5 miles until you meet up with Death Hollow. Access here is straightforward, with a couple of places where you'll need some Class 3 type scrambling.

Once in, the water flows pretty well, but is never too strong to be a problem. The hike down involves a mixture of walking in the stream coupled with multiple crossings to paths on either bank. Death Hollow becomes more overgrown as you hit the confluence to the Escalante River. There are lots of little side canyons to explore and some deep pools to swim in. Hike out to the Overlook for Death Hollow Parking Area.

Upper Escalante River

Moderate to Strenuous – (13.0 mi / 20.9 km), one-way, elev. Δ: 500 ft / 152 m, trailhead along river at Escalante, UT

There aren't many hikes in the world where you can literally close the door to your hotel room and just take a long walk down a river canyon and when you are done, get picked up with ease right from the highway. This hike exists and it is one of the gems of the Southwest in terms of beauty. It meanders gently downstream and passes arches and natural bridges, thick wonderful canyon walls, and even some swimming holes.

First off, for hikers, this description can be followed during the dry season when the river is low enough to wade down. During the wet season, the route is more suitable for river rafting, inner tubing, and kayaking.

The hike starts just about anywhere within the town of Escalante where you can access the river. If you want to reduce the amount of river wading whilst in town, find your way to the Pine Creek Escalante River Confluence at the northeast end of town. Not much in the way of parking here, but you'll soon be in the thick of the riparian desert wilderness from here.

Once inside the canyon, the river meanders almost as a rule, snaking along one bend after the other, giving to the curious the wonder of what could be around the next bend. The meanders allow for constantly changing views as well. One of the first notable formations to see is the Escalante Natural Arch, which sits high up on the south wall and is super easy to miss. Look for it after the confluence with Sand Creek. Less than 0.5 miles further on is Escalante Natural Bridge, a humbling and beautiful sight as well as the largest formation in the park. The bridge also marks the home stretch of the hike. Look for the UT 12 Bridge and your ride to home base back in Escalante. Your ride will pass by the Kiva Koffeehouse, which serves espressos seasonally from April to October in a very nice rustic building with great views.

Escalante Natural Bridge

Easy – (3.5 mi / 5.6 km), round trip, allow 2 hours, elev. Δ: 100 ft / 30 m, trailhead at Highway 12 bridge over Escalante River

For those that don't have the time to hike downstream from the town of Escalante, it is possible to see the Escalante Natural Bridge and do a bit of river trail hiking coming from the UT 12 Bridge that crosses over the Escalante River. Look for signs that indicate Escalante River trailhead access about 14 miles from the town of Escalante, heading south. The Escalante Natural Arch is about 0.5 miles further upstream (add 1.0 mile to your round trip distance).

Fortymile and Willow Gulch Loop

Moderate – (11.0 mi / 17.7 km), round trip, allow 6 hours, elev. Δ: 540 ft / 165 m, trailhead at Sooner Wash Trailhead off Hole in the Rock Road

Narrow canyons, bold rock faces, and a maze of seemingly endless hiking possibilities, this is Fortymile and Willow Gulch. There are many ways to explore this area, but in this description, the route starts at Sooner Wash Trailhead. Folks can start out at the adjacent Dance Hall Rock Campsite and check out the cool looking Sooner Rocks. The trailhead and the campsite are off Hole in the Rock Road. Note that this hike has spots where you will need to wade through waterholes and depending on water levels, may even require some swimming to get past the water obstacles.

From Sooner Wash Trailhead hike for 1.5 miles into the confluence of Sooner Wash and Fortymile Gulch. This portion will have some areas that require wading through canyon water pockets.

Continue for several miles to the Willow Gulch confluence. Here you can keep going down Fortymile Gulch as it meets up with Lake Powell, however the going is muddier. This description heads up Willow Gulch, which avoids the mucky bits and takes the hiker to Broken Bow Arch, which is about 0.5 miles up Willow Gulch from the confluence.

Devils Garden at night

Willow Gulch is definitely the more pristine of the two choices at the juncture. To exit, hike up any of the three main streams that feed the tributary. The northernmost stream is the most convenient of the three as it passes by a parking area near Hole in the Rock Road. Either hike back to your car from here or be thankful you brought two cars and parked one at the exit site. If you do have a second car, the total trip is 8.2 miles.

Hole in the Rock Trail

Strenuous – (1.0 mi / 1.6 km), round trip, allow 1 hour, elev. Δ: 600 ft / 182 m, trailhead on Highway 12 , just southeast of Escalante

Early Mormon pioneers used this steep but marginally passable draw as the route down to the Colorado River. The first thing one thinks when coming to the rim of the steep and narrow gully is something along the lines of, "They took their wagons and animals down that??"

The pioneers blasted the crevice to make it wide enough for wagons.

Today, this old supply route can be hiked down to what is now Lake Powell. It's very steep and very rocky, but fortunately only about a half mile. The trail has a plaque at the bottom commemorating the tenacity of these early settlers.

Devils Garden

Easy – (0.5 mi / 0.8 km), round trip, allow 30 – 60 minutes, elev. Δ: 10 ft / 3 m, trailhead on Hole in the Rock Road

This is a great family trail just off the Hole in the Rock Road. Here there be hoodoos and arches, of all manner of shapes and sizes, oddly misshapen things, every last one of them. To get to this garden of the devil himself, simply head east five miles on UT 12 from Escalante to the unpaved Hole in the Rock Road, which is suitable for 2WD vehicles in dry weather. Another 13 miles on Hole in the Rock takes you to a signed turnoff to Devils Garden. Park and roam around. There are picnic tables, BBQ grills and a pit toilet here, making this a nice lunch spot. This is a great place to make a deal.

Golden Cathedral

Moderate – (9.5 mi / 15.3 km), round trip, allow 5 - 6 hours, elev. Δ: 1,260 ft / 384 m, trailhead in Egypt area off Hole in the Rock Road

Golden Cathedral is a strikingly beautiful and unworldly set of three arches. Together they form a line of holes that resemble a massive rock spine. There is great light play here, that helps give the formation its name. The hike requires some decent navigational skill, winding down Fence Canyon into the confluence of Neon Canyon and the Escalante River.

Take Hole in the Rock Road to Egypt Bench Road and follow it for 9.9 miles. High clearance vehicles recommended here, as there are several washes to cross. At 2.9 miles, you will pass the trailhead for Twentyfive Mile Wash. At 6.4 miles, the road will turn sharply right into a wash and one mile later, you will need to navigate up a short but rocky and steep incline. Take the fork at 9.3 miles and turn right, parking the car at the Egypt trailhead after 9.9 miles.

From here, while there isn't much in the way of official trail, there are plenty of cairns to follow. You are at the highest point in the hike and will now drop down into Fence Canyon. Keep to the left of Fence Canyon as you come to it in order to head down into the wash and the confluence of the Escalante River and Fence Canyon. Also, be sure to note the route as you head down so you can find it on your way back.

From here, pull out your water shoes and follow the Escalante River downstream one-mile south from the confluence with Fence Canyon to Neon Canyon, which is the first side canyon on your left.

Head up Neon Canyon for another 0.9 miles to Golden Cathedral. This last stretch and the triptych of arches is serene and majestic and worth the trek to get there. Heading further up Neon Canyon requires ropes and technical skills.

Peek-a-Boo Gulch

Moderate – (2.0 mi / 3.2 km), round trip, allow 1 – 2 hours, elev. Δ: 100 ft / 30 m, trailhead at Dry Fork area off Hole in the Rock Road

Peek-a-Boo is a really fun little slot canyon. The trailhead is 26 miles northeast on Hole in the Rock Road and then take Dry Fork Turnoff, staying left. Take the short hike from Dry Fork Overlook to the bottom of Dry Fork. Peek-a-Boo is just ahead to the north. Dry Fork Road is barely passable by 2WD vehicles, but is better for high clearance rigs.

What makes this slot canyon fun is all of the little scramble puzzles that need to be figured out. Lots of little dry falls and chockstones. Finding the right route

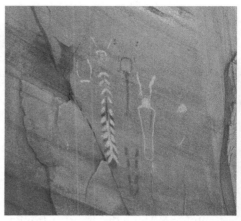

In Coyote Gulch

up the dry fall or figuring out whether to go under the big rock in the way or climb over it makes this a fun canyon to solve. A great hike for kids as none of the scrambling is that technical, though smaller children may need the occasional boost up.

The slot canyon is very narrow, though Spooky Gulch, which is typically combined with a hike through Peek-a-Boo, makes this gulch seem wide and spacious by comparison. Most folks scramble up Peek-a-Boo and then cross over and head into Spooky Gulch.

To combine the two slot canyons and make it a loop hike, scramble up Peek-a-Boo and then head overland through sandy red open terrain to the wide dry wash of Spooky Gulch. From there, head through Spooky back to Dry Fork and your car. This loop is 3.5 miles total.

Spooky Gulch

Moderate – (3.2 mi / 5.1 km), round trip, allow 2 -3 hours, elev. Δ: 100 ft / 30 m, trailhead at Dry Fork area off Hole in the Rock Road

Spooky Gulch is another short slot canyon that can be done alone or by combining with Peek-a-Boo Gulch. To get to Spooky Gulch, take the same route as to Peek-a-Boo from the Dry Fork Road.

Spooky Gulch is very different from Peek-a-Boo, though they are right next to each other. Whereas Peek-a-Boo is essentially a fun series of scramble puzzles to solve, Spooky is an extremely thin and deep slot canyon. It is so narrow that in some places there is only room for one person at time to pass. The canyon can make it feel like you are being compressed by the walls and some folks hit the narrow section at first thinking that it is too narrow to enter. You can and it does go all the way through, but it is definitely more of a spooky slot canyon than a soulful one. Those that are claustrophobic might want to take a pass on this one.

Coyote Gulch

Strenuous – (11.5 mi / 18.5 km), round trip, allow 5 - 6 hours or two-night backpacking trip, elev. Δ: 970 ft / 296 m, trailhead, see below

Coyote Gulch offers incredible scenery and some unique formations along the way. The trek is strenuous and it is recommended to make this a two-day jaunt. There is one section, Crack-in-the-Wall, that makes an argument for the day hike option if you don't have two days to spare, simply because it such an amazing and cool way to get down a cliff face.

The hike starts at some water tanks located 4.4 miles up Fortymile Ridge Road after coming from Hole-in-the-Rock Road in Escalante. The trail climbs up to Crack-in-the-Wall (or Crack-in-the-Rock), which is the first obstacle to surmount. The crack in question is a massive section of sandstone cliff that has broken off from the main section and moved outwards just enough for a grown person to shimmy in between. For the uninitiated, this may sound terrifying but it is easier than it may sound. Start by following the cairns to the very edge of the cliff and head right and down to what looks like the end of the cliff. Here you will find a crack that you shimmy in between to work to the canyon floor.

There are two areas of exposure, but for the most part, the crack is safe and is an exhilarating means of getting down to the river and upstream from there. If you are backpacking, it is recommended to lower your packs down by rope.

The scenery is amazing throughout and Coyote Gulch itself does not disappoint. Here one can fine one of the largest arches in the United States, Stevens Arch, standing 160 feet tall and spanning 225 feet. This is a hulk of an arch, simply massive. Then there is Coyote Bridge, a very picturesque natural bridge with water flowing underneath it year round.

Finally, there is Jacob Hamblin Arch, which marks the exit point for the hike. This is for some the hardest part of the hike. Hikers must be able to navigate up a 100-foot section of very steep slickrock to exit onto Fortymile Ridge. If you have anyone in the group that has doubts about this section, have the leader ascend and drop a rope down to aid in the climb up. This section is very exposed and at 45 degrees, is very steep. Once at the top of the ridge, head back to the water tanks and your vehicle.

Little Death Hollow

Easy – (16.0 mi / 25.7 km), round trip, full day or backpacking trip, elev. Δ: 600 ft / 183 m, trailhead: see description below

Grand Staircase has not one but two areas named Death Hollow. This hike refers to the beautiful slot canyon of Little Death Hollow. No one is sure what the relationship is between the Hollows, father and son perhaps? Whatever the connection, you can discuss this as you travel through this remote canyon. Little Death Hollow is popular for its long and narrow slot canyon, which is for the most part, obstacle free. The hike heads into the canyon and slot canyon further up with a turnaround point at the confluence with Horse Canyon. As with all hikes that involve narrow slot canyons,

Little Death Hollow Slot Canyon

National Park, but without the crowds. Be courteous to all of the generations ahead of you and refrain from picking up any pieces. From the petrified wood area, continue on the loop. It will cut east and then south into a valley before the entrance to Little Death Hollow. As remote as this is, there is a trail register and official trailhead. If you gotten this far, "Woot!" Let the hiking begin.

The canyon of Little Death Hollow starts out wide at first with cattle tracks paralleling the trail at first. The canyon continues to narrow and at some point, you realize you are in the slot canyon. In some sections, the canyon is just two feet wide and the water cut sandstone produces multiple lines horizontal to the ground. Depending on the season, there are pools of standing water that need to be crossed. These can be more like quicksand at times, especially after a rainstorm, so be careful.

be well aware of the weather to avoid being caught in a flash flood.

Little Death Hollow is in a more remote and generally less accessible part of the park, east of UT 12. To get there drive 19 miles east from Boulder, UT along Burr Trail Road and then turn right and head south on the unpaved Wolverine Loop Road. From this junction you will see a signpost indicating that the trailhead for Little Death Hollow is 12 miles on. This road is recommended for high clearance vehicles and even then, is impassable when wet. The main problem areas are at the two streambed crossings, Horse Canyon and Wolverine Creek. It will look level and inviting at the junction, but the road has some steep and sandy parts that are designed by nature to get 2WD cars stuck.

Once the turnoff for Wolverine Loop Road is found, take the right junction, heading counter-clockwise around the loop. This will allow for checking out the Wolverine Petrified Wood Natural Area, which is as amazing as Petrified Forest

The route ends at the confluence with Horse Canyon. From here, you can continue downstream to the Escalante River (about 3 miles further on) or head upstream to Wolverine Creek. If you take the upstream route, you can head up Wolverine Creek and hike the length of it to the head of the canyon, which sits just below the Wolverine Petrified Wood Natural Area. This adds another 1.5 miles to the hike, but gives a completely different view on the way back. Wolverine Creek is the first canyon on the right as you head up Horse Canyon. There is one junction as you head up Wolverine, stay to the right to exit closer to the Little Death Hollow Trailhead.

Cottonwood Canyon Road
Easy to Strenuous – Distance Varies

Cottonwood Road loosely follows the Paria River through Grand Staircase-Escalante NM from Highway 89 to Cannonville 46 miles to the north. The road offers incredible scenery, with views of

Cottonwood Canyon Road

river canyons, fins, and barren alien lands that look as if not of this planet. The road is impassable when wet, but is otherwise a great way to see a decent cross section of the park. Along the stretch are seemingly endless hiking opportunities. Sites to explore include Hackberry Canyon, Yellow Mountain, Cottonwood Canyon Narrows, the Cockscomb, and Grosvenor Arch.

The road also leads to Kodachrome State Park. Cottonwood Canyon Road can be picked up near milepost 18 on Highway 89 or from Kodachrome State Park Road.

Round Valley Draw

Moderate – (4.3 mi / 6.9 km), round trip, allow 2 -3 hours, elev. Δ: 400 ft / 122 m, trailhead is 1.5 miles on Rush Beds Road

Off Cottonwood Canyon Road and close to Grosvenor Arch is another slot canyon called Round Valley Draw. This slot canyon has some beautiful striations and in some areas is covered by suspended rock fall held in place above by the canyon walls.

From the north end of Cottonwood Canyon Road, drive south, then east for 14 miles. There is a signed spur road that heads south and winds up the Round Valley Wash to the mouth of the slot canyon. Off roaders can take the creek bed right up to the mouth, use good judgment on when to get out and start hiking otherwise.

From here, descend into the slot from the mesa top. There is a tree stump at the initial descent point to help navigate down into the slot. The total elevation down is about 15 feet. When the canyon opens up again, climb out back onto the mesa and hike out the way you came. For a longer journey, continue down the draw to Hackberry Creek. Round trip from Hackberry Creek is 5.5 miles.

Note that this slot canyon has contained obstacles that are best navigated with canyoneering skill and equipment (a good length of rope). There is one boulder that can sometimes be navigated by going under while at other times, the 15-foot obstacle requires a rope or good free climbing skills.

Paria Rimrocks Trail

Moderate – (1.5 mi / 2.4 km), round trip, allow 30 minutes, elev. Δ: 100 ft / 30 m, trailhead: see description below

Some of the coolest rock features in the area; Paria Rimrocks has to be seen to be believed. The trail follows a wash and then cairns to a goblin and hoodoo garden. The area is laden with hoodoos and toadstools, including one known as ET

Paria Rimrocks - Toadstool Trail

(aka Red Toadstool). Bring your camera; this is one of the more amazing hikes in the area.

Paria Rimrocks are near Highway 89 near mile marker 19. If driving north from Glen Canyon Dam, there will be a dirt parking area on the right just past the marker. There are maps available at the Grand Staircase-Escalante NM Visitor Center.

Harris Wash

Moderate – (21.2 mi / 34.1 km), round trip, full day or backpacking trip, elev. Δ: 700 ft / 213 m, trailhead is 4.5 mi south of Escalante on Hole-in-the-Rock Road

Harris Wash is one of the more accessible areas of Grand Staircase-Escalante NM and is also one of the most rewarding. It is the longest tributary of the Escalante River and can be done in full to the river as an overnight backpacking trip or as a day hike, going as far one's spirit of adventure takes them. There are many tributaries to explore, including Zebra and Tunnel Slot canyons, making this one of those hikes where there is seemingly something new around every bend.

Upper Harris Wash offers little in terms of scenery. The beginning of the route is as a small child, shy at first and not showing its true self until deeper into the draw. Big Horn Canyon joins from the north about 1.8 miles in and holds many interesting branches and narrow sections to explore.

At 4.3 miles one reaches Zebra Slot canyon, known for its orange sandstone layers striped with thin bands

of white. This tributary is well worth exploring. There are some dryfall obstacles to overcome as well as water filled pools, especially in wet weather.

Going downstream in Harris Wash another mile from Zebra Slot canyon leads to Tunnel Slot canyon. This is a short and cave like section, that follows for about 50 yards with high cliff walls surrounding a narrow passage. One typically will need to wade or even swim through a deep pool at start. The canyon then opens up to a scene of riparian brush and trees. The tunnel is just a few minutes from the main canyon.

There is another tributary about a half mile further downstream, containing serene vistas, several small springs and a simply pleasant vibe all around. Further down is Red Breaks, a seldom explored side canyon with deep passages and some shallow slot canyons. Opposite Red Breaks is the Harris Wash trailhead, used as a short cut to Escalante River from Halfway Hollow. It is possible to take Halfway Hollow back to Hole-in-the-Rock Road and north 3.5 miles to your car.

Harris Wash

Capitol Reef National Park

Quick Facts

Official Park Website: http://www.nps.gov/care

Visitor Center: (435) 425-3791

Park Accessibility:

- Okay for 2WD and RVs
- 4WD recommended in some areas
- Day and Overnight Use

Experience Level:

- Family Friendly to Backcountry Hiker

Camping in Park:

- Fruita: 71 T/RV, drinking water, restrooms, dump station, no hookups, first come-first served

Lodging and Dining in Park:

- Gifford's Pie Shop, serves fresh baked pie, ice cream, snacks

Nearest Town with Amenities:

- Torrey, UT is 11 mi / 18 km from park

Getting There:

- From Moab, UT: Take US-191 North, I-70 West-and UT-24 West 146 mi / 235 km to park entrance
- From St. George, UT: Take 1-15 North, UT-20 East, US-89 North and UT-24 East 215 mi / 346 km to park entrance

Capitol Reef NP is a mix of moonscape and magic

What Makes Capitol Reef Special

- The Waterpocket fold, the single largest monocline in the world. We are talking a 150-mile stretch of vastly different rock layers a full mile and half thick, titled at an angle and exposed in dramatic fashion

- Fruita, a once Mormon communal homestead turned to peaceful campground that serves pie and ice cream against the backdrop of the Fremont River

- Cathedral Valley, which sets a new standard in stunning during the day and the darkest skies you will likely ever see at night

The park gets its name because pioneers were faced with one cliff "reef" after the other as they headed westward. Given the Waterpocket Fold stretches for some 150 miles from north to south, it was just as tough to go around. The vast monocline represented a daunting challenge to pioneers, but this same ruggedness is what makes Capitol Reef NP so special. There is nothing else out this way except for a couple of towns and a couple of roads. Plus, this means that the night skies of Capitol Reef are top notch. In some areas, there are no soft glows of distant towns, let alone any other man made light. It is just you and the night sky.

Hiking in the Fruita Historic District

Chimney Rock Loop

Strenuous – (3.6 mi / 5.8 km), round trip, allow 2 -3 hours, elev. Δ: 800 ft / 244 m, trailhead on Highway 24, 3 mi west of visitor center

Chimney Rock Loop, located near the park's western boarder along Highway 24, offers some great views of Chimney Rock and the surrounding landscape.

Gifford Barn near Fruita Campground

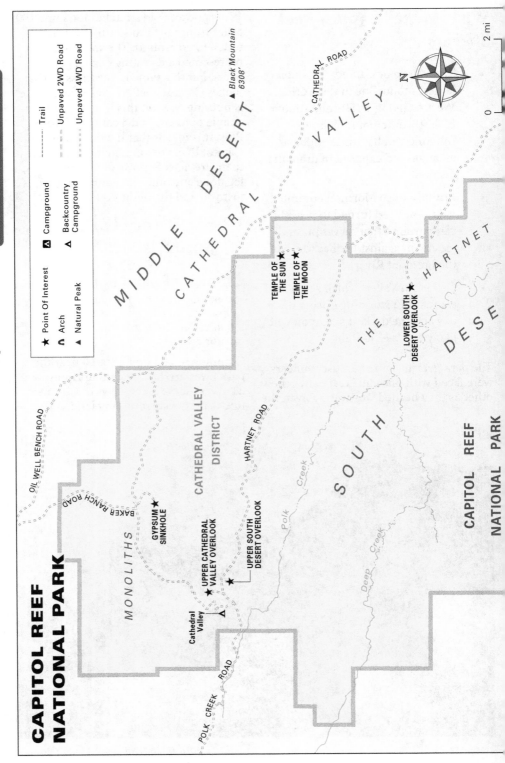

CAPITOL REEF
NATIONAL PARK

Legend:
- ★ Point Of Interest
- ∩ Arch
- ▲ Natural Peak
- ⬟ Campground
- ▲ Backcountry Campground
- ------ Trail
- = = = Unpaved 2WD Road
- ===== Unpaved 4WD Road

MIDDLE DESERT

CATHEDRAL

CATHEDRAL VALLEY

▲ Black Mountain
6308'

HARTNET

CATHEDRAL ROAD

★ TEMPLE OF
THE SUN

★ TEMPLE OF
THE MOON

★ LOWER SOUTH
DESERT OVERLOOK

THE

DESE

CATHEDRAL VALLEY
DISTRICT

HARTNET ROAD

SOUTH

OIL WELL BENCH ROAD

BAKER RANCH ROAD

MONOLITHS

★ GYPSUM
SINKHOLE

★ UPPER CATHEDRAL
VALLEY OVERLOOK

▲ Cathedral
Valley

★ UPPER SOUTH
DESERT OVERLOOK

Polk Creek

Deep Creek

POLK CREEK ROAD

CAPITOL REEF

NATIONAL PARK

N

0   2 mi

164

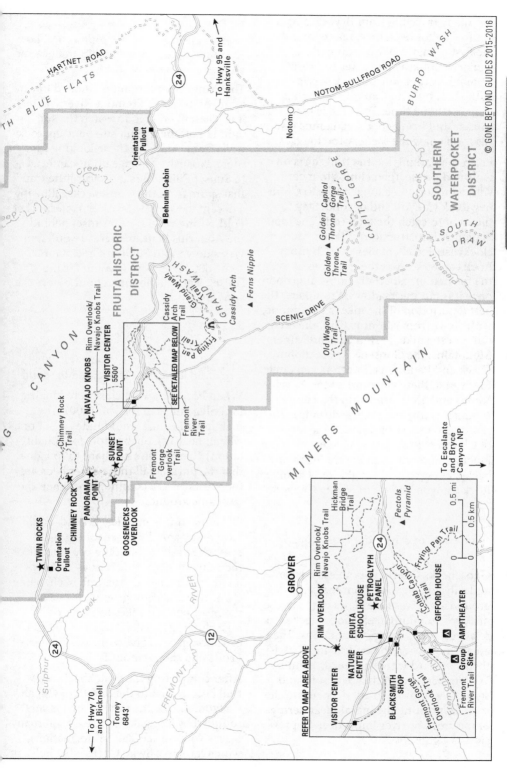

© GONE BEYOND GUIDES 2015-2016

HARTNET ROAD

NORTH BLUE FLATS

To Hwy 95 and Hanksville

24

NOTOM-BULLFROG ROAD

BURRO WASH

Notom

SOUTHERN
WATERPOCKET
DISTRICT

Orientation
Pullout

Behunin Cabin

Creek

FRUITA HISTORIC
DISTRICT

Golden Throne Trail

Capitol Gorge Trail

CAPITOL GORGE

SOUTH DRAW

Pleasant Creek

Golden
Throne
Trail

Golden
Throne ▲

▲ Ferns Nipple

CANYON

Rim Overlook/
Navajo Knobs Trail

Cassidy
Arch
Trail

Cassidy Arch

GRAND WASH

GRAND WASH

Trail

NAVAJO KNOBS

VISITOR CENTER
5500'

SCENIC DRIVE

Old Wagon
Trail

MINERS   MOUNTAIN

SEE DETAILED MAP BELOW

★ Chimney Rock

Chimney Rock
Trail

★ SUNSET
POINT

Fremont
River
Trail

Fremont Gorge
Overlook Trail

PANORAMA
POINT ★

★ CHIMNEY ROCK

GOOSENECKS
OVERLOOK

To Escalante
and Bryce
Canyon NP →

★ TWIN ROCKS

Orientation
Pullout

Sulphur Creek

24

To Hwy 70
and Bicknell

Torrey
6843'

12

FREMONT RIVER

GROVER

REFER TO MAP AREA ABOVE

Rim Overlook/
Navajo Knobs Trail

Hickman
Bridge
Trail

▲ Pectols
Pyramid

0.5 mi

0.5 km

0

24

RIM OVERLOOK ★

FRUITA
SCHOOLHOUSE

★ PETROGLYPH
PANEL

Cohab Canyon Trail

Frying Pan Trail

GIFFORD HOUSE

NATURE
CENTER

VISITOR CENTER

BLACKSMITH
SHOP

Fremont Gorge
Overlook Trail

Fremont River

▲ AMPITHEATER

▲ Group
Camp Site

Fremont
River Trail Site

165

For many traveling from Bryce Canyon NP to Capitol Reef, this area represents the first of many "Wow" moments as you drive into the park. Regardless of which direction you entered, this is one of the best trails in Capitol Reef and is well worth the time. This trail is great for sunsets, but bring good headlamps just in case you enjoy the scenery too long.

From the parking lot, the trail starts off wide and gentle, then climbs to meet with a junction to a longer hike to Chimney Rock Canyon and beyond. Stay to the right to catch the loop trail. The loop is slightly less strenuous if taken counter-clockwise. Excellent views of Chimney Rock can be seen as the trail rises above the formation, especially in the afternoon once it is out the shadows. From here, the best description of the hike is panoramic, with views from Mummy Cliff, the high point of the hike, to Boulder and Miners Mountains, the Goosenecks of Sulphur Creek and Panorama Point. As you circle to the east, there are views of the Navajo Knobs and The Castle with the Henry Mountains towering in the distance. The route then descends down to the mouth of Chimney Rock Canyon. Stay left at the junction and return to the trailhead or if backpacking, take the right into Chimney Rock Canyon and on to Spring Canyon.

Goosenecks Overlook
4 mi / 6.4 km drive from Fruita Campground

Goosenecks Overlook is an easy drive and subsequent walk from the campground and gives nice views of the goosenecks of Sulphur Creek. Goosenecks are relatively rare geologic formations. They are formed when the underlying rock is thrust upward where a creek is running. With the creek running over soft sandstone, it is allowed to cut deeper into the rock, imprinting the initial meanderings of the creek or river into a deep impression as a gooseneck.

Sunset Point
Easy – (0.7 mi / 1.1 km), round trip, allow 30 minutes, elev. Δ: negligible, trailhead at Goosenecks parking area

The Fruita campground is situated low in a canyon near the Fremont River. While it is pleasant enough to watch the sun light fall off the distant surrounding rock walls from camp, for those looking for a more expansive vantage point can head to Sunset Point. This is a short little trail that spurs from the Goosenecks, allowing a decent view of the broader Waterpocket Fold. Along with a great sunset behind the Aquarius Plateau, there are different views down into Sulphur Creek Gorge, some 600 feet below. If going for the sunset, start out about an hour before the sun sets.

Cohab Canyon Trail
Moderate– (1.7 mi / 2.7 km), one way, allow 90 minutes, elev. Δ: 402 ft / 123 m, trailhead just across Fruita Campground

When Federal law officials were looking for polygamists in the late 1800's, the men folk of Fruita would hide all but one wife in nearby Cohab (short for cohabitation) Canyon. It's not hard to imagine that the phrase, "all those other beds are for guests", was a common one when the law came around.

Of course this is pure legend and would have many a park ranger rolling their eyes when asked about the provenance of the canyon's name, but it does make for an interesting story. The trail itself, being close to Fruita campground, is one of the most popular hikes in the park. The hike climbs 22 switchbacks for 400 feet elevation gain to give some great views of Fruita and the Fremont River.

After completing the switchbacks, the trail become flat to the mouth of Cohab Canyon. Inside the canyon, one is surrounded by Wingate Sandstone. In many places you can see "tafoni" formations, which look like Swiss Cheese like holes in the rock walls. Tafoni are formed when the calcium carbonate holding the sand together into sandstone dissolves, leaving a sponge like system of holes.

Inside Cohab Canyon are several side canyons worth exploring, locally referred to as the "Wives". In the main canyon, look for the Cohab Arch and some solitary hoodoos. If you want to add a little more to the hike, take the spur trail from the Cohab Arch to the Fruita Overlooks. This side trip is well worth taking, providing some excellent views of the Fremont River Canyon and Walker Peak. There are two overlooks, named North and South respectively. The spur trails add an additional 1.2 miles and an hour to the hike.

Back on the main trail, continue heading up Cohab Canyon. Along the way, the trail passes Frying Pan Trail and onwards to Highway 24 a little more than a half mile further on. This final leg gives some great views of the Fremont River Canyon and Capitol Dome off in the distance. Hikers can opt to get picked up from here, head on to Hickman Bridge or turn around and head back.

Hickman Bridge

Moderate – (0.9 mi / 1.4 km), round trip, allow 1 – 2 hours, elev. Δ: 379 ft / 116 m, trailhead on Highway 24, 2 mi east of visitor center

This is a great little hike and a comfortable add on to the Cohab Canyon trail. It is one of the most hiked trails in the park and for good reason, as it offers great views along the way to a 133-foot natural bridge. The trail starts at Highway 24 or from Fruita Campground via Cohab Canyon. The lighting in this hike can be exceptional in the morning, plus getting an early start will also ensure a parking space during peak season. The trail starts along the Fremont River for a small stretch before climbing a series of switchbacks. Elevation gain here is about 100 feet, coming out onto a small grassy shelf. At this point, look for an informal looking spur trail that quickly ends at the remains of a pit house built by the Fremont people somewhere between 600-1300 AD.

After a very short distance, the trail meets with the junction to the Rim Overlook and Navajo Knobs. Stick to the left and climb again, passing the cone shaped Navajo Dome to the north. Capitol Dome is to the east and is where the park gets half of its name. The trail then descends through pinyon juniper forests, giving a good feel of immersion into the wilds of the park. After a short distance, the trail passes a small bridge in a wash, known as Nels Johnson Bridge. The trail ends at a 1/3-mile loop that passes under and around Hickman Bridge.

A couple of things about Hickman Bridge, it is pretty tough to photograph since it is surrounded by cliff walls. It is 125 feet high and 133 feet long. Arches and bridges both have water as one of the erosional elements that help create them.

Hickman Bridge

Bridges are distinguished from arches in that they are created from the direct result of free flowing water. Arches on the other hand are caused by the indirect effects of water, wind, and time on sandstone fins.

Rim Overlook / Navajo Knobs Trail

Strenuous – (4.6 mi / 7.4 km), round trip for Rim Overlook, (9.4 mi / 15.2 km), round trip for Navajo Knobs), elev. Δ: 540 ft / 165 m to Rim Overlook, trailhead at Hickman Bridge trailhead

The Rim Overlook starts from the Hickman Bridge trail. The full hike is strenuous due to elevation gains. The Rim Overlook is 4.5 miles (7.2 km) round trip, climbs 1,110 feet and gives great views of Fruita and the surrounding valley. The Navajo Knobs trail extends from the Rim Overlook trail. The Knobs are a collection of Navajo sandstone hills that are uniquely formed. The trail leads to one of the smaller knobs, though it is possible for a skilled scrambler to scale the other formations as well. The Navajo Knobs give 360-degree views as the reward for climbing an additional 500 feet over 2.5 miles (4.0 km).

Frying Pan

Strenuous – (2.9 mi / 4.7 km), one way, allow 1 – 2 hours, elev. Δ: 810 ft / 247 m, trailhead at Grand Wash Trailhead

Frying Pan Trail is a connector trail linking Cohab Canyon and Cassidy Arch Trails and beyond to the Grand Wash Trail. The trail travels along high and scenic ridgetops offering great and expansive views. There is a spur trail into Frying Pan Canyon, which starts about 2.2 miles in from Cassidy Arch Trail junction. This little canyon is fun to explore, with water pockets and high walls at the end of the canyon. Add another mile to the trip if going into the Frying Pan (Canyon, that is).

Fremont Gorge Overlook

Strenuous – (4.6 mi / 7.4 km), round trip, allow 3 - 4 hours, elev. Δ: 1,090 ft / 332 m, trailhead on Scenic Drive

This is a great hike. There is a short ascent of about 1/3 of a mile that puts the hiker on a wonderful mesa trail. If you enjoy being on a lone single track within a mesa top of desert brush, high up with the blue sky yet above you, the grassy shrubs below and thick red rock cliffs looming grand in the front, this is the hike for you. Look for rounded and varnished volcanic black boulders along the way.

After the gentle stroll across the mesa, the trail ascends steeply to Fremont Gorge Overlook. This last stretch is strenuous at times leading to a solitary formation of Moenkopi rock. Once past this formation, the trail juts left to the rim of Fremont Gorge. The overlook gives spectacular views down into the deep gorge. From here, enjoy a snack and head on back the way you came.

Fremont River

Easy to Moderate – (2.6 mi / 4.2 km), round trip, allow 1.5 – 2 hours, elev. Δ: 400 ft / 122 m, trailhead near Fruita Campground, loop B

As the name of this trail suggests, this little path follows along the Fremont River. The first stretch is flat and open to dogs and bikes and is ADA accessible. After about 0.4 miles, the trail switches into more of a rugged single track, with a gated passage that asks that all but hikers turn back. From here, the trail climbs steadily, ending at absolutely stunning views of the Fremont Gorge and river as well as the Waterpocket Fold. At trails end, it is possible to wander around the area. Look for Fern's Nipple, a cone shaped formation that stands out in the southeast.

Cassidy Arch

Strenuous – (3.4 mi / 5.5 km), round trip, allow 2 -3 hours, elev. Δ: 670 ft / 204 m, trailhead at Grand Wash trailhead

The arch is named after none other than Butch Cassidy, the leader of an infamous band of thieves known as the "Wild Bunch" in the 1890's. It is reputed that Butch had dinner at the cabin of area pioneer Elijah Cutler Behunin along the Fremont River and that the group frequented the area. For a hike through land good enough for outlaws to an arch worthy of Butch Cassidy himself, look no further than Cassidy Arch trail.

Cassidy Arch

The hike begins at the end of Grand Wash Road and immediately starts into a 600-foot ascent. Along the climb, the ledges of Kayenta sandstone are quite evident. As elevation is gained, the ecology of the trail changes to more densely packed pinyon juniper forest with stunning views of the surrounding sandstone. At the juncture to Frying Pan Trail, Cassidy Arch Trail juts to the left, down a gradual grade of slickrock to the canyon's rim and Cassidy Arch.

Once at your destination, look for the western themed Starbucks served by the great-great grandson of Butch Cassidy himself at the apex of the arch. As one hiker put it, "It was a delightful end to the hike", while another hiker has been quoted as saying, "The apex of the arch? Seriously? The author has clearly been out in the desert too long." Anyway, you get back to me with *your* experience.

Grand Wash

Easy – (4.8 mi / 7.7 km), round trip, allow 2 hours, elev. Δ: 200 ft / 61 m, trailhead on Scenic Drive, 4.7 mi from visitor center

This there and back trail is one of the flattest hikes in the park. It's a great walk for children (even small kids part way) and can be accessed from either the Scenic Drive or Highway 24. One of the highlights is the Narrows, which is found about 0.7 miles in from the Highway 24 trailhead. This half-mile narrow stretch is banded by sheer walls of Navajo red sandstone, towering 500 feet on either side, with dark stains of desert varnish running down the cliffs. Farther into the hike, the canyon widens, allowing the hiker to take in the views at a leisurely pace. This section also contains more plant life than the regularly scoured sections of the Narrows.

Old Wagon Trail

Strenuous – (3.8 mi / 6.1 km), round trip, allow 2 -3 hours, elev. Δ: 1,080 ft / 329 m, trailhead on Scenic Drive, 6.5 mi from visitor center

Perhaps the best part of this hike is its closeness to the Fruita Campground yet relatively unused aspect of the trail. While most of the trails along Scenic Drive take the hiker into the canyons and washes, Old Wagon Trail heads west away from them. This dishes up a hike that is more pinyon juniper in terrain. The trail is as persistent as it is straight as it climbs the 1,000 feet upwards, but does reward with some great views once elevation is reached. The Old Wagon Trail is not Capitol Reef's darling, sometimes the views are obscured by forest and the elevation gain can feel more like a dull march up alluvium, but it does offer unique views and hikers will likely have the entire journey to themselves.

Golden Throne Trail

Strenuous – (4.0 mi / 6.4 km), round trip, allow 2 - 3 hours, elev. Δ: 1,100 ft / 335 m, trailhead at Capitol Gorge parking area off Scenic Drive

Golden Throne

Golden Throne trail is a short but steep trail that winds through the backcountry of the Waterpocket Fold. It takes the viewer to the base of a large monolith known as the Golden Throne. This up-then-down hike gets the hiker up in elevation quickly, climbing 800 feet and following a series of well-marked switchbacks. This is a great hike to climb up into the higher realms of the backcountry in short order and still leave time to take in the amazing views.

Capitol Gorge

Easy – (2.0 mi / 3.2 km), round trip, allow 1 hour, elev. Δ: 100 ft / 30 m, trailhead at Capitol Gorge parking area off Scenic Drive

Until 1962, this was the only road that passed through the Waterpocket Fold. The road passes through a high cliff-walled gorge that displays pleasant shadows in the late afternoon. For those up for a short hike, continue to the Pioneer

Register, which contains the names of early Mormon pioneers etched into the side of the canyon. Across the wall where the pioneers "signed in," and all over, one can find petroglyphs as well. Also visible are the remains of old telephone lines. The trail officially ends at "The Tanks", a set of water pockets set in a row above the canyon floor. The natural curvature of these pools makes for a great resting spot. Those with more time can continue through Capitol Gorge to the eastern boundary of the park.

Hiking in Cathedral Valley District

Getting to all of the hikes in the Cathedral Valley area requires traveling on the unpaved 28 mile Hartnet Road as part of a 59-mile loop. Much of the road is okay for most cars; however, there are a couple of spots, including a river crossing, which bumps up the need for a high clearance vehicle. This northern section of the park is very different than the rest of the park, being cooler, more densely forested in pinyon juniper and with the fluted monolithic spires collectively referred to as the Cathedrals.

Upper South Desert Overlook

Easy – (0.4 mi / 0.6 km), round trip, allow 15 minutes, elev. Δ: 80 ft / 24 m, trailhead is 39 mi NW of visitor center on Hartnet Road to South Desert trailhead

This overlook provides wide expansive views of the Upper South Desert, a region dominated by a wide expansive valley of grasslands banded by sloping sandstone and some volcanic intrusion. Off in the distance, the Henry Mountains, the last mountain range in the contiguous United States to be mapped, lie as a centerpiece to this natural diorama. To the northwest lie the Thousand Lake Mountains, a wholly different world of Aspen trees, rambling creeks and even a bit of snow.

Upper Cathedral Valley

Take the obvious trail from the parking area and take the short hike to the overlook. The last portion does have a very short but steep ascent to the final viewing area.

Cathedral Valley Overlook

Easy – (0.2 mi / 0.3 km), round trip, allow 15 minutes, elev. Δ: 50 ft / 15 m, trailhead on Hartnet Road

The Cathedral Valley is special. Within it are 400-foot sheets of monolithic rock, distinctly orange in color, standing vertical right to their pointed tips. They look like curtains of rock, being a juxtaposition of fluidity and motion standing against an impression of eternal stillness. The Cathedral Valley Overlook is a little hike that gives one of the best views of this valley. Standing at the end of a rock peninsula, as high as the monoliths themselves, the overlook gives one of the most majestic views in the entire park.

There are picnic tables with some shade at the start of the trail. From the picnic area, follow the obvious trail through some trees down to the end of the peninsula. Note that the trail becomes a narrower route towards the end, with very steep drop-offs on either side. Use caution here.

Cathedrals Trail

Moderate – (2.2 mi / 3.5 km), round trip, allow 90 minutes, elev. Δ: 375 ft / 114 m, trailhead on Hartnet Road

Given the amount of time needed to undertake the 59-mile loop through Cathedral Valley, this trail often is overlooked. That said, what a wonderful little hike this is, hiking through arguably the heart of the Cathedrals, with some elevation gain to help give proper perspective to these unique and magical spires of Entrada Sandstone.

The trail starts in the Upper Cathedral Valley a couple miles prior to making the climb up to the primitive Cathedral Valley Campground (or down from the campground, depending). As the road climbs a small hill look for a sign that says, "Cathedral Trail Trails End 1.1". Park near the sign and head out on the trail, which starts to climb at a descent rate. As you round a corner past some trees, look for Needle Mountain and other Cathedrals. It will be easy to spot Cathedral Mountain, the largest of the monoliths. The trail levels out from here, giving up pleasant hiking and great views, and then climbs steeply to the final viewpoint at the end. If one looks closely, the Morrell Cabin can be seen along the trail.

Morrell Cabin Trail

Easy – (0.4 mi / 0.6 km), round trip, allow 30 minutes, elev. Δ: negligible, trailhead on Hartnet Road

This little cabin still contains a few artifacts just laying around to examine. They are still around because folks leave them be, so please keep with the sentiment of past hikers. The cabin is part of a ranch owned by a cattle rancher by the name of Lesley Morrell in the 1930's. For many, it became a way station for ranchers looking for a place to bed down for the night until the 70's, when it was placed into a preservation mode by the park. The little one room cabin is now listed on National Register of Historic Places

For those that make it out to Cathedral Valley, this becomes one of the must do hikes along the way as it hard to justify coming all this way and NOT seeing the cabin. The hike itself is straightforward with no real elevation gain and is accessed along a very well maintained path. It is possible to go inside the cabin, where there are tons of old relics found around the area. The views along the way are impressive and peaceful to the eye. Wildlife is often spotted along the trail.

Hiking in the Southern Waterpocket District

This is the least visited section of the park and as such, the trails are often more rugged and unmaintained. For most that

Old Ford at Fruita

make it out here, the Waterpocket District offers a more immersive experience, where the route taken is defined only by one's skill. The section below outlines the various trails in this region of the park. Consult with a ranger at the visitor center for more detail on any of these hikes.

Burro Wash

Strenuous – (3.4 mi / 5.5 km), round trip, allow 3 -4 hours, elev. Δ: 350 ft / 107 m, trailhead is 9 mi south on Notom-Bullfrog Road

The "stubbornest" of the three slot canyons in this area. Expect many chockstone obstacles and two sets of narrows that confine the hiker to shoulder width. It is not unheard of in some places to climb out of the slot canyon briefly to reengage it at wider spot or to navigate a chockstone.

Cottonwood Wash

Strenuous – (3.3 mi / 5.3 km), round trip, allow 3 -5 hours, elev. Δ: 350 ft / 107 m, trailhead is 9 mi south on Notom-Bullfrog Road

This is the most obstacle laden and wettest of the slot canyons in this area. Start by scrambling up and over or around a set of large chockstones as the canyon narrows. Continue to a thin lens of water that must be waded through to continue. If you decide to continue (first off congrats, most folks turn around here), you will be rewarded with yet more chockstones that need to negotiated often and even more pools of water. Finally, gaze upon an impassable 35-foot dry fall and either turn around or get out the ropes and continue deeper into the canyon for more. After all this hard work, just think how good dinner will taste when you get back to your camp!

Sheets Gulch

Strenuous – (6.7 mi / 10.8 km), round trip, allow 5-7 hours, elev. Δ: 500 ft / 152 m, trailhead is 13 mi south on Notom-Bullfrog Road

A rough around the edges slot canyon in three sections. Plenty of chockstone and waterpocket pool obstacles to navigate, making this a nice scramble puzzle, and potentially wet fun.

Red Canyon Trail

Moderate – (4.5 mi / 7.2 km), round trip, allow 2 - 3 hours, elev. Δ: 400 ft / 122 m, trailhead is 21 mi south on Notom-Bullfrog Road

This hike offers wide-open expanses to slot canyons; Red Canyon Trail showcases the varied aspects of Capitol Reef National Park.

Upper Muley Twist Canyon

Strenuous – (9.0 mi / 14.5 km), round trip, hard day hike or 2-3 day backpacking trip, elev. Δ: 800 ft / 244 m, trailhead is 2.9 mi south on Strike Valley Road

Freedom, surprise, and possibly even a little wonder combine in this multi-faceted citadel of red rock, white rock, arches, double arches, and even narrows. Some of the best views of the Waterpocket Fold to be seen are on this trail.

Strike Valley Overlook

Moderate – (0.8 mi / 1.3 km), round trip, allow 30 minutes, elev. Δ: 100 ft / 30 m, trailhead is 2.9 mi south on Strike Valley Road

A great hike for those looking for that picture perfect view of the Waterpocket Fold. This is a short hike but gives views of the classic picture of the monocline that is seen in brochures.

Lower Muley Twist Canyon

Easy – (8.0 mi / 12.9 km), round trip, allow 4 -5 hours, elev. Δ: 600 ft / 183 m, trailhead at Burr Trail, 2 mi west of Notom-Bullfrog Road junction

For this description, the trail starts at the Lower Muley Twist Canyon and ends at the Post Cut Off Junction. A great canyon hike, more wonder and scenic charm

The Waterpocket Fold from Strike Valley Overlook

than slotted narrows, but well worth the effort. Lots of red rock in all its varieties to be seen along the way.

Surprise Canyon

Easy – (2.0 mi / 3.2 km), round trip, allow 90 minutes, elev. Δ: 240 ft / 73 m, trailhead is 34 mi south on Notom-Bullfrog Road

Surprise Canyon is the next-door neighbor to Headquarters Canyon. The biggest difference between the two canyons is Surprise opens up wide at the end versus Headquarters, which remains narrow throughout.

Headquarters Canyon

Easy – (3.4 mi / 5.5 km), round trip, allow 2 hours, elev. Δ: 400 ft / 122 m, trailhead is 35 mi south on Notom-Bullfrog Road

Headquarters Canyon is a narrow slot canyon with a sandy floor and tan water

Upper Muley Twist

carved walls. This is a good hike for families, though be sure to check the weather before entering.

Oak Creek Canyon Trail

Moderate – (5.0 mi / 8.0 km), round trip, allow 2 -3 hours, elev. Δ: 200 ft / 61 m, trailhead is 4 mi east on Oak Creek access road

Waterfalls, diversions, dams, and scenic expanses can all be found on this hike with only 200 feet in elevation gain. Pleasant and peaceful, with a little alcove at the end to stop and have a snack while peering out into the canyon. A very worthwhile hike.

Lower Muley Twist Canyon and Hamburger Rocks

Strenuous – (17.0 mi / 27.4 km), round trip, hard day hike or 2-3 day backpacking trip, elev. Δ: 900 ft / 274 m, trailhead at Post Corral off Notom-Bullfrog Road

A dreamland of rock with unreal curvatures, heights, colors, and form. Akin to hiking in a museum of art for the day, where even the corridors to the next gallery are impressive. One highlight is the Hamburger Rocks, a study in erosion creating a series of logic defying toadstool like formations that just have to be seen to be believed. Allow another 3 hours to take the spur trail to these rocks.

Halls Creek Narrows

Strenuous – (22.4 mi / 36.0 km), round trip, hard day hike or 2-3 day backpacking trip, elev. Δ: 1,000 ft / 304 m, trailhead is 3.6 mi south of Halls Creek Overlook on airport road

The hike is like combining the Narrows of Zion with the purity of Capitol Reef. Towering rock walls bend and turn on the whims of the watercourse that created this slot canyon, all coming together to create one of the best-kept secrets in the entire park.

Natural Bridges National Monument

Quick Facts

Official Park Website: http://www.nps.gov/nabr

Visitor Center: (435) 692-1234 ext. 16

Park Accessibility:

- Okay for 2WD and RVs
- Day and Overnight Use

Experience Level:

- Family Friendly to Casual Hiker

Camping in Park:

- Natural Bridges Campground: 13 T/RV, no water, vault restrooms, no dump station, no hookups, first come-first served
- Several backcountry campgrounds

Lodging and Dining in Park:

- None

Nearest Town with Amenities:

- Blanding, UT is 44 mi / 71 km from park

Getting There:

- From Blanding, UT: Take UT-95 North to UT-275 North 44 mi / 71 km to park entrance

As above, so below. The Owachomo Bridge

NATURAL BRIDGES NATIONAL MONUMENT

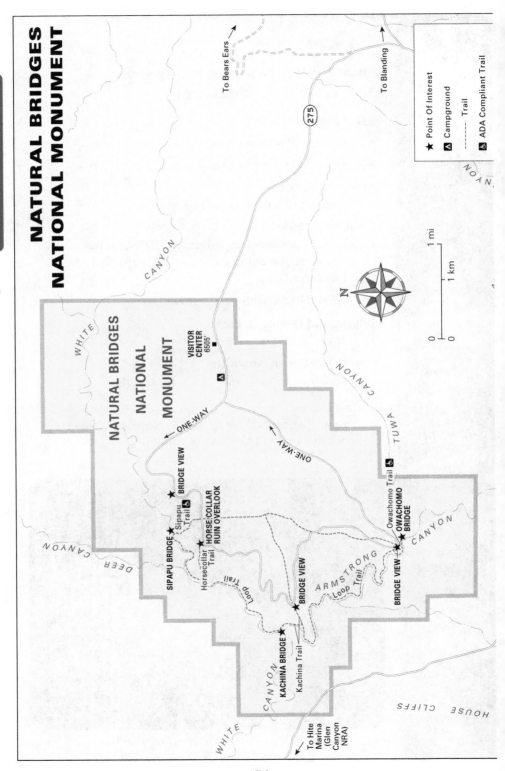

NATURAL BRIDGES NATIONAL MONUMENT

To Bears Ears

To Blanding

275

VISITOR CENTER 6505'

WHITE   CANYON

DEER CANYON

ONE-WAY

ONE-WAY

Sipapu Trail   BRIDGE VIEW

SIPAPU BRIDGE

HORSECOLLAR RUIN OVERLOOK

Horsecollar Trail

Loop Trail

BRIDGE VIEW

Loop Trail

ARMSTRONG

CANYON

Owachomo Trail

OWACHOMO BRIDGE

BRIDGE VIEW

KACHINA BRIDGE

Kachina Trail

WHITE   CANYON

TUWA   CANYON

CANYON

HOUSE CLIFFS

To Hite Marina (Glen Canyon NRA)

N

1 mi
1 km
0
0

Legend
- ★ Point Of Interest
- △ Campground
- ----- Trail
- ♿ ADA Compliant Trail

What Makes Natural Bridges Special

- The reverence of seeing three massive stone bridges that cross over deep canyons in a lush pinyon juniper forest setting

- Knowing they were formed by a gooseneck that is so close together that it eroded through and pinched off the lower portion of the "neck", leaving the top layer of rock intact as a true natural bridge

- One of the easier side trips if you just want to peer over from the top and see what a natural bridge looks like

Natural Bridges National Monument is a unique place in that there are a total of three natural bridges here. From above, the overlooks peer down to the canyon below, which seems to be a confusing maze of twists and turns with huge spans of rock arching across streambeds of pale white sandstone. In reality, the area has had a number of gooseneck meanders, where the stream has created a U-shaped canyon into the strata. At three places, the water eroded through the bottom layer of the meander, leaving the top layer as a natural bridge.

Most folks take the short trips to the various overlooks and peer down to the bridges below. The scenic drive takes about an hour to see all three, not including the trip to the visitor center to get all the necessary brochures. Hiking down below is more immersive and more strenuous, as the canyon floor is about 500 feet below. All of the trails as well as the bridges themselves have awesome mythological names from the Hopi tradition, which adds to the overall ambiance of this park.

Hiking Natural Bridges National Monument

Horsecollar Ruin Overlook Trail

Easy – (0.6 mi / 1.0 m), round trip, allow 30 minutes

A fairly level trail leading to the edge of White Canyon where an Ancestral Puebloan cliff dwelling can be seen in a large alcove. This ruin is best known for its two granaries, which look like large circular barrels with doorways that look like horse collars (hence the name).

Horsecollar Ruins

Sipapu Bridge Trail

Easy – (1.2 mi / 1.9 km), round trip, allow 1 hour

Sipapu Bridge is the second largest natural bridge in the world, second only to Rainbow Bridge at Rainbow Bridge NM. The name Sipapu is a Hopi term for the gateway of souls into the spirit world. The trip down is steep but once on the canyon floor, the going is easier, though a bit uneven. The elevation gain/loss here is 500 feet and there is a staircase and three wooden ladders to help hikers get down safely. At the top of the stairway, look for a set of logs reaching from the cliff wall to a large fir. Early visitors used this fir, climbing up and down it to get to the canyon floor. At the base of the tree, you can still see remnants of the earlier staircase.

SOUTHERN UTAH

Natural Bridges

Kachina Bridge Trail

Easy – (1.4 mi / 2.3 km), round trip, allow
1 hour

Kachina Bridge is considered the youngest formed of the three bridges and is also the least dramatic from the overlook above due to the angle. Take switchbacks down 400 feet to the bridge.

Owachomo Bridge Trail

Easy – (0.4 mi / 0.6 km), round trip, allow
30 minutes

The easiest of the bridges to get to, Owachomo, meaning "rock mound" in the Hopi language is also the most delicate of the three bridge formation. The bridge's form suggests that it is eroding more quickly than the others. It is also considered the most pleasing to the eye, due to its thin span of rock that stretches across the sky.

Loop Trail

Strenuous – (8.6 mi / 13.8 km), round
trip, allow 4 -5 hours

The Loop Trail gives the complete package of all three bridges with return options along the mesa top. At the mesa, the loop has a juncture that allows for a shorter hike. Start the hike at any of the parking areas. Starting at Sipapu gives the most flexibility if you need to return early as you pass by Sipapu and Kachina before climbing back out. If you do continue to Owachomo Bridge, follow the trail up the left side of the canyon after Kachina Bridge in order to more easily navigate past the Knickpoint pour-off, a dry fall that pours water runoff into a pool below when it rains.

Sipapu Bridge

Kachina Bridge

Goosenecks State Park

Quick Facts

Official Park Website: http://stateparks.utah.gov/parks/goosenecks/

Visitor Center: none, contact park at (435) 678-2238

Park Accessibility:

- Okay for 2WD and RVs
- Day Use Only

Experience Level:

- Family Friendly – Experienced Hiker

Nearest Town with Amenities:

- Mexican Hat, UT is 8 mi / 13 km from park

Getting There:

- From Page, AZ: Take AZ-98 East to US-160 East to US-163 North to UT-261 North to UT-316 West. Total distance is 151 mi / 243 km to park

What Makes Goosenecks State Park Special

- Peering over the edge to see the neatly layered rock cut like artwork by the deep meander of the San Juan River

- Driving away from the general viewing area down a dusty dirt road to hike the Honaker Trail to the river's shore and becoming for a brief moment, part of this artwork

- Learning about and seeing a gooseneck

Goosenecks State Park is an easy side trip for those traveling from the Moab area parks south towards Arizona. The park has its own state highway, UT-316, which travels 3.5 miles from its juncture with UT 261 to the Goosenecks overlook and parking area. What to do once you are there is limited.

At a modest 10 acres of park, most folk's park, head to the railing and look down at the meandering San Juan River. In this section of the river, there are a number of U shaped river course ways that have been cut dramatically and deeply into the underlying strata. The view is well worth the five minutes to get there. There is also one trail that takes the more adventurous traveler down to the San Juan River shoreline.

By the way, if you are asking yourself why the river doesn't just carve a straight line, the answer has to do with the river itself. The flow of water erodes the outer banks at a faster rate, while simultaneously depositing sediment on the slower moving inner course of the river. The result of this erosional process causes a snaking pattern to form as the river cuts through the valley. Any flowing body of water can carve out a meandering course, as the principles are the same no matter the volume of the water. In the course of sandstone, this process starts very early and then essentially sets in place, eroding straight down thereafter.

Hiking Goosenecks State Park

Honaker Trail

Strenuous – (5.0 mi / 8.0 km), round trip, allow 3 - 4 hours

This is a steep route built in 1893 by prospectors during the short-lived gold rush in this territory. Honaker Trail proved too steep even for pack animals or so the legend goes, so if you do take this trail and make it the bottom, you'll have the bragging rights that you out hiked a mule. The trail is 1.5 miles northeast from the Goosenecks SP parking lot. Look for a water tank and a metal sign that says Honaker. The road travels below the first rim to the non-descript cairn-marked trailhead. From here, it's 1,000 feet over 2.5 miles to the bottom. At about 1.5 miles down, you'll notice an abundance of fossilized brachiopods (fossilized shells). It is nearly impossible to avoid walking on them in this spot. Once at the bottom, take a look up to where you came from. As a sign at the Grand Canyon reminds us hikers at times like these, "Down is optional. Up is mandatory". Keep this mind as you take the strenuous hike back up.

View from Goosenecks State Park Overlook

Eastern Nevada

NEVADA

Mesquite

95 Indian Springs

VALLEY OF FIRE SP

LAS VEGAS ●

127

Henderson

LAKE MEAD
NRA   Lake
               Mead

95

93

15

Valley of Fire State Park

Quick Facts

Official Park Website:

- http://parks.nv.gov/parks/valley-of-fire-state-park/

Visitor Center:

- (702) 397-2088

Park Accessibility:

- Okay for 2WD and RVs
- Day and Overnight Use

Experience Level:

- Family Friendly to Casual Hiker

Camping in Park:
There are 2 campgrounds in the park plus 3 group sites.

- Combined total of 72 T/RV, drinking water, restrooms, showers, dump station, power and water hookups, first come-first served, contact visitor center to reserve group sites

Lodging and Dining in Park:

- None

Nearest Town with Amenities:

- Echo Bay Resort and Marina on Lake Mead is 21 mi / 34 km from park.

Getting There:

- From Las Vegas, NV: Take I-15 North to Valley of Fire Highway. Total distance is 52 mi / 84 km to park.

Valley of Fire State Park

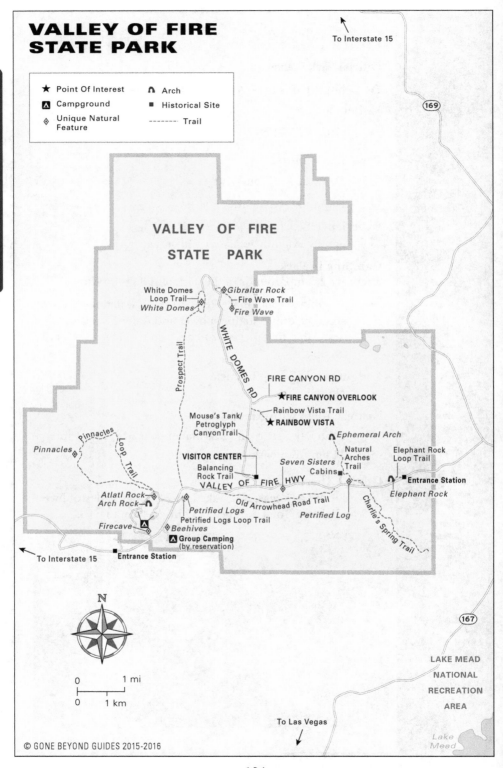

VALLEY OF FIRE STATE PARK

To Interstate 15

169

Legend:
- ★ Point Of Interest
- ⚑ Arch
- 🏕 Campground
- ◼ Historical Site
- ◈ Unique Natural Feature
- ------- Trail

VALLEY OF FIRE STATE PARK

White Domes Loop Trail
White Domes
◈ Gibraltar Rock
Fire Wave Trail
Fire Wave

Prospect Trail

WHITE DOMES RD

FIRE CANYON RD
★ FIRE CANYON OVERLOOK
Rainbow Vista Trail
Mouse's Tank/ Petroglyph Canyon Trail
★ RAINBOW VISTA

⚑ Ephemeral Arch

Pinnacles Loop Trail
Pinnacles

VISITOR CENTER
Balancing Rock Trail
Natural Arches Trail
Elephant Rock Loop Trail

Seven Sisters
Cabins

VALLEY OF FIRE HWY
⚑ Entrance Station
Elephant Rock

Atlatl Rock
Arch Rock
Old Arrowhead Road Trail
Petrified Log
Charlie's Spring Trail

Firecave
🏕
Petrified Logs
Petrified Logs Loop Trail
◈ Beehives
🏕 Group Camping (by reservation)

To Interstate 15
◼ Entrance Station

N

0   1 mi
0   1 km

167

LAKE MEAD NATIONAL RECREATION AREA

To Las Vegas

Lake Mead

What Makes Valley of Fire State Park Special

- Nevada's oldest and largest state park and one of the best park names ever!

- Breathtaking scenery of red sandstone features, all varied and unique

- Close to Las Vegas, makes a great side trip to refresh from the excesses of The Strip

What a park! If you are one of the many coming from California for a jaunt into Las Vegas, you have likely flown over Valley of Fire SP as you make your final descent. It's the beacon of intriguing red sandstone that stands out amongst the dry landscape of the Mojave Desert just before landing. If you can pry yourself away from the gaming tables, this park won't disappoint. Arches, slot canyons, petrified wood and candy caned striped rock formations greet the visitor. It's a no brainer as to why this was Nevada's first state park, because it is one of the coolest places in the Southwest.

Hiking Valley of Fire State Park

Old Arrowhead Road
Moderate to Strenuous – (6.8 mi / 10.9 km), round trip, allow 1 hour

The Old Arrowhead Road follows the remains of the first all-weather road connecting Salt Lake City to Los Angeles, by way of Las Vegas. There is a little historical marker dedicated to this "milestone of progress". The Arrowhead Road started in 1914 and began receiving motorists in 1915. This was a novel time for the automobile; roads were being built as fast as trains were declining as the means to get around the country. It was a time when the personal freedom of being able to "hit the road" and go anywhere your car could take you was a new thought. By 1924, Highways 91 and Interstate 15 took over as the main routes. This hike encompasses some beautiful scenery. Most walk the short extension near Elephant Rock and leave the longer trail for folks who can drop one car at one end and shuttle back to the other.

Petrified Logs Loop
Easy – (0.3 mi / 0.5 km), round trip, allow 15 to 30 minutes

This short interpretive trail is described for one reason; petrified logs are downright awesome. Simply put, this area was once part of a super continent called Pangea that sat near the equator. Mind you, this was 225 million years ago, but still, nothing puts context that there used to be an ancient pine forest here than a testimony of petrified logs. There are two locations where the logs can be viewed and interpretive signs along the way.

Pinnacles Loop
Moderate to Strenuous – (4.5 mi / 7.2 km), round trip, allow 1 hour

This is great remote hike, with possibilities of seeing no other hiker. From the trailhead near the Atlatl Rock parking area, head up the main wash, following marked signs. You'll enter into an area of sharp pinnacles, with tons of exploration possibilities. There is some scrambling and the trail does get faint in areas as you make your way through the pinnacles and back down an alluvial fan to the parking lot.

Prospect Trail
Moderate to Strenuous – (4.6 mi / 7.4 km), one way, allow 2-3 hours

The Prospect Trail is another there and back trail with one end starting at the White Domes parking area and the other end at Highway 169 near the Petrified Logs area. This trail is best done with

Valley of Fire

The remarkable colors of Valley of Fire State Park

two cars and is easier, (downhill), if you start from the White Domes parking lot. Prospect Trail gives a sense of deep immersion into the park's wilderness and is one of the best hikes for feeling remote and "away from it all". It starts by following nearly half of the White Dome Trail before continuing south at the White Dome/Prospect Trail fork. From here, the trail continues to navigate through cross channels and small canyons. There is some scrambling at a few stretches along this part, but nothing major. For the last stretch, the trail empties into an alluvial fan that is crossed to connect to the Valley of Fire Highway 169.

Balancing Rock

Easy – (0.1 mi / 0.2 km), round trip, allow 15 minutes

If you make a stop at the visitor center, be sure to take this short trail to a large precariously tilted square shaped rock that looks as if at any moment it will fall over, crushing any and all in its path. Great photo op!

Mouse's Tank

Easy – (1.4 mi / 2.3 km), round trip, allow 30 minutes

Mouse's Tank and Atlatl Rock together hold some of the largest concentrations of petroglyphs in Nevada, comprising of historical markings by different culture groups, with some being 3,000 years old.

The trail is quite sandy and typically very busy. Either try to go at sun up or just as the sun is setting to minimize crowds. Petroglyphs tend to be more noticeable in indirect light and with a fair amount of patience. It is easy to miss the less obvious ones. Pay particular attention to the north face of canyon walls, there are literally thousands of various symbols and artistic figures. Some are closer to eye level, while others are high up on cliff faces, as if as a test of bravery.

The trail ends at a natural round stone tank that holds water year round in all but the driest of years. It is named after a Southern Paiute Indian named "Little Mouse", who used this location to hide out in the 1890's. Little Mouse was known for thievery and general local nuisance, going on occasional drunken bouts of craziness. He hid out in the area because he was accused of murdering two prospectors. Whether he actually did or not is not actually known, though it is known he was surrounded a few miles away and in refusing to give up, was shot and killed.

Rainbow Vista

Moderate – (2.1 mi / 3.4 km), round trip, allow 1-2 hours

Most take this hike to get a great view of Fire Canyon from the overlook at the end of this there and back trail. This trail offers full immersion up a small canyon, with stunning rock formations along the way. The trailhead itself is a great pull off spot to take pictures of the landscape to the north, which can be quite inviting under mixed lighting conditions, especially in the spring after a storm. The one downside to this trail is that for the most part, the trail floor is deep sand, making the going a bit harder. Once inside the canyon and towards the end point at Fire Canyon overlook, there are caves and other nooks and crannies to explore.

White Domes Loop

Moderate – (1.0 mi / 1.6 km), round trip, allow 45 minutes to 1 hour

The White Domes Loop showcases the diversity of the park's contrasting rock, with just about every color in the sandstone palate. There is a bit of minor rock scrambling involved that leads to a little slot canyon. The slot canyon is just 0.25 miles long, but is pleasantly narrow. As you make your way back on the loop, look for an arch.

The one other aspect of this trail is the ruin of a stone building, which was used in the 1966 movie, "The Professionals", staring Lee Marvin and Burt Lancaster. The movie was about a kidnapped wife of a Texas millionaire, who hires four rough and tumble characters to get her back. It was nominated for three Academy Awards.

Fire Wave Trail

Moderate to Strenuous – (1.3 mi / 2.1 km), round trip, allow 1 hour

This hike is certainly one of the top picks in terms of great hikes. It's the unique sandstone formations that really make this hike outstanding, which is saying something, as there are many unique rock formations in Valley of Fire SP. The highlights of the hike are swirls of red and white rock layers that have then been eroded into graceful curves of slickrock. The formations here defy the imagination and are a photographers dream. While the hike itself can be done in an hour or less, give yourself more time to take in the vividly crisp colors of rock as natural art.

Natural Arches

Moderate – (5.0 mi / 8.0 km), round trip, allow 2 to 4 hours

The first thing to know about this trail is that the main attraction, a natural arch that looked like a dragon feeding it's young, collapsed in 2010. It fell from natural causes and no one was hurt. Now just the broken remnants remain. The good news is the views on this hike are stunning in their own right. The trail is on the trail map but isn't given much attention in the brochure covering the main hikes, making Natural Arches a great hike to get away from it all, even during crowded weekends.

The trail follows a sandy wash of pink and white canyon sand, deep enough in spots to test the hiker. Heading up canyon, the wash narrows after about a mile with a few short scrambles. This portion is not well marked, but is obvious enough, despite a couple of side canyons that quickly become dead ends if you should take a wrong turn. The trail gives the hiker ample views of this amazing landscape, and while the showcase dragon arch is gone, there are a few arches to be seen that are cool in their own right.

A nice place to hang out

There is a humongous balancing rock 2.4 miles that makes for a pleasant stop before heading back.

Elephant Rock Loop
Easy – (1.2 mi / 1.9 km), round trip, allow 30 minutes

This is a super family friendly trail that is fairly flat and easy to navigate for all ages. It is 0.4 miles round trip if you just want to see the Elephant Rock or 1.2 miles for the whole loop. The rock is just off the main highway, however there is no parking here, so head first to the East Entrance parking lot. From there, hike from the self-pay station and about 0.1 miles into the trail take a left to lead you right on up to Elephant Rock. The loop continues parallel to the road before bearing right and looping back around past some interesting rock formations.

Charlie's Spring Trail
Moderate to Strenuous – (6.7 mi / 10.8 km), round trip, allow 3-4 hours

This trail is seldom traveled and leads to a nice watery oasis fed by an underground spring. You will see tamarisk and cattails downstream of the spring before the water is reclaimed by the earth. For the most part, the trail follows an obvious wash, with one small dry waterfall and an equally small slot canyon before the reveal of the watery oasis. One half mile into the trail is a large memorial for John Clark, an honorably discharged Sergeant who died in route to Salt Lake City in 1915, presumably from thirst.

The journey to the spring is 2.75 miles. From here, you can either turn around or continue up the wash and bushwhack your way back. To do the latter, continue up the wash until you reach a power line road on your right coming into the wash. Take this road and continue until you see the road cross on your left and follow it up a hill and over to the next wash north of you. Continue on this wash in a northwesterly direction looking for a large solitary sandstone monolith as a marker. Once you see this outcrop, head towards it back to the highway. Head left on the Valley of Fire Highway back to your car.

Photo Attributes

Attributions and permissions given where indicated.

- All Grand Circle Maps and Park Maps copyright Gone Beyond Guides

Front Cover

- Vermilion Cliffs, by Bob Wick, BLM California, CC-BY-2.0

Back Cover

- All Grand Circle Maps and Park Maps copyright Gone Beyond Guides

In order of appearance.

Title Page

- E. S. Curtis (1904): Canon de Chelly – Navajo. Seven riders on horseback and dog trek against background of canyon cliffs., PD US

Table of Contents

- Grand Canyon at Winter Solstice, NPS photo by M. Quinn, CC-BY-2.0

General Information

- All Grand Circle Maps copyright Gone Beyond Guides
- Reverse Handprint, by NPS photo by Jacob W. Frank, CC-BY-2.0
- Monument Valley, by Christian Mehlführer, CC-BY-2.5
- Vermilion Cliffs NM, by Erik Voss, CC-BY-SA-2.5,2.0,1.0
- Painted Desert, by katsrcool, CC-BY-2.0
- Grand Canyon, by Tobi 87, CC-BY-SA-4.0,3.0,2.5,2.0,1.0

Northern Arizona

- Grand Canyon, by Chensiyuan, CC-BY-SA-4.0,3.0,2.5,2.0,1.0

Grand Canyon National Park

- Canyon Mid Day, by Realbrvhrt, CC-BY-SA-3.0-migrated
- Grand Canyon Panorama, by Roger Bolsius, CC-BY-SA-3.0
- North Rim, by Scott Catron, CC-BY-SA-3.0-migrated
- Grand Canyon North, by Khlnmusa, CC-BY-SA-3.0
- Lower Ribbon Falls, by Kkaufman11, PD-self
- South of Point Imperial, by NPS, PD US Government
- Ewe in Canyon, by Ronthemon2, PD-self
- Grand Canyon Geology, by NPS, PD-USGov

Havasu Falls

- Havasu Falls, by Moondigger, CC-By-SA-2.5

Canyon de Chelly NM

- Canyon de Chelly, by katsrcool, CC-BY-2.0

Four Corners

- Four Corners, by Rich Torres, CC-By-SA-3.0
- Canyonlands - Needles District by Famartin, CC-By-SA-3.0

Monument Valley

- Monument Valley, by Luca Galuzzi (Lucag), CC-BY-SA-2.5

Navajo National Monument

- Betakin, by Diego Delso, CC-BY-SA-4.0,3.0,2.5,2.0,1.0
- Betakin Ruins, by John Fowler, CC-BY-2.0

Antelope Canyon

- Antelope Canyon, by Moyan Brenn, CC-BY-2.0
- Antelope Canyon, by Moyan Brenn, CC-BY-2.0
- Antelope Canyon, by Eric Henze, copyright Gone Beyond Guides

Vermilion Cliffs NM

- Coyote Buttes South, by John Fowler, CC-BY-2.0
- Condors on the Rise, by Bob Wick, BLM California, CC-BY-2.0
- The Wave, by Lobineau, CC-BY-SA-3.0-migrated-with-disclaimers
- Vermilion Cliffs, by Bob Wick, BLM California, CC-BY-2.0
- Sunrise at Cottonwood Cove, by Bob Wick, BLM California, CC-BY-2.0

Pipe Springs National Monument

- Pipe Spring, by Nikater, PD-self
- Pipe Spring, by John Fowler, CC-BY-2.0

Grand Canyon-Parashant NM

- Grand Canyon-Parashant, by NPS, PD-NPS
- Mt Trumbull Wilderness, by Tainter, PD-user

Lake Mead NRA

- Historic Railroad Trail, by Lake Mead NRA Public Affairs, CC-BY-SA-2.0
- Redstone, by Lake Mead NRA Public Affairs, CC-BY-SA-2.0
- Muddy Mountains, by Lake Mead NRA Public Affairs, CC-BY-SA-2.0

Central Arizona

- Rainbow at Petrified Forest, by NPS, PD-NPS

Petrifed Forest

- Slice at Petrified Forest, by Michael Gäbler, CC-BY-2.0
- Blue Mesa, by Akos Kokai, CC-BY-2.0
- Agate House, by NPS, PD-NPS
- Sunset at Petrified Forest, by NPS, PD-NPS
- Jasper Forest, by Andrew Kearns, CC-BY-2.0

Hubbell Trading Post NHS

- Hubbell Trading Post, by Nikater, PD-self
- Hubbell Trading Post, by National Park Service Digital Image Archives, PD US NPS
- Hubbell Trading Post, by National Park Service Digital Image Archives, PD US NPS

Tonto National Monument

- Tonto NM looking west - edited, by Steven C. Price, CC-BY-SA-4.0

Agua Fria National Monument

- Agua Fria, by BLM, PD US BLM

Montezuma Castle NM

- Montezuma Castle, by SonoranDesertNPS, CC-BY-2.0
- Montezuma Castle, by Bernard Gagnon, CC-BY-SA-3.0,2.5,2.0,1.0

Dead Horse Ranch State Park

- Dead Horse Ranch Marshes, by AIBAP, PD-user
- Dead Horse Ranch, by Benjamin Cody, CC-BY-SA-3.0-migrated

Tuzigoot National Monument

- Tuzigoot, by Jhugg, CC-BY-SA-3.0-migrated-with-disclaimers

Red Rock State Park

- Cathedral Rock, by Wendy from Pennsylvania, USA, CC-BY-SA-2.0
- Red Rock SP Panorama, by Michael Wifall, CC-BY-SA-2.0

Slide Rock State Park

- Slide Rock, by Don Graham, CC-BY-SA-2.0
- Oak Creek Canyon, by Don Graham, CC-BY-SA-2.0
- Broken Arrow Trail, by Brady Smith. Credit: USDA Forest Service, Coconino National Forest, CC-BY-SA-2.0

Walnut Canyon NM

- Cliff Homes, by Irish Typepad, CC-BY-SA-2.0
- Walnut Canyon, by Mike Peel, CC-BY-SA-4.0

Sunset Crater Volcano NM

- Sunset Crater, by NPS, PD US NPS
- Sunset Crater Terrain, by Mark Turner, PD-author

Wupatki NM

- Clouds over Crack in the Rock, by NPS, PD US NPS
- Wupatki Panorama, by Stephen McCluskey, CC-BY-SA-2.5

Southwest Utah

- Kolob Canyons, by Gmhatfield, CC-Zero

Zion National Park

Coral Pink Sand Dunes SP

Snow Canyon State Park

Bryce Canyon National Park

Grand Staircase-Escalante National Monument

Capitol Reef National Park

Goosenecks State Park

Eastern Nevada

Valley of Fire State Park

FIND YOUR PARK

In Celebration of a Birthday

In 2016, the National Park Service will turn 100 years old. The national parks have always held a very special place in my heart. They represent some of the best of the best in terms of the natural wonders that America holds. I like the robustness that a national park offers, being fully wilderness in so many different ways, the architectural and historical significance of its buildings, and the educational aspects that the rangers play; including the junior ranger and other programs. Each park protects something that is unique to the world, continually inspiring poets, painters, and patrons every single day. They bring that amazement to all that visit them and connect in a way that we should experience more often.

There was an ask of the national park system to share something and bring a gift to this grandest of birthday celebrations. These books are my gift. Happy birthday NPS, for me you represent America at its best! Here's hoping we can continue to enjoy and protect these lands as a nation for many centuries to come.

The Grand Circle Series Project

This series of hiking guides started from a passion for the area itself. I started visiting the Grand Circle while still in diapers, coming along with my dad on fishing trips up Oak Creek Canyon in the 60's. I have lived within the Grand Circle for much of my life and have hiked many of these places multiple times and through all seasons. I have explored this land for over three decades and each time I went out on a trail or off trail; it was with the same childlike wonder. If a person can fall in love with a place, that is me. Each time I went out, I wanted to share the experience. This sharing started with my friends and then my family, but still, I continued to want to share. Therefore, in that spirit of sharing, I decided to write about my experiences.

The project started by writing my first book on the area, called *A Family Guide to the Grand Circle National Parks*. This travel guide describes a vacation around seven national parks, Zion, Bryce Canyon, Capitol Reef, Canyonlands, Arches, Mesa Verde, and the Grand Canyon. I had fun with the book. I worked with the rangers on the park descriptions and even wrote semi fictional stories to go along with each park. It was great fun sharing the Grand Circle with others.

Describing the national parks along the "main route" was awesome, but I had this larger idea. What if I described every park within the Grand Circle? I had no idea how large such a project would be or how long it would take. I simply started by writing about every park I knew of and then followed up with firsthand accounts for the ones that I hadn't. I received multiple accounts for each trail. Where I had hiked, I wrote my account, researching, and fact checking along the way. Where I hadn't hiked, I worked with others who had, incorporating firsthand accounts from a strong and amazing network of hiking experts and other folks passionate about the area. A tremendous amount of fact checking and support went into this work because while it is nearly impossible for one person to have hiked every trail in this book, I wanted to make sure every trail was described accurately and robustly.

The intent of this work is simple. The Grand Circle Series attempts at gathering every trail for every national park, national monument, national historic park, national recreation area, tribal park, and state park within the Grand Circle. I am certain that there are trails and possibly even parks yet that need to be included. The Browns Canyon National Monument is a great case in point. It was just recently added to the national park system in 2015. That said, after describing nearly 500 trails and after crossing the 100,000-word mark, I realized I was at a stopping point. (This was my 'Forest Gump at Monument Valley' moment).

When it was all done I had described 12 national parks, 31 national monuments, including national historic sites and preserves, 3 national recreation areas, 29 state parks and 4 tribal parks. These 79 parks in all cover 480 hikes and the truth is there are still hikes left to be defined, especially in the larger and more remote parks. I left out unofficial hikes within parks and also left out secret areas only known to locals, as I believe some land is so special that it should be preserved, that if it wants you to visit it, it will call you, it needs no introduction.

So what to do with all these trail descriptions? The intent originally was to put everything into one book, but then I realized that wouldn't be very useful. It would be too big to fit into a daypack and most folks would not make full use of a book covering such a large area. In the end, I decided to split the content into four guides, one each for Nevada, Utah, Arizona and finally one more collectively covering Colorado and New Mexico. These four kept everything to a manageable area of interest.

Each book spills over in its surrounding states just a bit, because that's how I would use such a book. This way if you are planning to hike Black Canyon of the Gunnison National Park using the Colorado/New Mexico trail guide, you can read on to the chapter that describes Canyonlands National Park in nearby Utah, because it's just as amazing, but in a completely different way. For the one person who buys all four books, first off, thank you! Secondly, hopefully you understand why you have four copies of the Four Corners Monument chapter.

I am always looking for feedback on improving these books and for any accuracy, misspellings, gripes, wants, and of course kudos. Please send to gonebeyondguides@gmail.com. I write, design, and publish these works myself.

Happy hiking!

Acknowledgments

First off, I want to thank MRoy Cartography for their wonderful map making, headed by Molly Roy. I came in with a request to make these the best maps out there and she fully delivered.

I am extremely thankful for the constant ebb and flow of feedback from my growing focus group, whom I used day in and day out as a sounding board for ideas, research, and pretty much for every aspect of this book. This is never a one-man shop; I couldn't do what I do without them. These include Ernie, Chris, Frank, Joel, George, Geoff, Jeff, Peggy, John, and Angela.

A special thanks to the National Park Service and its employees. There has never been a time when you weren't able to support this effort, which is remarkable given how much you all do. I truly appreciate all that you do for us as a nation and for all the help and assistance you have given me. To NPS - - Happy 100th birthday!

I also want to thank the states of Utah, Arizona, New Mexico, Colorado, and Nevada. Each of you protects some of the best and most remote lands in the United States. Each state, I commend you for your efforts here.

To my wife Angela and two boys, Everest and Bryce, thank you. The time you have given me to create these books is a true blessing, both in the adventures we have taken and in the many hours writing and editing away you have given me.

You can reach the author through our FaceBook page:

www.facebook.com/GBG.GoneBeyondGuides

ISBN-10:   0-9971370-3-7

ISBN-13:   978-0-9971370-3-3

Eric Henze began his writing career at the age of twelve with a sci fi short titled "5:15", tackling a plot around a timepiece that could end the world. His passion for hiking started in Sedona, Arizona where he lived in his youth. It expanded to peak bagging in the Sierra Nevada Mountains and then the Andes of South America, where he lived as a Peace Corp volunteer for two years, climbing many of the peaks of Ecuador and Peru. A highlight was climbing Sangay, an active volcano that often shoots VW size rocks at climbers to maintain their attention. In his own words, "It was a delight".

His passions for writing, hiking, and adventure have led to a series of guidebooks for both the National Park Service and the California State Parks. A portion of the proceeds of all of his books will go towards directly supporting these parks.

By day, the intrepid author works for a Fortune 50 company helping large enterprises navigate towards, within and beyond the digital revolution. He is lives his family, two awesome boys, a lovely wife, and a blue-eyed merle named Sedona.

His children have noted that his last words will be while driving through the Southwest and seeing some point of interest. Those last words will be, "I'll be right back, I'm going go check that out".

Also Available Within the Grand Circle Series

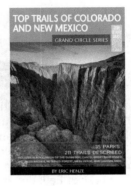

Top Trails of Utah

Top Trails of Nevada

Top Trails of Colorado and New Mexico

A Family Guide to the Grand Circle National Parks

Follow us on Facebook and Twitter!

 facebook.com/GBG.GoneBeyondGuides

 twitter.com/GoneBeyondGuide

All titles published by Gone Beyond Guides

CPSIA information can be obtained
at www.ICGtesting.com
Printed in the USA
LVHW081255100223
738951LV00001B/2